PERSONAL INSOLVENCY LAW, REGULATION AND POLICY

Markets and the Law

Series Editor:
Geraint Howells
Lancaster University, UK

Markets and the Law is concerned with the way the law interacts with the market through regulation, self-regulation and the impact of private law regimes. It looks at the impact of regional and international organizations (e.g. EC and WTO) and many of the works adopt a comparative approach and/or appeal to an international audience. Examples of subjects covered include trade laws, intellectual property, sales law, insurance, consumer law, banking, financial markets, labour law, environmental law and social regulation affecting the market as well as competition law. The series includes texts covering a broad area, monographs on focused issues, and collections of essays dealing with particular themes.

Other titles in the series

Information Rights and Obligations
A Challenge for Party Autonomy and Transactional Fairness
Geraint Howells, André Janssen and Reiner Schulze
ISBN 0 7546 2432 3

Cyber Consumer Law and Unfair Trading Practices
Cristina Coteanu
ISBN 0 7546 2417 X

Consumer Protection Law
Geraint Howells and Stephen Weatherill
ISBN 0 7546 2338 6 (Pbk)
ISBN 0 7546 2331 9 (Hbk)

Personal Insolvency Law, Regulation and Policy

DAVID MILMAN
Lancaster University, UK

ASHGATE

Published by
Ashgate Publishing Limited
Gower House
Croft Road
Aldershot
Hampshire GU11 3HR
England

Ashgate Publishing Company
Suite 420
101 Cherry Street
Burlington, VT 05401-4405
USA

Ashgate website: http://www.ashgate.com

British Library Cataloguing in Publication Data
Milman, David
   Personal insolvency law, regulation and policy. - (Markets and the law)
   1. Bankruptcy - England 2. Bankruptcy - Wales
   I. Title
   346.4'2078

Library of Congress Cataloging-in-Publication Data
Milman, David.
   Personal insolvency law, regulation and policy / by David Milman.
        p. cm. -- (Markets and the law)
   Includes bibliographical references and index.
   ISBN 0-7546-4302-6
 1. Bankruptcy--England. I Title.

   KD2139.M55 2005
   346.4207'8--dc22

ISBN 0 7546 4302 6

2005005676

Printed and bound by Athenaeum Press Ltd, Gateshead, Tyne & Wear.

Contents

Foreword

Personal insolvency law has enjoyed a renaissance in modern times. The 1985-86 reforms did much to stimulate recourse to personal insolvency procedures both by creditors and (more significantly) by debtors themselves. The legislature has been kept busy, initially through fine tuning but more recently with radical statutory reform. There has been a boom in litigation and, as the Cork Committee recommended way back in 1982 (see Cmnd 8558, para 1030), a specialist series of law reports on the subject has emerged (*Bankruptcy and Personal Insolvency Reports*, 1996). Scholarship on the subject has mushroomed and this monograph hopefully will, in some small part, reflect that tradition.

My personal interest in bankruptcy law goes back many years. As a doctoral student in the 1970s working in the area of corporate insolvency law, it was necessary on occasions to trespass into this more established body of jurisprudence in order to track the origins of certain concepts which had informed the development of bankruptcy's sibling. A real opportunity to dig deeper came in the wake of the 1985-86 reforms when I was required to familiarise myself with the personal insolvency provisions for the purposes of producing a guide to the new legislation. Subsequently, I gained more experience of contemporary judicial thinking via a combination of editorial and law reporting roles.

This particular project has experienced a protracted genesis. The initial impetus came in 1999. At that stage the law was fairly well settled; the 1986 reforms had bedded down and from an exterior perspective not much was happening. The *Landau* ruling ([1998] Ch 223) on the treatment of private pensions in the event of bankruptcy, however, showed the potential for major disruption where principles of bankruptcy law clashed with the dictates of government policy. Certainly, this episode gave me the idea for a new text on this area. The intention was to review the boundaries of personal insolvency law in the light of changing social needs. Work on the book proceeded fairly smoothly over the course of the next year. The reforms to IVA law ushered in by the Insolvency Act 2000 were not too intimidating to accommodate within the parameters of the project as originally conceived. However, the publication of the Consultative Document, *Bankruptcy: A Fresh Start* in April 2000 caused me to reconsider the wisdom of an early completion. The reform proposals contained therein were so radical that it was necessary to hold breath to see whether they did materialise. Well, these proposals (albeit in watered down form) did provide the basis for major legislative change via the medium of the Enterprise Act 2002, reform which was introduced with effect from April 2004.

During the years 2000-2002 other developments added spice to the recipe of personal insolvency regulation. The frequent (and usually unsuccessful) challenges to established bankruptcy principles by claimants citing the Human Rights Act 1998 provided a steady source of copy for law reporters. On the economic front the inexorable rise of consumer credit debt pushed personal insolvency law more towards the political spotlight. All of the available statistics, whether they deal with bankruptcy petitions presented, orders made, numbers of mortgage repossessions or levels of personal debt, point to personal insolvency operating at record levels. Personal debt in the UK (including secured and unsecured debt) is now estimated to have passed the £1 trillion mark! Another pointer to current usage can be found in the fact that it is estimated that someone becomes bankrupt in this country every 15 minutes. This socio-economic problem is not unique to the UK. It has provoked profound debate in the USA and in comparable jurisdictions such as Canada and Australia. Previously viewed as an insignificant social problem within Continental Europe, it has risen to such prominence that European policymakers/legislators are beginning to exert a harmonising influence. At the end of the day this text may represent the swansong of personal insolvency law as we know it. The reforms on the horizon may completely change the topography of the subject, and in particular may radically reduce the role played by bankruptcy law proper.

My approach towards exposition in the subject may at times appear unorthodox. I have resisted the temptation to construct a rigid conceptual fence around IVAs; rather I have attempted to look at pervasive personal insolvency issues, such as procedural laxity, stewardship, balancing competing interests and rehabilitation with the result that there is some interchange between bankruptcy law proper and the IVA mechanism. I apologise to those readers who find this methodology irritating.

In undertaking this project I have received support from many quarters. Individuals worthy of particular mention are Sue Bate, David Brown, David Graham, Joseph Jaconelli, Peter Joyce, Andrew Keay, David Mond, Mike Norris, Ruth Pedley, Adrian Walters and Geoffrey Weisgard. Catherine Deering, as always, has contributed hours of unpaid research assistance. The debt I owe these individuals is non-dischargeable. The views expressed in this book are mine alone and should not be attributed to the aforementioned. I would also like to thank the staff at Ashgate for their understanding and patience in dealing with a quirky author.

I have attempted to state the law as it stood at 31 December 2004. Some developments occurring thereafter have been accommodated on an ad hoc basis. Readers should, however, note that lump sums (and costs) awarded in matrimonial proceedings have at last been made provable bankruptcy debts by the Insolvency (Amendment) Rules 2005 (SI 2005/527). This change is made by amendment to Insolvency Rule 12.3(2)(a). Looking to the future the Insolvency Service revealed its full NINA debt relief proposals in a consultative document published in March 2005 (see at 153–4 below for an early warning of these). In the USA the long-awaited swing of the pendulum towards creditor interests was manifested in the Bankruptcy Abuse Prevention and Consumer Protection Act 2005 which was signed into law in April. Unfortunately, these developments occurred too late in the day to be accommodated in the main text.

David Milman
Lancaster University

Table of Cases

European Court of Human Rights

Australia

Table of Legislation

Primary Legislation

United Kingdom

Selected UK Secondary Legislation

Abbreviations Used for Law Reports and Periodicals

AC	Appeal Cases
All ER	All England Law Reports
ALR	Australian Law Reports
Am Jo of L Hist	American Journal of Legal History
App Cas	Appeal Cases
BCC	British Company Cases
BCLC	Butterworths Company Law Cases
BPIR	Bankruptcy and Personal Insolvency Reports
Brit Jo of Crimin	British Journal of Criminology
Cam Hist Rev	Cambridge Historical Review
Can Jo of Hist	Canadian Journal of History
CBR	Canadian Bankruptcy Reports
CFILR	Company Financial and Insolvency Law Review
Ch	Chancery
Ch App	Chancery Appeals
CLJ	Cambridge Law Journal
CLR	Commonwealth Law Reports
CLWR	Common Law World Review
CLY	Current Law Yearbook
Co Law	The Company Lawyer
Col L Rev	Columbia Law Review
Conv	Conveyancer and Property Lawyer
DLR	Dominion Law Reports
Econ Hist Rev	Economic History Review
ER	English Reports
EWCA Civ	England and Wales Court of Appeal Civil Division (neutral citation)
EWCA Crim	England and Wales Court of Appeal Criminal Division (neutral citation)
EWHC	England and Wales High Court (neutral citation)
Exch	Exchequer Cases
FLR	Family Law Reports
Harv L Rev	Harvard Law Review
Hist Ty	History Today
IIR	International Insolvency Review
IL&P	Insolvency Law and Practice
Ins Intell	Insolvency Intelligence

Ins Law	Insolvency Lawyer
Ins Pract	Insolvency Practitioner
IR	Irish Reports
Ir Jur	Irish Jurist
JBL	Journal of Business Law
JCLS	Journal of Corporate Law Studies
Jo of Brit Stud	Journal of British Studies
Jo of Bus Eth	Journal of Business Ethics
Jo of Cons Pol	Journal of Consumer Policy
Jo of L Hist	Journal of Legal History
Jo of Law and Soc	Journal of Law and Society
KB	King's Bench
Law and Cont Prob	Law and Contemporary Problems
Law and Soc Inq	Law and Social Inquiry
Leg Stud	Legal Studies
LMCLQ	Lloyds Maritime and Commercial Law Quarterly
LQR	Law Quarterly Review
MLR	Modern Law Review
NI	Northern Irish Reports
NILQ	Northern Ireland Legal Quarterly
NLJ	New Law Journal
PL	Public Law
Pen L Rev	Pennsylvania Law Review
Pub Hist	Publishing History
QB	Queen's Bench
RALQ	Receivers, Administrators and Liquidators Quarterly
Recov	Recovery
SC	Session Cases
SJ	Solicitors Journal
SLT	Scots Law Times
UKHL	House of Lords (neutral citation)
Univ Chic L Rev	University of Chicago Law Review
US US	Supreme Court Reports
WLR	Weekly Law Reports

Series Editor's Introduction

Geraint Howells
Lancaster University, UK

This latest addition by David Milman to the *Markets and the Law* series is particularly opportune given that personal insolvency in the UK is running at an all-time high. It is a state of affairs that attracts great media attention and provokes much soul-searching amongst regulators and policymakers as to appropriate regulation of a variety of markets.

Insolvency regimes such as bankruptcy represent a market default mechanism, the relevant market being the *credit market*, which itself is made up of trade credit and consumer credit. The latter market has expanded exponentially in modern times and that growth is a major cause behind the prevalence of personal insolvency. Since Tudor times it has been necessary to provide procedures dealing with cases where one of the players in the market (the debtor) fails to perform repayment obligations to counterparties (the creditors). Over the ages these mechanisms have changed. Originally a dedicated procedure known as bankruptcy was made available to "traders" with a much harsher regime featuring imprisonment for debt being applied to non-traders. That schizophrenic approach began to break down with the gradual widening of the concept of "trader" and eventually by the mid 19th century personal insolvency for the most part became equated with bankruptcy.

In modern times we have seen a gradual rolling back of bankruptcy law. The use of alternative procedures such as the Individual Voluntary Arrangement (IVA) has become a significant trend, with as many as 25 per cent of all personal insolvencies being dealt with in that way. Moreover, the liberalisation of bankruptcy may have tempted many debtors to view it as an easy way out of their financial predicament. Such opportunistic behaviour has implications for the way the credit market operates and may affect the position of the general population by driving up interest rates as credit providers reassess their risk.

There is another market that plays a significant role in shaping the evolution of personal insolvency law; the *market for professional insolvency services*. Insolvency practitioners play an increasingly important role in the operation of insolvency regimes through their role as office holders. Insolvency practitioners play a constructive role in the system by contributing to policy debates, launching new initiatives (such as model IVA terms) and by supporting research. Questions arise as to what extent their duties should be prescribed by law and how remuneration practices should be controlled. More recently, the government, desirous of introducing greater competition into the market, has through the Insolvency Act 2000 permitted non-insolvency practitioners to play a role. That is only a minor intrusion and needs to be seen in the context of the fact that much personal insolvency work is currently being handled by debt management firms which operate in a largely unregulated climate.

A pervasive issue that is addressed in this monograph is whether (and, if so, to what extent) the state has a role to play in intervening in the market with regard to insolvency. It clearly does so to an increasing extent at the point of entry to the market where consumer credit is being provided and it also acts where the credit bargain is defaulted upon by providing a collective bankruptcy procedure. In reality the state through the office of the Official Receiver will undertake much insolvency work where the private insolvency service providers are not prepared to act because of the lack of an economic return. The relationship between public and private players in the insolvency services market is a controversial one that is discussed in this text.

There are other markets requiring comment. Bankruptcy law has traditionally operated through a *market in the provision of court services*, in that bankruptcy can only be activated by court order. Commentators have become increasingly aware of the inefficiencies of bankruptcy as a recovery device. Consequently, the IVA procedure, which involves minimal contact with the court, has prospered. Moreover, doubts have emerged recently as to the suitability of that mechanism with the result that we are now on the point of considering the introduction of largely bureaucratic procedures to deal with hopelessly insolvent estates. Such a transformation could have significant implications for those lawyers undertaking insolvency work through the courts or through the IVA procedure.

One of the central purposes of insolvency law is to permit the recovery of assets wrongfully dispersed from the estate. That will involve litigation instituted by a trustee in bankruptcy, who, by definition, will be short of funds. The trustee may be tempted to seek external funding for the prosecution of such a claim or even to sell it outright to a third party. Such considerations give rise to a concern on the part of traditionalists that a *market in litigation* is being developed. This aspect of the law is considered in Chapter 3.

Finally, the operation of personal insolvency law may impact upon markets beyond those involving the provision of credit. A perfect example is the *market for the provision of personal pensions*. If the rules of insolvency law develop in such a way as to take away from a bankrupt all the benefits of having made pension provision, that will clearly affect any incentive to take out such pensions. This issue has arisen in bankruptcy law and it is addressed again in Chapter 3.

I am delighted that this book is included in the *Markets and the Law* series. David Milman is a well-known insolvency lawyer and the fact that he has thought it relevant to reflect upon personal insolvency is evidence of the growing importance of this field. In Europe, but especially the UK, the bankruptcy rules are being liberalised along US lines at exactly the same time as US rules are becoming stricter on debtors. Bankruptcy rules are clearly linked to the type of economy one wants and the degree to which entrepreneurship is to be encouraged. This will be an increasingly important area for debate and I am confident this work will become a reference point in those discussions.

Chapter 1

Surveying the Topography of Personal Insolvency and the Law

Bankruptcy as a Phenomenon

There is much ground to cover in this introduction so let us begin with terminology. The word "bankrupt" first appears in the English language vocabulary in the early part of the 16th century.[1] Whatever the etymological origins of the word, bankruptcy[2] has been a distinctive feature of English law and society for centuries since then. In recent decades for the most part it has remained low profile, occasionally rearing its ugly head for public debate when some well-known figure is declared bankrupt.[3] In the previous centuries, however, it has been a central social/economic issue dominating political discourse and the legislative process.[4] It has provided the basic plot for many literary and artistic productions[5] and has led to the downfall of

---

[1]   The Oxford English Dictionary has identified its initial usage in 1533. It first featured in statutory language in 1542.

[2]   The most plausible origin of the word is that it is derived from the medieval Italian practice of breaking merchants' benches (in Latin *"banca rupta"*) when they were unable to meet their obligations. See T. Jackson *The Logic and Limits of Bankruptcy Law* (1986) at 1 (hereafter "Jackson") . Note also I. Treiman (1938) 52 Harv L Rev 189 and M. Radin (1940) 89 Pen L Rev 1. I.P.H. Duffy prefers the French heritage – *"banque rumper"* (to break the bank) – see (1980) 24 Am Jo of L Hist 283). The Oxford English Dictionary favours the Latin root but also suggests influence by French usage.

[3]   A number of notable literary, political, business and public figures have fallen foul of bankruptcy or equivalent financial misfortunes – Johann Gutenberg, the Renaissance printer (1455), Daniel Defoe, entrepreneur and author (1692), Joseph Smith, founder of the Mormon Church (1838), Charles Goodyear, the tyre magnate (1855), Mary Seacole, Crimean War nurse (1856), Jonathan Aitken, former Cabinet Minister (1999) (who recounted his self-imposed entry into bankruptcy in his autobiographical *Pride and Perjury* (2000)) and Neil Hamilton, former Minister for Corporate Affairs (2001). On a fictional level the reduction of *Eastenders'* mini-capitalist Ian Beale to a state verging on bankruptcy cheered the nation's TV soap addicts in the year 2000.

[4]   Holdsworth noted that bankruptcy was *the* commercial issue that most tested Parliament in the years 1833–75 – see *A History of English Law* (1965) Volume 15, Part I, Chapter V(III).

[5]   John Bunyan painted an unsympathetic picture of the bankrupt in *The Life and Death of Mr Badman* (1680). Subsequent literary treatment of bankrupts has been more caring. The outstanding review by Barbara Weiss, *The Hell of the English: Bankruptcy and the Victorian Novel* (1982) provides ample evidence of this. The most celebrated of these novels featuring bankruptcy or insolvency are *The Mill on the Floss* (1860) by George Eliot and to a lesser extent *Dombey and Son* (1848) and *Little Dorrit* (1857) by Charles Dickens. The machinations of players in the Bankruptcy Court are described by W.M. Thackeray in *The Newcomes* (1855). Numerous other novels during the Victorian period make use of insolvency, bankruptcy or the threat of bankruptcy for dramatic effect. In so doing they were partly reflecting contemporary social concerns and partly expunging personal angst (Dickens' father had, in the early 1820s, been imprisoned for debt for three months at Marshalsea Debtors' Prison, only securing his release after formally declaring

famous people.[6] Bankruptcy no longer enjoys this celebrity status within the hall of fame of legal institutions. To some extent this devaluation is due to the advent of the limited liability company in the mid 19th century; much of the debate on liability and moral responsibility for debt has switched focus to that concept.[7] The perceived success of Joseph Chamberlain's 1883 Bankruptcy Act must also be seen as a factor behind the dampening of the debate. A hundred years on, is the regime of bankruptcy still working satisfactorily? Recent reforms indicate that bankruptcy once again is becoming a burning social issue.

The purpose of this monograph is to evaluate the current state of bankruptcy law in the light of the demands of changing socio-economic priorities. If one can view bankruptcy law as a *product* which the state offers to its citizens (and increasingly foreign customers) the fundamental question to be asked is whether it provides the optimum balance between promoting justice between the various stakeholders and achieving the goal of economic efficiency. When considering the bankruptcy regime it is necessary to identify the formative perceptions on the part of society. These have developed with the course of history. The original view was that bankruptcy was a state of affairs that was to be deplored and bankrupts were to be treated with the utmost severity. In more recent times a perception that is less based upon fault has evolved in influential circles. In many cases today bankruptcy is due to an inability to handle credit. If we accept that credit is an integral element in a modern capitalist society[8] then we should recognise that bankruptcy is an inevitable consequence of dysfunctional credit-taking and an acceptable mode of discharging debts.[9] Bankrupts should not be punished, but rather assisted to return to a position of financial stability and social productivity. This gentler view has been a significant influence on policy reform but it is not without its critics who argue that we should return to a stricter approach towards those who incur debt that they are unable to discharge.

---

himself an insolvent debtor – see generally Weiss op cit at 15). Incidentally William Shakespeare's father was a bankrupt, though the influence on his son's literary work appears less pronounced. A telling point made by Weiss at the end of her monograph is that bankruptcy has virtually ceased to be a key plot element in modern novels of repute, though, as we have mentioned above in footnote 3, TV producers have found sufficient merit in the topic to use it as a storyline.

[6] The most notable and indirect judicial victim of a bankruptcy-related scandal was Richard Bethel, better known as Lord Westbury. He was compelled to resign as Lord Chancellor in 1865 partly as a result of severe Parliamentary censure relating to his handling of a scandal surrounding the Leeds Bankruptcy Registry – for a detailed (and sympathetic) explanation see T. Nash, *The Life of Lord Westbury* (1888). Conversely, there are others for whom the humiliation of being unable to pay one's debts has been the making of them – William Addis is reputed to have invented the toothbrush in 1780 whilst languishing in a debtor's prison. On his release he profited handsomely from this invention.

[7] Limited liability companies created by simple act of registration originated in English law in 1855. It quickly became apparent to those individuals wishing to engage in enterprise but without being prepared to accept personal risk that such vehicles provided an ideal opportunity to carry out their designs.

[8] The Bankruptcy Commissioners had already reached this conclusion by 1840. J.K. Galbraith would argue that the consumer debtors make a vital contribution to modern capitalist society by consuming its products – *The New Industrial State* (1967).

[9] The Cork Committee declared (Cmnd 8558, para 23): "Society facilitates the creation of credit, and therefore multiplies the risk of insolvency. We consider that it is incumbent upon society to provide machinery which, in the event of insolvency, is adequate to ensure a fair distribution of the insolvent's assets amongst his creditors." See also I. Ramsay, *Debtors and Creditors: Themes on Issues* (1986).

Before embarking on our study we need to clarify a terminological dichotomy. Some commentators might view this as a distinction without a difference, but the terms bankruptcy and insolvency are not synonymous in English law. Historically separate regimes existed for traders (bankruptcy) and non-traders (personal insolvency) and even with the abolition of that formal distinction in 1869 differences remain. Indeed recent trends point to a growing re-emergence of that bifurcation. Insolvency is an economic condition that may lead to bankruptcy (which is a formal legal status). An individual cannot be declared bankrupt without being insolvent.[10] Moreover, the concept of insolvency extends both to natural persons and companies. In English law (unlike many other jurisdictions) the law of bankruptcy deals only with individuals.

The Aim of Bankruptcy Law

The avowed purpose [11] of bankruptcy law is to provide a formal regime for the settlement of debt in circumstances where the creditor is unable to pay and where there exists a deficiency of assets. This bald explanation does not, however, address the underlying *social* goal. Blackstone, in his celebrated *Commentaries* of 1766, summarised the purpose of the law in terms of the desirability of promoting commerce by offering an unfortunate trader the opportunity to hand over his assets to creditors as an alternative to imprisonment.[12] Bankruptcy thus offered traders (and *only* traders) the opportunity of a fresh start free of old debt. Although the nature of the trade-off has changed in modern times (particularly with the advent of limited liability companies in 1855) the link between the bankruptcy regime and the promotion of commerce still holds true. Certainly, modern writers have highlighted the need for an enlightened bankruptcy law to cater for the inevitable casualties of the vicissitudes of commerce.[13] The April 2000 government Consultative Document "Bankruptcy: A Fresh Start" took this as its initial premise. This consultation lead to the White Paper, "Insolvency: A Second Chance" [14] and ultimately to the major reforms embodied in Part 10 of the Enterprise Act 2002.[15]

Recent judicial expositions of the aims of bankruptcy law have provided a more rounded picture of its function. Thus in *Storey v Lane*, Gibbs CJ sitting in the High Court of Australia stated:

---

[10] Having said that, "insolvent" may be ascribed a formal legal meaning in certain contexts (see for example s. 183 of the Employment Rights Act 1996) in which case the court has no role in extending the statutory definition – *Secretary of State for Trade and Industry v Key* [2004] BPIR 214.

[11] The fact that this is not the exclusive purpose is illustrated by *Re Field* [1978] Ch 371 where the debtor was bankrupted even though there was not the slightest chance of the creditors receiving anything from the estate. The point is also exemplified by *Shepherd v LSC* [2003] BCC 728. Compare *Amihyia v Official Receiver* [2004] EWHC 2617 (Ch).

[12] See *Commentaries on the Laws of England* (1766) Vol II p. 472.

[13] J. Hoppit, *Risk and Failure in English Business, 1700–1800* (1987).

[14] Cm 5234. Discussed by P. Bloxam and L. Tilbrook [2002] 5 RALQ 59 and by M. Rollings (2001) 17 IL&P 238.

[15] For a review of the implications of the Enterprise Act 2002 see D. McKenzie-Skene [2004] JBL 171, D. Flynn [2004] Recov (Summer) 4, A. J. Walters [2005] 5 JCLS 65.

An essential feature of any modern system of bankruptcy law is that provision is made for the appropriation of the assets of the debtor and their equitable distribution amongst his creditors, and for the discharge of the debtor from future liability for his existing debts.[16]

Thomas Jackson, the leading American scholar, would argue that creditor protection is the prime role of the bankruptcy regime and that the function of the law should be to provide a cost-efficient mechanism for the recovery of debt that disrupts as little as possible pre-bankruptcy expectations:[17]

... the basic role of bankruptcy law is to translate relative values of non bankruptcy entitlements into bankruptcy's collective forum with as few dislocations as possible.

This economic perspective draws support from the fact that bankruptcy can, for a group of creditors, reduce recovery costs and allow for the value of the estate to be maximised by preventing damaging "asset grabbing" actions by individual creditors. It is a strong part of Jackson's philosophy that bankruptcy law should adopt a what we might describe as "minimalist" role by interfering with pre-bankruptcy rights as little as possible. This aspect of his thesis has generated fierce debate on the grounds that it is too conservative in preserving the contractual claims of secured creditors whilst ignoring other competing social values.[18] Certainly, the Cork Committee would have no truck with the minimalist perspective (see Cmnd 8558, para 240). It is not part of this text to lend support to the narrow view on the proper role of insolvency law but rather to reflect the critical and wide ranging role of this regulatory regime.

Apart from promoting public order by taking control of this potentially fractious situation the state can offer favourable treatment to certain creditors.[19] Paternalism thus makes an appearance in bankruptcy law.[20] In some senses, as the Cork Committee recognised (para 23), the existence of a bankruptcy regime is seen as a form of atonement by the state for allowing credit business to operate. The system also has subsidiary aims. There is clearly an aspect of post mortem written into the procedure to enable abuses to be identified and countered. The state additionally recognises the importance of rehabilitation, and although the idea of a "fresh start" seems to be a more recent innovation it does have a long pedigree. It is not in the long-term interests of society to leave a bankrupt a destitute and broken man. This humane and pragmatic point was well made at the start of the 20th century by Vaughan Williams LJ in *Re Gaskell*:

---

[16] (1981) 147 CLR 549 at 556. As Gibbs CJ acknowledged, this explanation owed much to the comments of James LJ in *Ex parte Walton, Re Levy* (1881) 17 Ch D 746 at 756.
[17] "Jackson" at 253.
[18] See for example the criticisms put forward by E. Warren in (1987) 54 Univ Chic L Rev 775 and D. R. Korobkin in (1991) 91 Col L Rev 715. For comment by a leading UK scholar see V. Finch (1997) 17 OJLS 227.
[19] Witness here the soft spot for apprentices. Premiums paid by apprentices to now bankrupt employers rank as pre-preferential debts. Preferential treatment for employees dates back to the 1825 Act (6 Geo IV, c. 16).
[20] Paternalism has been manifested more recently in the idea (which was not implemented) of compulsory financial counselling for bankrupts about to be discharged – see April 2000 Consultative Document, "Bankruptcy: A Fresh Start".

The overriding intention of the legislature in all Bankruptcy Acts is that the debtor on giving up the whole of his property shall be a free man again, able to earn his livelihood, and having the ordinary inducements to industry.[21]

From an economic perspective it is clearly in the interests of society that the bankruptcy system works efficiently. A system that swallows up net assets in administration costs whilst leaving little to distribute to creditors should not be tolerated. Unfortunately, the statistics show that depressing scenario to be the norm with unsecured creditors recovering only a pittance in many cases. Nor indeed should a system that relies too heavily on subventions from the public exchequer be permitted. Finally, the performance of the legal system in dealing with bankruptcy disputes needs to be scrutinised; unfortunately on occasions it has been found to be sadly lacking. For example in *Mulkerrins v PricewaterhouseCoopers*[22] Lord Millett, commenting upon the plight of an individual embroiled in bankruptcy litigation, lamented:

> ... she has been shamefully ill-served by her former advisers, by the law of insolvency, and by the civil justice system.[23]

In modern times the economics of bankruptcy have provided a powerful impetus for reform. The Cork Committee (Cmnd 8558, 1982, para 192) saw bankruptcy as an element in a social contract under which society protected bankrupts from harassment at the hands of their creditors and in return they offered up their assets and income to repay creditors, agreed to subject themselves to investigation and to accept disabilities for the duration of their bankruptcy.

Historical Development [24]

Bankruptcy law in this jurisdiction has an ancient pedigree going back at least to the 16th century. Throughout that period it has been forced to adapt to changing economic conditions and new perceptions about social justice. In some senses bankruptcy law has become a mere tool of economic policy. The 1542 Act (34 and 35 Hen VIII, c. 4) is generally regarded as the first bankruptcy statute in English law.[25] It was specifically

---

[21]   [1904] 2 KB 478 at 482.
[22]   [2003] UKHL 41, [2003] 1 WLR 1937.
[23]   [2003] UK HL 41 at para 3, [2003] 1 WLR 1937 at 1939.
[24]   For most entertaining texts on the history of the subject see H. Barty-King, *The Worst Poverty: A History of Debt and Debtors* (1997) and Bob Pykett, *From Babylon to Bloomsbury* (2000). The regulation of debt and credit in the early medieval period (and in particular the use of debt actions and the role of debt registries) is described in detail in *Credit and Debt in Medieval England (1180–1350)* by P.R. Schofield and T.J. Mayhew (eds) (2002). See also L. Levinthal (1918) 66 Univ of Pen L Rev 223 and (1919) 67 Univ Pen L Rev 1, I. Treiman (1927) 43 LQR 230, A. Keay (2001) 30 CLWR 206. For a review from an Australian perspective see J. Duns, *Insolvency: Law and Policy* (2002) at 14–31.
[25]   It would be a mistake to perceive bankruptcy as a new phenomenon that first attracted legal attention in 1542. There are recorded instances of insolvencies in English law going back to medieval times. For one such insolvency episode which required delicate handling by both the courts and the state see P. Nightingale, *The Bankruptcy of the Scali of Florence in England, 1326–1328* in R. Britnell and J. Hatcher, *Progress and Problems in Medieval England* (1996), Chapter 6.

conceived as a criminal statute designed to combat debt evasion and apparently enacted to reassure traders having difficulty in recovering their debts from individuals who were skilled at avoiding payment. This was perceived as but one further aspect of the social problems posed by debt and poverty in Tudor England.[26] Unfavourable comparisons had been drawn with the debt recovery facilities available to merchants elsewhere in Europe. Another reason why bankruptcy legislation was deemed necessary was that the common law had failed to establish an adequate regime for dealing with debt recovery. Under English law a creditor could either seize the body of the debtor (pursuant to the writ of *capias ad satisfaciendum*) or the debtor's assets, but not both. Imprisonment for debt was in fact not a creature of the common law, but a statutory manifestation that could be traced back to 1263.[27] As far as the seizure of assets was concerned, the governing maxim was that "the first in time prevailed", a formulation that became a mantra in determining priorities. Unfortunately, the execution against assets option was inappropriate in the case of professional persons whose assets were in an intangible form (e.g. investments or future earning potential); the common law execution procedures (such as *elegit* or *fieri facias*) only worked in the case of land or tangible assets respectively with the result that debtors lacking such hard assets became prime targets for arrest.[28] The consensus amongst creditors was that the state was more interested in seeing debtors punished than providing an effective means for the recovery of debt. It was hardly surprising that this primitive self-help system was not conducive to good public order. Moreover, venerable rules on contractual consideration meant that arrangements whereby an individual creditor agreed to accept a lesser sum in discharge of a debt were not legally enforceable.[29] The 1571 legislation (13 Eliz I, c. 7) was more significant in terms of the future evolution of the bankruptcy paradigm. It introduced the concept of the act of bankruptcy and vested the management of the system in Bankruptcy Commissioners. The distinction between traders and non-traders, a pivotal aspect of bankruptcy law for the next three hundred years, dates back to this Act. The distinction ceased to operate under the terms of the 1861 Act (24 and 25 Vict, c. 124). In an Act of 1603 (1 Jac I, c. 15) the process of formally examining bankrupts was introduced. An important development in the history of bankruptcy law came via the 1705 Act (4 and 5 Anne, c. 17) with the advent of the facility of discharge. This mechanism became a bone of contention in the next 150 years as disputes raged over whether it was a prerogative of the law or should be regarded as a concession within the exclusive control of creditors. Having introduced a formal bankruptcy system by legislation the institution quickly fell under the control of the courts of equity with the formal transfer of

---

[26]   On the development of bankruptcy law in Tudor England see D. Graham [2000] 13 Ins Intell 36 and 44. For a general review of how the Tudors sought to handle the problem of poverty by coercing the poor who were seen as a threat to social stability, see J. Pound, *Poverty and Vagrancy in Tudor England* (1971). This harsh approach towards the able-bodied poor was mirrored throughout Europe at that particular time – see B. Geremek, *Poverty: A History* (1994).

[27]   See J. Cohen (1982) 3 Jo of L Hist 153.

[28]   For a comprehensive explanation see W. S. Holdsworth, *Charles Dickens as a Legal Historian* (1929) at 142–143.

[29]   *Pinnels Case* (1602) 5 Co Rep 1179, *Re C (a Debtor)* [1996] BPIR 535.

jurisdiction to the Lord Chancellor being effected by the 1732 Act (5 Geo II, c. 30).[30] Until the first bankruptcy court proper was set up in 1831, bankruptcy in the strict sense of the word fell within the province of the Chancery courts and in particular within the remit of the Bankruptcy Commissioners.[31] These Commissioners, who had the power to commence the bankruptcy regime through the issue of a *fiat* and to conduct hearings in public, essentially operated an administrative function and could not be regarded as fully fledged courts of record[32] – for example disputed points of law had to be dealt with in the painfully slow courts of Chancery[33] until the dedicated Bankruptcy Court was established in 1831 (1 and 2 Will IV, c.56). The 1732 Act was also notable for the beginning of the process of delegating day to day stewardship from public bodies (in the form of the Commissioners) to "assignees" appointed by creditors.

We have noted that a curious feature of early bankruptcy law introduced by the 1570 Act was that the regime only applied to insolvent traders. Individual debtors, characterised not as "bankrupts" but as "insolvents", were left to the tender mercies of the system of imprisonment for private debt. Figures for the early 19th century suggest that several thousand debtors were being imprisoned each year with the only redeeming statistic being that imprisonment was normally merely for a duration of a few months. One of the most obnoxious aspects of this regime was the so-called mesne process[34] by which the court could order the arrest of an alleged debtor without the creditor having first obtained final judgment against the arrested person – a bizarre form of interlocutory relief! In spite of public opprobrium this system persisted for many centuries and the mesne process was only abolished as a result of Lord Cottenham's Act (1 and 2 Vict, c. 110) in 1838.[35] Attempts were made by Parliament to counteract its worst features by enabling the court to intervene to prevent the imprisonment of genuine insolvents and by improving the scandalous conditions in

---

[30]   The Lord Chancellor was first given the power to appoint Bankruptcy Commissioners in 1571. In 1676 Lord Nottingham, the then Lord Chancellor, set a precedent by hearing bankruptcy cases personally.

[31]   For a graphic account of the down-at-heel conditions in which the Bankruptcy Commissioners worked see E. Welbourne (1932) 4 Cam Hist Rev 51. The reluctance of the courts to intervene with the discretion of the Commissioners is well reflected by the celebrated litigation *Ex parte King* (1805) 11 Ves Jun 417, (1806) 13 Ves Jun 181 and (1808) 15 Ves Jun 127. For a superb analysis of this affair see M. S. Servian, (1987) 3 IL&P 7.

[32]   See S. Marriner (1980) 33 Econ Hist Rev 351.

[33]   Brilliantly satirised by Charles Dickens in *Bleak House* (1853). See D. Graham and J. Tribe [2004] 17 Ins Intell 150.

[34]   For judicial explanation of this procedure and the duties of the sheriff holding the debtor see *Plank v Anderson* (1792) 5 TR 40.

[35]   Looking beyond imprisonment for debt through the mesne process it is estimated that in the early 1830s between 12,000 to 15,000 debtors were being imprisoned each year – see A. Manchester, *A Modern Legal History of England and Wales 1750–1950* (1980) at 132. For an account of the infamous debtors' prisons in London see P. Rock, *Making People Pay* (1973) Chapters 10 and 11. R.H. Condon offers an illuminating history of the Fleet Prison in (1964) 14 Hist Ty 453. This intimate study, supported by many perceptive contemporary illustrations, covers the period from the 12th century to the closure of the prison in 1842. The Marshalsea Prison was a central location for Charles Dickens' *Little Dorrit* (1857) (see the vivid description of this Southwark landmark in First Book, Chapter 6).

debtors' prisons.[36] It was further ameliorated by the advent of the Court for the Relief of Insolvent Debtors in 1813 established by Lord Redesdale's Act (53 Geo III c. 102). This judicial body[37] (constituted a court of record in 1838), which allowed for a moratorium on arrest and an ordered handling of debts, operated until 1861 when the system of bankruptcy law was extended to non-traders, having been progressively moving in that direction for over 100 years as a result of the widening of the concept of "trader".[38] Imprisonment for private debt was ostensibly abolished by the Debtors Act 1869, though as Rubin has noted,[39] this historic claim is misleading. Wilful failure to pay a judgment debt as defined by the notorious s. 5(2) of the Debtors Act 1869 could still lead to imprisonment for the next 100 years until the enactment of the Administration of Justice Act 1970.[40] The legal system therefore distinguished between bankrupt traders and insolvent debtors. This distinction has been seen by some commentators (such as Paul Johnson) as manifesting a form of class bias. In his analysis of legal discourse in the 19th century Johnson[41] paints a convincing picture of bankrupts being seen as unfortunate traders whereas debtors left to the mercy of the county courts were castigated as feckless. This thesis highlights another complication in that small debts were enforced originally through local "courts of request"[42] presided over by commissioners and which operated a series of predetermined sanctions (coupled with a fair slice of localised equity) against debtors. This system was developed through legislation at local level in the 16th and 17th centuries and continued until such courts were replaced by the county courts in 1846.

---

[36] Although conditions were generally poor the debtor with money could ironically provide for relatively congenial living conditions whilst imprisoned and in some cases could continue to operate in business – see W. S. Holdsworth, *Charles Dickens as a Legal Historian* (1929) at 138–9. In Charles Dickens' *Pickwick Papers* (1837) the character Sam Weller voluntarily arranged for himself to be imprisoned in order to wait on his master, surely an indication that some level of hospitality existed. Charles Dickens' own father was accompanied by the entire family (with the exception of Charles himself) during his sojourn in the Marshalsea in 1823.

[37] A graphic account of the sleazy environment of this court, which sat in Portugal Street, is provided by Charles Dickens in Chapter XLIII ("Showing How Mr Samuel Weller Got into Difficulties") of *The Pickwick Papers* (1836).

[38] See S. Marriner (1980) 33 Econ Hist Rev 351 at 357 and I.P.H. Duffy (1980) 24 Am Jo of L Hist 283 especially at 294 et seq. It is instructive to note that Daniel Defoe, who was a trader first and a writer second, was imprisoned in The Fleet and Kings Bench in 1692.

[39] See the article by G. R. Rubin, A5 in G.R. Rubin and D. Sugarman, *Law, Economy and Society* (1984). Imprisonment for debt owed to the state or state organs (such as local authorities) still persists. It is estimated that some 6000 persons were imprisoned in 1999 for non-payment of fines and council tax – CPAG (March 1 2000). It is typical of bankruptcy policy that the state reserves for itself a sanction deemed unacceptable for private creditors. Imprisonment can still be used for non-payment of maintenance or child support. Note that imprisonment for simple contract liability would breach the European Convention on Human Rights, Article 1 Fourth Protocol.

[40] The 1970 Act was the result of the Payne Committee on Enforcement of Judgment Debts (Cmnd 3909, 1969). Payne estimated that in the mid 1960s some 3000 civil debtors were still being imprisoned each year – see para 991. Paul de Berker offers an insight to the pathetic individuals imprisoned for debt in his study "Impressions of Civil Debtors in Prison" based upon imprisoned debtors in Brixton in 1961 which is published in (1965) 5 Brit Jo of Crimin 310.

[41] See "Creditors, Debtors and the Law in Victorian and Edwardian England" forming Chapter 19 in W. Steinmetz (ed), *Private Law and Social Inequality in the Industrial Age* (2000) pp. 485–504.

[42] See W.H.D. Winder (1936) 52 LQR 369.

The courts of request, although a commendable attempt to resolve the problem of small debt without troubling the Royal Courts, were of uneven quality and some developed a reputation for corruption.

The 19th century witnessed a struggle for the conscience of bankruptcy law. Merchants, politicians, intellectuals and popular writers all contributed to the debate over the future of bankruptcy.[43] The reputation of bankruptcy law within the commercial community fell to an all-time nadir.[44] In this climate the legislators were naturally kept busy; there were dozens of statutes dealing with bankruptcy and insolvency enacted during the century.[45] Reformers such as Basil Montagu[46] and Sir Samuel Romilly pushed for changes in the Acts of 1806, 1809 and 1820 designed to ameliorate the worst features of the law including the death penalty which was abolished by the last of these statutes. Lord Eldon sponsored a major consolidation of the increasing mass of bankruptcy laws in the celebrated 1825 Act (5 Geo IV c. 16). Subsequent violent policy swings were reflected in contradictory legislation. The key dispute centred on who should control the administration of bankrupts' estates. The prevailing view at the beginning of the 19th century was that the creditors should be at the helm by selecting the assignee and controlling the fate of the debtor by exercising a veto over discharge. The abusive actions of private assignees were notorious. That lamentable state of affairs was challenged by reformers such as Bentham (who was firmly wedded to the idea that the state had a responsibility to police bankruptcy) and Brougham; the latter in particular argued that the state should exercise this function via the new office of official assignee, introduced in the 1831 Act (1 and 2 Will IV, c.56). The role of the court thus changed from being a mere arbiter in bankruptcy disputes to a managing position. Funds realised by assignees were lodged (belatedly) with the Bank of England and eventually the idea was developed that if these sums were invested the income could be used to fund the system. This model was typified by the structures set in place by the 1861 Act (24 and 25 Vict, c. 134). Lester has characterised this development in favour of greater

---

[43] Many commentators took the view that the law was too harsh. Bentham was a leading protagonist for this view. Others took a more moral stance – Carlyle for example viewed bankruptcy as a symptom of moral decline in Victorian England where the pursuit of mammon had been a corrupting influence. J.S. Mill was a firm supporter both of the institution of bankruptcy and also of imprisonment for debt – see, for example, his view that irresponsible debtors deserve punishment because they are in breach of duty to their dependants (*On Liberty* (1859), Chapter IV).

[44] See A. V. Dicey, *Law and Public Opinion in England During the Nineteenth Century* (1930) (Lecture V) at 122 quoting contemporary comment in 1837.

[45] See Weiss (op cit at 41) for the complaints of Parliamentarians and others about the confusing profusion of bankruptcy laws. For a review of the position in this period see D. Graham and J. Tribe [2004] 17 Ins Intell 85. A contemporary indication of the complex mixture of statutory provisions governing bankruptcy is to be found in the 8th edition (1823) of Gifford's, *The Complete English Lawyer* (Chapter 16) where numerous statutes are cited as authoritative sources of the law. The tensions between the business community and the legislators during the mid 19th century are expertly charted by V.M. Batzel (1983) 18 Can Jo of Hist 171. The repeal of the usury laws in 1853 also contributed to the development of the use of credit in society at large.

[46] See M.S. Servian (1986) 2 IL&P 45.

state participation as one of creeping "officialism".[47] Further reforms occurred during this period. Notable amongst these was the attempt in the 1849 Act (12 and 13 Vict, c. 106) to distinguish between culpable and non-culpable bankrupts with regard to discharge. Thus certificates of discharge were graded first class, second class and third class depending upon the perceived moral culpability of the bankrupt. This experiment in moral categorisation was dropped in 1861. There were also other attempts to offer some further protection to creditors (who had lost their right to veto discharge in 1842). However, this effort to mollify criticism did not work and creditor groups, alarmed at the costs of the 1831 bureaucratic model of administration, rebelled and in 1869 secured the passing of legislation in the form of the Bankruptcy Act of that year (32 and 33 Vict, c. 71) that once again gave them control over the running of bankrupt estates. This return to deregulation did not succeed. Creditors displayed remarkable apathy when it came to small bankruptcies and complaints were raised that the investigation aspect of bankruptcy was no longer being enforced. Joseph Chamberlain, the new President of the Board of Trade, was convinced that there was a public role to be played in the administration of bankruptcy and he developed proposals for a Bill that became the landmark 1883 Act (46 and 47 Vict, c.52). This Act[48] effected a compromise based upon a combination of public/private control and the removal of the administrative function from the courts. The immediate management of the insolvency system was vested in trustees (or official receivers) who themselves operated under tight regulation from a burgeoning bankruptcy department within the Board of Trade which was generously funded by interest earned on insolvency estates whose funds were lodged at the Bank of England. The 1883 Act also introduced the possibility of deregulated bankruptcy regimes for small bankruptcies.

Further minor reforms were introduced with regard to discharge in the 1890 Act (53 and 54 Vict, c.71) and also the 1913 Act (3 and 4 Geo V, c. 34), which were immediately consolidated into the Bankruptcy Act 1914 (4 and 5 Geo V, c.59). The present system is still very much founded upon Victorian attitudes towards debt and inability to pay, attitudes exemplified by the 1883 Act. Those censorious attitudes moderated during the course of the 20th century. The Muir MacKenzie Committee[49] in 1908, the Hansell Committee[50] in 1925 and the Blagden Committee[51] in 1957 recognised little need for radical change in the prevailing system. The Deeds of Arrangement Act 1914 (4 and 5 Geo V, c. 47) was introduced on the back of the first of these reviews and some changes were made to discharge procedures by the 1926 Bankruptcy (Amendment) Act (16 and 17 Geo V, c. 7). The secondary regulations were found in the Bankruptcy Rules 1952 (SI 1952/2113).

This basic legislative structure persisted for six decades until the Insolvency Act 1976 came on the scene with its innovative provisions introducing *automatic* discharge after five years. This legislation, which was influenced by a JUSTICE report[52] in

---

[47] See M. Lester, *Victorian Insolvency* (1995) at 2 where the point is made that this was both a contemporary and pejorative term.

[48] For background to this legislative landmark see H.L. Smith, *The Board of Trade* (1928) at 169 et seq.

[49] Cmnd 4068 (1908).

[50] Cmnd 2326 (1925).

[51] The Blagden Committee (Cmd 221) (1957) did express concerns about the rules on discharge.

1975, ushered in a new era of debtor-friendly statutory reform. The law was recast in 1985–86 as a result of the implementation of many of the recommendations of the Cork Committee (Cmnd 8558, 1982). The Cork Committee was established in 1977 with the remit of undertaking a general review of Insolvency Law and Practice. The final Report was published in 1982[53] and after much delay many of its recommendations found their way into the Insolvency Act 1985, a piece of legislation that was quickly repealed and reconsolidated into the Insolvency Act 1986.[54] The Cork Committee addressed central issues and laid down broad policy aims. The verdict on the current system was damning:

> Despite the fundamental changes in society and commercial life which have occurred since then, the system for dealing with the problems created by insolvency has been tinkered with, patched and extended by false analogies, so that today it is replete with anomalies, inconsistencies and deficiencies. We are convinced that the systems (for they are numerous) no longer work satisfactorily. They do not accomplish what is required of them; moreover, they no longer accord with what the general public conceive to be the demands of fairness and justice to all in a modern society (para 9).

Cork added that the current regime was obsolescent and at times positively harmful. Aims for the future were set forth in Chapter 52. Thus, there were calls for procedural simplification, for greater use of income to settle a bankrupt's debts (instead of simply selling up assets), for improved mechanisms to promote administration of bankrupt estates, for providing unsecured creditors with a better deal and for the reduction of preferential claims. Finally, there was a consensus that the current system was too draconian on bankrupts. As far as bankruptcy was concerned the Cork Committee conceived it as only one piece in a complex jigsaw relating to personal insolvency. If all of the radical Cork recommendations for completely new procedures to deal with insolvent individuals had been implemented, bankruptcy would have only occupied a residual role dealing with the more serious cases (para 554). That vision did not materialise.

At the end of the 20th century new political priorities began to exert an influence on the shape of bankruptcy law. A return to the enterprise and risk culture, ironically under a Labour government, necessitated reform of bankruptcy law. The driving influence for these changes was the so called enterprise culture that existed in the

---

[52] *A Report by the British Section of the International Commission of Jurists ("Justice") on Bankruptcy* (JUSTICE, 1975).
[53] A brief interim report was produced in 1980 (Cmnd 7968) – for comment see I. Fletcher (1981) 44 MLR 77. This five-year gestation period seems positively precipitative when compared with the 11-year period (1962–73) taken by the Budd Committee in Ireland which produced recommendations (Prl 2714) leading to the Bankruptcy Act 1988. The Harmer Committee in Australia was put to work in the early 1980s with its report, *General Insolvency Inquiry* (ALRC 45) finally being published in 1988. The previous review of the subject was carried out by the Clyne Committee whose 1962 Report provided the basis for the 1966 Bankruptcy Act which, although much amended, still constitutes the foundation stone of Australian bankruptcy law.
[54] For the genesis of the new legislation in the aftermath of the Cork Report see I. Fletcher [1989] JBL 365. The Cork Report is frequently referred to by the courts when interpreting the insolvency legislation – see for example Peter Gibson LJ in *Cork v Rawlins* [2001] EWCA Civ 202, [2001] BPIR 222 at [9].

US. In its Consultative Document of April 2000, "Bankruptcy: A Fresh Start", the government raised the possibility of radical reform. An attempt would be made to distinguish between honest but unlucky bankrupts and those who might be said to be responsible for their plight. The former (suspected of being in the great majority and perhaps 90% of all bankrupts) would benefit from greatly liberalised rules including discharge after six months and the right to retain a greater proportion of their assets from the clutches of the trustee in bankruptcy. The latter (the remaining 10%) would be stigmatised and would suffer greater degrees of disqualification. This consultation exercise produced an overwhelming preponderance of negative responses.[55] These centred on various common criticisms: lack of practicality; failure to recognise resource implications; poor underlying research. The response was so hostile that it was surprising that the initiative was persisted with. Nevertheless the government refined its proposals in its White Paper, "Insolvency: A Second Chance"[56] and these were converted into statutory reform by the Enterprise Act 2002. Although this new statutory regime (which took effect on 1 April 2004) makes radical changes, those reforms are more moderate than had originally been intended. Essentially the reforms of bankruptcy law allow for early discharge after a maximum interval of one year, remove obligations on the Official Receiver to investigate all bankrupts, offer greater protection to stakeholders in family home and remove certain disabilities from undischarged bankrupts. Significant changes are also introduced into the IVA model. The detailed discussion of these changes is reserved for later sections in this work. Further reform is currently being considered to address the burgeoning problem of over-indebtedness.[57] At the time of writing a consultation exercise is underway at the Department of Constitutional Affairs. More of this in the concluding chapter. Thus has the law evolved over the past five centuries.

Bankruptcy Usage

What do the statistics tell us about the operation of the bankruptcy regime over that timescale? The 17th century witnessed a steady rise in bankruptcies to the point where at the end of that period the numbers of bankruptcies were beginning to approach four figures.[58] On any reading of the available figures bankruptcy is shown to have increased substantially during the mid Victorian period.[59] Early statistics however, suffer from the deficiency arising from the fact that debt arrangements and

---

[55]   See V.S. Dennis (2000) 16 IL&P 179, K. Howells [2000] Recov (March) 12 (a government perspective), C. Haig [2000] Recov (June) 16, R. Robinson [2000] Recov (Aug) 31.

[56]   *Enterprise and Productivity: Insolvency: A Second Chance* (Cm 5234) discussed by C. Brougham and J. Briggs [2002] 15 Ins Intell 17. See also P. Bloxam and L. Tilbrook [2002] 5 RALQ 59.

[57]   See *A Choice of Paths: Better Options to Manage Over-indebtedness and Multiple Debt* (CP 23/04), Department of Constitutional Affairs (July 2004).

[58]   See J. Hoppit, *Risk and Failure in English Business 1700–1800* (1987) at 46.

[59]   See the Appendix to Weiss (op cit) for an attempt to rationalise the figures for the Victorian period.

compositions did not require registration until the latter half of the 19th century. The consensus seems to be that such arrangements outnumbered official bankruptcies by a factor of three. One problem with the statistics in the mid 19th century is that the consumers of bankruptcy law changed. Prior to that date the system was reserved to traders. After 1855 traders could freely incorporate and in some senses limited liability began to fulfil the role occupied by bankruptcy law prior to that date by allowing entrepreneurs the opportunity to free themselves of commercial obligations. After 1869 the bankruptcy system was opened up to non-traders with the result that by the end of the 19th century they were becoming some of the major consumers of the regime.[60]

Modern statistics show bankruptcy's continued popularity both amongst creditors and debtors. These figures need to be set against a population for England and Wales of some 52 million. Figures in the Insolvency General Annual Report for 2003–2004 disclosed that there were 28,021 bankruptcies initiated by creditors and debtors, with the later group of petitioner now predominating.[61] This latter insight is important because it shows how the 1985–86 reforms have succeeded in attracting debtors to use this method of debt discharge; under the old regime very few debtors were prepared to petition for their own bankruptcy. That trend has accelerated in recent years to the point where debtor initiated bankruptcy is now the prevalent species. Judicial Statistics for the early 1970s show that only 3% of bankruptcy petitions were initiated by debtors. The modern topography as revealed in the official statistics needs to be digested in the context of a rollercoaster pattern for the 1990s showing about 30,000 bankruptcies at the start of the decade increasing to 40,000 in the mid 1990s and then retreating back towards 20,000 by the turn of the century. The latest trend is very much upwards with the 30,000 barrier likely to be breached in the current year.[62] By way of comparison in 1984, in the last year before major legal reforms were introduced the figure was a mere 7726. Bankruptcy has thus become a popular institution and that may be regarded in some quarters as a measure of success. Another key statistical feature has been the growth of individual voluntary arrangements. As we shall see in Chapter 7 these were introduced in 1985 as a constructive alternative to bankruptcy. Their popularity has exceeded expectations with the 2003–4 figures disclosing 8307 IVAs, a figure that represented some 25% of all personal insolvencies. Interestingly, that percentage has been higher and the long-term future of the IVA is now uncertain. Although the Enterprise Act 2002 has opened up an IVA option to undischarged bankrupts,[63] the great liberalisation of the general bankruptcy regime by that legislation

---

[60]   For discussion of this see W. R. Cornish and G. Clark, *Law and Society in England 1750–1950* (1989) at 236. In similar vein J. Cohen describes bankruptcy as a "surrogate for the modern corporate form" in (1982) 3 Jo of L Hist 153 at 162.

[61]   Debtors were only given the right to initiate their bankruptcy in 1824. Not surprisingly this particular act of bankruptcy was not common! A rare instance of it happening is provided by the case of the bookbinder William Pickering in 1853 recounted by B. Warrington in (1990) 27 Pub Hist 5. At the other end of the spectrum under US law some 90% of bankruptcies are now initiated by debtors!

[62]   This latter statistic needs to be evaluated in the light that there were in addition some 7195 IVAs entered into in 1999.

[63]   See now Insolvency Act 1986 ss 263A–G as inserted by the Enterprise Act 2002.

may render the IVA solution comparatively unattractive in the years to come. This critical issue will be reviewed in Chapter 7.

Looking more closely at the detailed statistics for bankruptcy one can discern certain constant patterns. Particularly vulnerable types of business, e.g. construction, provide much bankruptcy fodder. The law can afford to take a relaxed view here lest it discourage commercial enterprise in these sectors. But equally there is a large constituency (more than half of all bankrupts) of bankrupts who are not in business in any shape or form. There must be real concern on the part of society here as to how bankruptcy should cater for such individuals. Consumer indebtedness has continued to rise since the Cork Committee reported nearly 20 years ago and there are believed to be more than 55 million credit cards in issue. These differences in the consumers of bankruptcy law used to be reflected in considerable divergence in the substantive law between traders and non-traders. That dichotomy has now largely (but not entirely) disappeared. Some commentators would argue that the merits of a twin track approach need to be reasserted in modern conditions.[64] Of course, statistics on bankruptcy orders tell only part of the picture. Information on petitions presented can add another dimension. Such data used to be found in the Lord Chancellor's Judicial Statistics but are now published by the Department of Constitutional Affairs.[65] The statistics for 2003 (published in 2004) indicate that in the year under review 10850 petitions were issued in the High Court (representing a seven per cent increase on the previous year). Of these 9679 were creditor petitions with 1171 being petitions presented by debtors. In response to these creditor petitions 4449 orders were granted. Virtually all of the debtor petitions succeeded with only two petitions proving unsuccessful. A much larger number of petitions originate in the county courts; the statistics here (which indicate an 11% increase on 2002) show that in 2003 there were 7579 creditor petitions and 18152 debtor petitions. The Judicial Statistics also show the the type of bankruptcy work in the High Court. Some 13,174 other applications were dealt with by registrars (mainly set aside applications and interim orders).

Other Debt Enforcement Regimes Available in English Law

Bankruptcy is not (and never was) the exclusive method of enforcing debt.[66] There

---

[64] See *Consumer Debt Report: Report on Findings and Recommendations* (INSOL, 2001) Recommendation 3.

[65] Judicial Statistics 2004 (Cm 6251), Department of Constitutional Affairs (July 2004).

[66] For an account of these other procedures see J. Ford and M. Wilson in Chapter 6 of H. Rajak (ed) *Insolvency Law: Theory and Practice* (1993), I. Loveland (1990) 17 Jo of Law and Soc 363 and R. Clements (1987) 3 IL&P 115. For a more recent study see P. Walton [2003] CLWR 179. Note also J. Baldwin and R. Cunnington [2004] PL 305 on reform issues. As these commentators point out such alternative procedures play a vital role in dealing with small debt and in the case of the poorest debtors where bankruptcy is not a realistic option. For a classic piece of descriptive sociology recounting debt enforcement procedures in the 1970s see P. Rock, *Making People Pay* (1973). The role of bailiffs in enforcing debts has been the subject of a major review carried out by the Cambridge Centre for Public Law on behalf of the Lord Chancellor's Department as part of the wider review on Enforcement of Civil Justice – see J. Beatson, *An Independent Review of Bailiff Law* (2000) which is available on the Lord Chancellor's Department (now Department of Constitutional Affairs) website *http://www.dca.gov.uk/enforcement/beatson.pdf.*

are other significant court based regimes dealing with attachment of earnings,[67] garnishee proceedings (now third party debt orders[68]) and charging orders under the Charging Orders Act 1979 (which replaced the ancient writ of elegit). Judicial Statistics provide invaluable information on the extent to which these mechanisms continue to be used.[69] The use of debt enforcement procedures where bailiffs were involved was recently reviewed by the Beatson Study[70] which recommended consolidation and the placing of the various procedures on a modern footing. A casual observer is forced to conclude that the approach of English law in this area has been piecemeal at best and ramshackle at worst.[71]

The county court administration order procedure (not to be confused with the corporate rescue procedure of the same name) allows for a cheap method of dealing with debts[72] where the debtor's total liabilities do not exceed £5000 and there is an outstanding county court judgment against the debtor. Under the procedure the court is responsible for collecting monthly payments from the debtor and distributing these pro rata between creditors. There is no seizure of assets involved. Judicial Statistics published by the Department of Constitutional Affairs in July 2004 (Cm 6251) show 4448 orders granted in 2003, which represents a massive fall of 30% on the previous year. Clearly this statutory regime, which is now[73] found in s. 112 of the County Courts Act 1984, has a number of limitations. These had been recognised a decade ago when Parliament enacted amending legislation in s. 13 of the Courts and Legal Services Act 1990. Unfortunately (and inexplicably) this remedial legislation has never been brought into force. The issue (and very future) of county court administration orders is very much in the spotlight at present with a major review of how best to deal with multiple debt underway.[74] An important research

---

[67]   Attachment of Earnings Act 1971. This procedure can be used against fluctuating earnings – *R v York Magistrates ex parte Grimes* [1998] BPIR 642.

[68]   The rebranding with effect from 25 March 2002 by SI 2001/2792 as third party debt orders represents a functional denomination but one which lacks the mystique of the more archaic terminology. For the current rules see CPR Pt 72.2(1) and *Fraser v Oystertec plc and Yorkshire Bank plc* [2004] EWHC 1582 (Ch) where a final third party debt order was refused as third party interests had intervened since the making of the interim order.

[69]   The Judicial Statistics for 2003 (Cm 6251) show some 40,384 attachment of earnings orders used to recover judgment debts (up one % on 2002), charging orders were up 14% to 34,756 and third party debt orders also increased by 9% to 6019.

[70]   J. Beatson, *Independent Review of Bailiff Law* (2000).

[71]   Compare the system in Northern Ireland which is organised on a much more effective basis through an Enforcement of Judgments Office – see D. Capper, *The Enforcement of Judgments in Northern Ireland* (2004) (SLS).

[72]   Debts for these purposes are widely defined – *Preston BC v Riley* [1999] BPIR 284 (poll tax arrears covered).

[73]   County court administration orders were developed in the late 19th century, (they are credited as the brainchild of Joseph Chamberlain and first appeared in section 122 of the 1883 Act). They were based upon the Scottish concept of *cessio bonorum*. They have never proved popular.

[74]   *A Choice of Paths: Better Options to Manage Over-indebtedness and Multiple Debt* (CP 23/04), Department of Constitutional Affairs (July 2004) (available on *www.dca.gov.uk*). This report will be reviewed in Chapter 8.

report[75] produced by Kempson and Collard as part of that review offers invaluable insights into the usage of the procedure, its strengths and weaknesses. The report, based upon some 550 cases, shows that it tends to be used by low income debtors (predominantly female, and often single parents) who have difficulty in handling a range of modest debts. An administration order is preferred by such debtors as it avoids some of the stigma of bankruptcy and is cheaper than an IVA. Monthly payments required of debtors tend to be about £29 and, even at this modest level, there is a considerable degree of payment lapse. Payment lapse might lead to the order being revoked; a common occurrence. Apart from the personal difficulties experienced by debtors this report indicates that payment methods are partly responsible for this systemic fault. When the court makes an administration order it can supplement it with a composition, thereby scaling back the overall debt burden. It appears to do this in a quarter of cases. In recommending reform Kempson and Collard suggest that the £5000 upper limit should be substantially increased (possibly to a figure of £25,000) and, for very poor debtors, an alternative debt relief scheme considered.

Secured creditors, well protected by the primacy given to freedom of contract, have additional options to facilitate debt recovery. Mortgage repossessions do not at first instance require the assistance of the court, though the court can be asked to intervene on an application by the mortgagor under s. 36 of the Administration of Justice Act 1970 seeking relief against repossession.[76] Ancient remedies like landlord's distress[77] and *fieri facias* have survived the test of time and are still used. The old writ of *ne exeat regno* might also be pressed into action to restrain a debtor who might be tempted to abscond from the jurisdiction.[78]

Debt enforcement procedures have always been a source of grievance, capable of generating social disorder.[79] A perusal of the current procedures would reveal a lack of consistency and an abundance of anomaly. This was exactly the situation that presented itself to the Payne Committee, "Report of the Committee on the Enforcement

---

[75] E. Kempson and S. Collard, *Managing Multiple Debts. Experiences of County Court Administration Orders Among Debtors, Creditors and Advisers* (DCA Research Series 1/04, July 2004).

[76] For discussion of the jurisprudence on s. 36 see M. Haley [1997] 17 Leg Stud 483 and M. Dixon [1998] 18 Leg Stud 279.

[77] Distress by landlords has long been a glaring anomaly in English law made worse by the fact that related jurisdictions have long discarded it – see P. Walton [2000] 64 Conv 508. In spite of recommendations from the Payne Committee (Cm 3909, para 924) and the Law Commission (Report No. 194, 1991) it continues to survive. Indeed, it has only been as a result of amendments introduced in the Insolvency Act 2000 that the levying of distress has been brought within the IVA moratorium. A similar power of distress is conferred on local authorities in respect of unpaid council tax (formerly community charge) – see *Evans v South Ribble Borough Council* [1992] 2 WLR 429.

[78] These writs (which represented a form of equitable relief for a creditor seeking the arrest of a debtor) are extant and issued under the conditions specified in s. 6 of the Debtors Act 1869 – for a recent illustration see *Al Nahkel For Contracting and Trading Ltd v Lowe* [1986] 1 QB 235 where the writ was issued against an alleged debtor. The conditions in s. 6 were not met to the satisfaction of the court in *Felton v Kallis* [1969] 1 QB 200. The Payne Committee (Cm 3909, para 1259) recommended the abolition of such writs as part of its overhaul of debt enforcement procedures but this recommendation was not implemented.

[79] This fact is apparent from the inclusion of Royal promises about the future operation of distraint procedures in the Magna Carta in 1215 (see articles 9 and 26).

of Judgement Debts" (Cm 6909) in 1969. This Committee made radical proposals for the coordination of the law. Central amongst the proposals was the establishment of an Office for the Enforcement of Judgments which would seek to regulate the current free for all and would operate a *pari passu* principle of distribution. There were also enlightened proposals for the extension of social services to cover debt counselling and the abolition of imprisonment for debt. The attachment of an earnings mechanism was to be made generally available to enforce civil debts and a more efficient Register of Judgment Debts was to be established. Unfortunately, some of these recommendations were too drastic (or too expensive) for the legislature; the proposals for an Office for the Enforcement of Judgment and for a debt counselling regime fell into this category, whereas action was taken with regard to imprisonment for debt and new procedures for the attachment of earnings.

Deeds of arrangement, now governed by the 1914 Act of that title, have also survived but in name only with barely one deed per annum being entered into in recent years. A nil return was recorded for 1999. Such deeds fell into disuse under English law because the mere act of entry into a deed constituted an act of bankruptcy which a dissenting creditor could exploit to mount bankruptcy proceedings. The Cork Committee recommended their abolition (see para 399) but for some reason they survived the cull. As it happens, statistics in recent years show that they have completely disappeared off the personal insolvency radar screen.

Causes of Bankruptcy

If one is to properly understand the institution of bankruptcy it is necessary to grasp the causes behind an individual becoming insolvent. This is an aspect of the law that until recently has not been adequately researched in this country (unlike other jurisdictions such as Canada).[80] Much more effort has gone into detecting the causes of corporate failure. Having said that, the surveys carried out by the body formerly known as the Society of Practitioners of Insolvency offer some useful insights,[81] as do the findings contained in the Insolvency Service Consultative Document, "Bankruptcy: A Fresh Start" with regard to bankruptcies caused by enterprise failure. When one is considering causes of insolvency one must distinguish between general macro-economic factors, such as the state of the economy and prevailing interest rates, and special circumstances arising in particular cases relating to individual debtors. Such general influences then have to be read in the light of the peculiar circumstances affecting particular debtors.

---

[80]   For an illuminating discussion of the causes of bankruptcy in 18th century England see I.P.H.Duffy, *Bankruptcy and Insolvency in London During the Industrial Revolution* (1985), Chapter V and also J. Hoppit, *Risk and Failure in English Business 1700–1800* (1987). For the Canadian position see J. Ziegel, Ch 10, in J. Ziegel, *New Developments in International, Commercial and Consumer Law* (1998).
[81]   The 7th SPI survey on personal insolvency is summarised by T. Grundon in [1998] (Nov) Ins Pract 20. This survey suggests that 72% of personal insolvencies might be classified as "commercial" with the remainder being classed as "domestic". However, this headline figure needs to be treated with caution because, as the survey concedes, it only covers cases dealt with by private insolvency practitioners. The official receiver is likely to deal with those bankrupts with few assets and therefore the percentage of consumers of domestic bankrupts in this unknown group is likely to be much higher.

Failure of a business may clearly be one factor; indeed if the R3 (formerly SPI) figures are accepted this is the cause of the majority of bankruptcies. If the business is operating in sole trader format, business failure will almost inevitably result in bankruptcy. Critical underlying factors might be loss of market, failure to manage tax liabilities, bad debts and poor management. If a partnership option is used or even a limited corporate model adopted then there is still the distinct possibility that business failure will impact personally upon the participator. Thus in the partnership scenario it must be remembered that each partner is jointly liable for all of the debts of the firm (Partnership Act 1890 s. 9). This draconian rule has caused many users of partnership to be concerned and the government has responded with the introduction of the Limited Liability Partnerships Act 2000. In theory if a corporate vehicle is used the participators should benefit from limited liability. In practice, particularly in the context of small businesses, large creditors will have extracted personal guarantees and, when these are called in, personal insolvency is often the result.[82] The research carried out by the Insolvency Service contains valuable insights into the causes of a business failing and resulting in bankruptcy. The critical problems revolve around poor management, bad debts and an inability to manage tax liabilities. Late debt payment is also clearly a problem, a fact that the government recognised when enacting the Late Payment of Commercial Debts (Interest) Act 1998.[83] This statute, which has been updated in the intervening years, created a statutory entitlement to interest where commercial debts are not paid on time. Unfortunately, real questions exist as to the effectiveness of this well-intentioned legislation.

Many bankrupts are not entrepreneurs. For want of a better label they may be characterised as "consumer bankrupts". Official figures for 1999 suggest that in the UK this group might constitute some 40% of all bankrupts. The White Paper, "Insolvency: A Second Chance" (Cmnd 5234) disclosed (at para 1.46) that in 1992 some 39% of all bankrupts were regarded as consumer debtors whereas this figure had shot up to 53% in 2000. This constituency arrives at the door of the bankruptcy court for a myriad of reasons including non-economic factors such as ill health and marital breakdown. Two economic factors, however, stand out as common. Firstly, unemployment. In 1999 some 4357 of all bankrupts were recorded as having no occupation or unemployed. This is clearly a significant cause, but in the past decade, with the number of jobless persons declining, the stark fact is that the number of bankruptcies has grown. We need therefore to look further afield for causes of personal insolvency. It may well be that changes in the labour market with the move towards short-term and part-time working and away from stable employment for a working lifetime with a single employer offer more fruitful lines of speculation. The second common ground for insolvency is excessive consumer credit (including secured credit obtained through a mortgage). In the USA major research embodied in *The Fragile Middle Class: Americans in Debt*[84] indicates that five common factors may be identified in order of significance – job disruption (the major problem), divorce, medical bills, consumer credit, and the cost of house ownership. All of these are

---

[82] This all too common scenario is well reflected by *Sullivan v Montagu* [1999] BPIR 316.
[83] For the wider campaign against late debt payment see EC Directive 2000/35/EC.
[84] Authored by T.A. Sullivan, E. Warren and J.L. Westbrook (2000).

relevant to the UK with the possible exception of medical bills, though this is an expense that is growing in social importance. Research in Canada[85] has shown that the intervention of unemployment accounts for a third of all consumer bankruptcies whereas consumer credit is responsible for another 25% of cases. Taking an overview of these surveys, the common causes are therefore self evident.

The Players

Bankruptcy may be viewed on one level as an intricate game designed to enable players who have been parties to a credit transaction to snatch or retain assets. The central figures are thus the debtor and his or her creditors. Creditors tend to be repeat players, whereas for debtors insolvency is often a new experience. Debtors have families and creditors (such as banks) have stakeholders whose interests merit consideration.

There are other participants. The game must be managed by operation of the law. The legislature and the courts are clearly central figures in the scheme of things. Legislative reform may be on the grand policy level or on the micro technical plane. In this respect the Insolvency Rules Committee[86] deserves mention. It was set up pursuant to authority in s. 413 of the Insolvency Act 1986 to keep under constant review the operation of the new Insolvency Rules. Matters have been referred to it, often by the courts,[87] and in some cases follow up action has resulted.[88] The courts play their part both in applying the law and developing it to meet changing needs. The overriding power of the courts, as expressed in s. 363 of the Insolvency Act 1986 cannot be overestimated.[89] It is clear from s. 373 that bankruptcy cases will be dealt with either by the county court or the High Court. The former, which since their inception in 1846 have always been a forum for debt collection, acquired much of their bankruptcy jurisdiction in 1861, whereas the jurisdiction of the High Court can be traced back to the early days of bankruptcy law when the Court of Chancery was the dominant influence. The division of functions is mapped out by Insolvency Rule 1986 r. 6.9 with the more serious/problematical cases being dealt with (as one might expect) by the High Court. There is still no specialist Insolvency Court in existence, a state of affairs that attracts a mixed response.[90] The Insolvency Court Users

---

[85] On this issue see *Personal Insolvency Task Force: Final Report* (2002) at 6. The PITF was set up in 2000 by the Canadian Superintendent of Bankruptcy. See generally J. Ziegel, *Comparative Consumer Insolvency Regimes: A Canadian Perspective* (2003) Chapter 2.

[86] The composition of this committee, which is heavily skewed in favour of the judiciary, is detailed on the Insolvency Service web page – see *www. insolvency.gov.uk.*

[87] See *Woodley v Woodley* (No. 2) [1994] 1 WLR 1167 (status of lump sums on divorce as provable debts and IR 12.3) – but note the comments of the Court of Appeal in *Ram v Ram* [2004] EWCA Civ 1452 at [18] as to the lack of progress here. In *Re Austintel Ltd* [1997] 1 WLR 616 the court invited the IRC to look at the issue of mass searching of court records.

[88] Insolvency Rules 1986 Part 6A (public register of bankrupts).

[89] See *Hardy v Buchler* [1997] BPIR 643.

[90] The Cork Committee (Cmnd 8558) favoured such an innovation – see para 1003. Muir Hunter, a member of the Cork Committee, has lamented the lack of a specialist tribunal – see (1985) 1 IL&P 102. Having said that, some judges have stated their opposition to being pigeon-holed into a court with a very

Committee does exist but does not appear particularly active from the viewpoint of the outside world.[91] Behind the scenes however it performs a valuable task.

The state has a legitimate interest to ensure that the institution of credit, the lifeblood of the economy, is not abused. More selfishly it may have rights as a creditor that need to be safeguarded. Figures put to the Cork Committee suggested that a third of all creditor petitions for bankruptcy emanated from state departments such as the Inland Revenue and Customs and Excise. In its analysis of *Insolvency Law and Practice* the Cork Committee (at para 1734) characterised the insolvency law regime as a compact between debtors, creditors and the State. The public interest is usually protected through the activities of the Official Receiver, an institution viewed by the Cork Committee as vital for maintaining public confidence (para 716). The role of this civil servant has been reduced in recent times with the private sector increasingly dominating[92] but that pattern of development was reversed by the Enterprise Act 2002 by offering the Official Receiver a monopoly on managing post-bankruptcy IVAs for undischarged bankrupts. If this initiative succeeds one might anticipate the Official Receiver competing more aggressively for other work currently reserved for private practitioners. The bankruptcy system as a whole is affected by the role played by the Insolvency Service, in which the Official Receiver is based. The key provisions here are found in the Insolvency Act 1986 ss. 399–401 and Part 10 of the Insolvency Rules 1986. The position of the Official Receiver will be considered in Chapter 6.

Looking to the private sector the contribution of insolvency practitioners to the system is vital. The growth of the profession, particularly since the introduction of compulsory qualification in 1985, has been most impressive. Insolvency work was for many years seen as the poor end of the accountant's trade.[93] It is now high profile with leading insolvency practitioners becoming national celebrities, a tendency further boosted by the role played by insolvency practitioners in the running of football clubs! The self-regulatory bodies such as the ICAEW and the ACCA would provide the regulatory base for the bulk of insolvency practitioners in England and Wales.

---

specific jurisdiction – see the comments of Neuberger J in response to an interview with Richard Floyd recorded in (2003) 19 IL&P 216. Arden J (as she then was) proposed a compromise solution in [1994] 10 Ins Law 11 at 14. There are precedents for specialist tribunals in this area – the Court for the Relief of Insolvent Debtors was in existence 1813–1861.

[91] This group seems to have been particularly concerned with the teething difficulties that might be caused with the advent of the major reforms in 1985–86 – see The Times April 8 1987 and (1988) 4 IL&P 188.

[92] In its 1980 "Bankruptcy: A Consultative Document" (Cmnd 7967) the government, in a drive to reduce the public sector, recommended the virtual removal of the Official Receiver from the bankruptcy arena. This proposal attracted furious criticism and was dropped. The Cork Committee (para 856) favoured financing the system through general taxation rather than by depriving creditors of interest on funds which had to be lodged in the Insolvency Services Account. However, the desire to cut back on the public input still remains strong and the Insolvency Service has had to fight off various subsequent efforts to marginalise it. For a fierce exchange of views see the caustic piece by R. Floyd and the robust response from D. Flynn in (1999) 15 IL&P at 85 and 90 respectively. Indications are that the Insolvency Service stood up well to government scrutiny and as a result was earmarked to operate on an exclusive basis the post–bankruptcy IVA scheme – see Chapter 7.

[93] For discussion see S. Wheeler (1994) 21 Jo of Law and Soc 350 at 370.

The Insolvency Practitioners Association[94] serves a coordinating function. The investigation of practitioners belonging to these organisations is vested in the hands of the Joint Insolvency Monitoring Unit,[95] which is empowered to make spot checks and to report upon irregularities which may then be the subject of disciplinary proceedings by the appropriate professional body. The Society of Practitioners of Insolvency (set up in 1990 but recently renamed as the Association of Business Recovery Professionals or "R3") plays a more general role; its work in collecting statistics[96] and in developing model terms for individual voluntary arrangements (see Chapter 7) deserves particular praise. The Insolvency Lawyers Association has also played its part in developing good practice.[97] Disciplinary sanctions may be exercised by the Insolvency Practitioners Tribunal.[98] Much day to day activity in the distressed debtor market is handled not by insolvency practitioners, but rather by debt management companies. These players are largely unregulated, a state of affairs that has attracted much criticism.[99] At the other end of the spectrum of perceived virtue invaluable advisory assistance is offered by a range of charitable agencies specialising in offering help to distressed debtors.

Lawyers (as private practitioners) play a very limited role, mainly because personal insolvency work is not seen as profitable. This compares dramatically to the position in the US where the lawyer has always occupied a central position. Having said that, lawyers do still have a role to play, particularly when reform is being discussed. The constructive role of the Insolvency Lawyers Association (mentioned above) should also be noted here.

The Bankruptcy Association, which was founded by John McQueen in 1983, is a private association that acts as a pressure group on behalf of bankrupts. In spite of its limited resources it is vociferous in policy discussions and has done much to put forward the arguments for a less draconian treatment of debtors.[100] Its work has been developed by the Bankruptcy Advisory Service[101] headed by Gill Hankey. This latter organisation appears to have played a significant role in promoting reforms embodied in the Enterprise Act 2002.

---

[94]   For background see R.W. Hellyer (1985) 1 IL&P 166. The origins lie in informal contacts in the early 1960s with the IPA being formally constituted in 1973.

[95]   JIMU was set up in 1994 by various recognised professional bodies in an effort to standardise regulation and to achieve economies of scale in reviewing the practices of licence holders. It employs full-time inspectors. For background see V. Finch [1998] JBL 334 at 338 and [1999] Ins Law 228, I. Poyntz [2002] (Sept) Ins Pract 14. On regulation of the profession see Consultative Document *Ten Years On* discussed by J. Stanner in (1998) 14 IL& P 3. For future regulatory options see V. Finch [2005] 18 Ins Intell 17.

[96]   See for example the 9th Personal Insolvency Survey described by P. Sargent in [2002] Recov (March) 32.

[97]   For example the ILA developed a model conditional fee agreement in 1995 – its terms were reproduced in (1996) 12 IL&P 163.

[98]   See R. Clements and G. Broadbent (1987) 3 IL&P 34.

[99]   For an expose of the scams perpetrated by unlicensed debt advisers see R. Oldfield [2002] Recov (Sept) 20. See also L. Wilkinson [2002] (Dec) Insolv Pract 14.

[100] See for example the pieces by John McQueen in (1987) 3 IL&P 81 and (1997) 13 IL&P 197. An intriguing insider's account of the work of the Association is to be found in J. McQueen, *Boom to Bust: The Great 1990s Slump* (1994). The Insolvency Aid Society is less high profile – for an indication of its role see J. Wollaston in (1985) 1 IL&P 152 and (1987) 3 IL&P 9.

[101] See G. Hankey [2001] Recov (Feb) 26.

In spite of recommendations to that effect the idea of introducing an Insolvency Ombudsman[102] has not found approval with the powers that be, though an Insolvency Practices Council[103] was set up in 2000 to advise on general professional issues. This body provides a forum for discussion. Issues examined include IVA performance, communication with creditors and the treatment of the family home. The Insolvency Service does now maintain (and publicise) a complaints procedure involving the use of an independent Adjudicator.[104]

Regulatory Mechanisms

Regulating bankruptcy is a major policy objective in all developed jurisdictions. In countries with federal arrangements it is often seen as so important as to justify regulating at the federal level.[105] From a formal perspective the basis of the English law on bankruptcy is to be found in the Insolvency Act 1986, a piece of consolidation that was much needed. This has been subject to some amendment, notably by the Insolvency (No. 2) Act 1994, the Trusts of Land and Appointment of Trustees Act 1996, the Welfare Reform and Pensions Act 1999, the Insolvency Act 2000 and most recently by the Enterprise Act 2002. This primary legislation is supported by the Insolvency Rules 1986 (SI 1986/1925), a major piece of delegated legislation authorised by section 412 of the Act.[106] The new legislative provisions, although borrowing much from the 1914 regime, were meant to represent a clean break with the former legislative model. Thus, in *Re A Debtor (No. 1 of 1987)*[107] the Court of Appeal felt able to pioneer a new approach to deal with defects in statutory demands by pointing to the legislative sea change that had occurred. Nicholls LJ declared:

> I do not think that this new bankruptcy code simply incorporates and adopts the same approach as the old code. The new code has made many changes in the law of bankruptcy, and the court's task, with regard to the new code, must be to construe the new statutory provisions in accordance with the ordinary canons of construction, unfettered by previous authorities.[108]

---

[102]   The Cork Committee (para 1772) called for an Insolvency Ombudsman to be introduced to deal with complaints against practitioners. Lightman J (as he then was) supported the idea in [1996] 16 Ins Law 2 at 5. Australia makes use of the device of an Ombudsman in its bankruptcy system.

[103]   For the IPC, which was established in early 2000 see D. Harrison [2002] Ins Law 175 and [2004] 17 Ins Intell 108. See R. Robinson for the impact of the IPC study of bankruptcy and the family home [2002] Recov (June) 34. The website *www.insolvencypractices.co.uk* should also be visited.

[104]   Details may be found in an April 2003 Insolvency Service publication entitled Complaints Procedures. The 2003–4 *Insolvency Service Annual Report* (HCP 812) at page 27 also contains useful information on the role played by The Adjudicator (Dame Barbara Mills). It appears that access to the Parliamentary Commissioner for Administration is now possible via a complaint channelled through an MP. On the question of whether the Insolvency Service itself is subject to PCA scrutiny see V. Finch [1998] JBL 334 at 345.

[105]   Witness the USA – Art 1, para 8, clause 4 of the US Constitution.

[106]   Occasionally questions have been asked as to whether the secondary legislation is ultra vires the primary Act but such challenges usually fail – *R v Lord Chancellor ex parte Lightfoot* [2000] 2 WLR 318.

[107]   [1989] 1 WLR 271.

[108]   Ibid at 276 per Nicholls LJ.

Again in *Smith v Braintree DC*[109] the House of Lords justified taking a fresh look at a piece of established legislation by pointing out that the legal regime in which it was now located had drastically changed. Lord Jauncey, specifically supporting the approach adopted by the Court of Appeal in the passage quoted above, explained:

> ... the Act of 1986, although re-enacting many provisions from earlier statutes, contains a good deal of fresh material derived from the Insolvency Act 1985. In particular, the legislation now emphasises the importance of the rehabilitation of the individual insolvent, it provides for automatic discharge from bankruptcy in many cases, and it abolishes mandatory public examinations as well as enabling a bankrupt to be discharged without public examination. Thus not only has the legislative approach to individual bankruptcy altered since the mid-19th century, but social views as to what conduct involves delinquency, as to punishment and as to the desirability of imprisonment have drastically changed ... In these circumstances, I feel justified in construing ... the Act of 1986 as a new piece of legislation without regard to 19th century authorities or similar provisions of repealed Bankruptcy Acts.

The common law, never a substantial component of bankruptcy law, has been reduced largely to the function of statutory interpretation. Nevertheless this is a mission that can still spring surprises.[110] Apart from this role there are historical instances offering rare glimpses of judicial creativity, most obviously in the development by Lord Mansfield in the late 18th century of the concept of a preference in cases such as *Alderson v Temple*[111] and *Rust v Cooper*,[112] this concept being later largely overtaken by statute. A similar evolutionary pattern could be detected in the context of the doctrine of reputed ownership; developed by the courts, consolidated into statute and then repealed by legislation. The introduction of a mens rea element for acts of bankruptcy was also a significant judicial input[113] but once again this contribution has become redundant. The common law heritage is also to be found reflected in the curious rule of professional ethics laid down in *Ex parte James*,[114] in the prohibition on admission of double proof of debts,[115] in the hotchpot rule of distributional justice[116] and in the now superseded rule in *Cohen v Mitchell*.[117] The clearest modern example of the continuing role of the common law in personal insolvency law is afforded by the case of *Cadbury Schweppes v Somji*[118] where a 19th century rule (developed in

---

[109] [1990] AC 215 at 237–8 per Lord Jauncey.

[110] Witness *Mountney v Treharne* [2002] EWCA Civ 1174, [2002] BPIR 1126 where the Court of Appeal reluctantly admitted that an old and forgotten equity authority could intrude to completely upset a previous understanding of priorities in the vexed interface of matrimonial law and bankruptcy law. See Chapter 6 post and D. Milman, "The Challenge of Modern Bankruptcy Policy: The Judicial Response", Chapter 13 in S. Worthington (ed), *Commercial Law and Commercial Practice* (2003).

[111] (1768) 4 Burr 2235. The persistence of the common law principles governing preference in spite of discrete statutory provision was confirmed by the Privy Council in *Lewis v Hyde* [1998] 1 WLR 94.

[112] (1777) 2 Cowp 629.

[113] *Fowler v Padget* (1798) 7 Term Rep 509. For analysis see M.S. Servian (1988) 4 IL&P 117.

[114] (1874) LR 9 Ch App 609.

[115] *Deering v Governor of the Bank of Ireland* (1886) 12 App Cas 20. The durability of this common law rule was confirmed by Neuberger J in *Re Glen Express Ltd* [2000] BPIR 456.

[116] See *Selkrig v Davis* (1814) 2 Rose 291 and *Banco de Portugal v Waddell* (1880) 5 App Cas 161. In the US, for example, this rule has taken statutory form – s. 508(a) of the Bankruptcy Code.

[117] (1890) 25 QBD 262 – see now Insolvency Act 1986 s. 307(4).

[118] [2001] 1 WLR 615.

the context of deeds of arrangement) which enabled the courts to set aside arrangements in circumstances where one creditor had been induced to vote for the arrangement by the promise of additional benefits not disclosed to other creditors was applied to individual voluntary arrangements. The court felt that this rule of commercial ethics still had a valuable role to play and there was no indication from the IVA statutory regime that it would be inappropriate to incorporate it.

Until recently personal insolvency law in the UK remained largely uninfluenced by developments in Europe. That position began to change in the 1990s with the European Convention and Human Rights and Fundamental Freedoms being cited in many a case. That trend accelerated when the Human Rights Act 1998 came into force in October 2001. As far as the EU was concerned it did not achieve a significant breakthrough until the EC Regulation on Insolvency Proceedings 1346/2000 took effect on 31 May 2002. Essentially that Regulation determines jurisdiction in cases of cross-border insolvency. Since 2002 there have been a number of insolvency cases where its impact has been felt but most of these have featured insolvent companies. This matter will be discussed in Chapter 8.

For the most part bankruptcy law falls within the province of civil law and procedure. Within that segment of law the private law aspect predominates. However, public law issues can come into play – e.g. the funding of the system and the consistency of the law with fundamental rights expectations. These matters will be investigated in Chapters 6 and 5 respectively.

There is, and always has been, a criminal law aspect to bankruptcy. In the past bankruptcy offences were sanctioned with the greatest severity. Under the 1706 Act concealment of assets worth more than £30 exposed the debtor to a capital penalty. Death continued to be prescribed as the penalty for certain serious bankruptcy offences which involved fraud until 1820, though Duffy tells us that only five unfortunates suffered that fate.[119] There are still offences associated with bankruptcy. Although imprisonment for private debt has been abolished, a debtor whose conduct falls below certain levels of prudence may incur criminal liability as a result of entering bankruptcy. The best example of this until recently was the offence of gambling (s. 362). Similarly failure to maintain proper business records[120] until this year could also have rendered a person who later becomes bankrupt subject to criminal sanction (s. 361). These offences were abolished by the Enterprise Act 2002,[121] though the conduct in question may be relevant when determining whether a bankruptcy restrictions order (see Chapter 5) should be imposed. The criminal law can continue to come into play to regulate the conduct of a person whilst undergoing bankruptcy – there are many offences concerned with failure to disclose assets or even to cooperate with the trustee (ss. 353–355). Moreover obtaining credit without disclosing one's status as an undischarged bankrupt is an offence (s. 361). The imposition of criminal sanctions to combat perceived abuses by bankrupts and would-be bankrupts is reinforced by the fact that some of the above offences are treated as crimes of strict liability requiring

---

[119] I.P.H. Duffy (1980) 24 Am Jo of L Hist 283 at 287.

[120] This offence could only be committed by those bankrupts who might be expected to keep such records – see *Re Mutton* (1887) 19 QBD 102.

[121] See Enterprise Act 2002 s. 263.

no mens rea.[122] There is to be noted an anomalous[123] notion of criminal bankruptcy which was used under the Powers of the Criminal Courts Act 1973 as a sanction in cases of offences causing damage to property in excess of £15,000 and which was imported into bankruptcy law via ss. 264(1)(d) and 277 of the Insolvency Act 1986. However, that mechanism (additionally regulated by IR 1986 rr. 6.229–6. 234) has fallen into disuse as no new orders have been made since 1989. The White Paper, "Insolvency: A Second Chance" estimated that prosecution (or the threat of it) only played a role in some three percent of bankruptcies. Another indication of the relative importance (or lack of it) of the criminal side of bankruptcy may be gleaned from the statistics in the Annual Report. In 1984 the total number of convictions for bankruptcy offences was 143. The latest figures gleaned from the 2002–03 Annual Report show an increase to a total of just over 200. Most of the offences listed result in single figure convictions. There are about 67 convictions each year for breach of ss. 353 and 354, whereas the s. 360 offence of obtaining credit without status disclosure generates approximately 50 convictions. The most common bankruptcy offence is that of failing to keep proper accounting records (s. 361) and the rate of conviction here in 1999 was 98. The Cork Committee supported the retention of this criminal component and urged (para 1900) that more prosecutions be undertaken. The Insolvency Service has taken this point seriously and the latest official statistics reflect greater use of the criminal law[124] but it is still believed that criminal prosecutions are invoked in only three percent of bankruptcy cases.[125] Moreover, the changes introduced by the Enterprise Act 2002 will further marginalise that constituency.

Whatever the precise source of bankruptcy law, whether it be legislative or common law, civil law or criminal law, one constant remains; the mandatory nature of the bankruptcy code. The courts have constantly set their face against attempts to contract out of the code prescribed by law.[126] Most recently Chadwick LJ in *Dennison v Krasner*[127] stressed the public interest in maintaining this constant in the controversial area of bankruptcy and pension rights, an issue that will be reviewed in Chapter 3. Having said that, the policymakers are aware of the limitations (and inefficiencies) of enforcing bankruptcy goals through the courts. Thus, in the Enterprise Act 2002 we see the advent of income payment agreements as an alternative to formal court orders. Moreover it will be possible in the future to penalise those whose conduct falls short of accepted standards by persuading them to agree to a bankruptcy restrictions undertaking rather than imposing an order on them to the same effect. When considering the effectiveness of the current regulatory matrix one has to sympathise

---

[122] See *R v Salter* [1968] 2 QB 793 (offence of gambling) and the Australian case of *R v Scott* [1998] BPIR 471(credit). The offences relating to non-disclosure/concealment are not, however, crimes of strict liability as they are covered by the general defence in section 352.

[123] Criminal bankruptcy was introduced in 1972 as an experimental development in sentencing. See *R v Garner* [1986] 1 WLR 73 *seriatim* per Hodgson J where the point was made that for the court to grant a criminal bankruptcy order against an offender did not necessarily mean that the Crown would then pursue bankruptcy; the making of the order was in old parlance a mere act of bankruptcy. The Cork Committee had grave doubts about this hybrid – see Chapter 41, especially para 1722.

[124] See 2002–03 Annual Report (HCP 846) at 14.

[125] See White Paper, "Insolvency: A Second Chance" (2001) (Cm 5234) at para 1.25.

[126] See *Re Fitzgerald* [1903] 1 Ch 933.

[127] [2000] BPIR 410.

with the legislators. That sympathy is derived from the fact that the system is designed to serve many aims. It is also seeking to deal with different types of debtor ranging from the feckless credit card addict to the genuine entrepreneur who is reduced to bankruptcy as a result of a business failure that may be due to prevailing economic conditions. This "one size fits all" approach is misguided and at last there is encouraging evidence that the policymakers are moving towards a more discriminating treatment of different types of debtor.[128]

The Disunited Kingdom

There are significant differences in the personal insolvency regimes operating within the UK. Although the same system applies throughout England and Wales there is an entirely different procedure operated in Scotland (which is specifically exempted from Part 5 and 6 of the Insolvency Act 1986 by s. 440); that procedure is known as sequestration and governed by the Bankruptcy (Scotland) Act 1985, as amended. Trust deeds are used in Scotland as an alternative to IVAs.[129] Although there are many similarities to the English model of bankruptcy there are significant points of departure, particularly in the procedural sphere. When the new law on sequestration was introduced in the 1980s it was seen by debtors as such a beneficial procedure that there was an explosion in the number of cases coming before the courts and steps had to be taken to dampen down usage. A key reason for these amendments was the need to control public expenditure.[130] There is unlikely to be great harmonisation between these two constituencies in Great Britain, particularly as personal insolvency clearly falls within the powers of the Scottish Parliament under the terms of the Scotland Act 1998 because it is not a reserved matter for Westminster.[131] Having said that, there is unlikely to be a complete parting of the ways. For instance although the personal insolvency provisions in Part 10 of the Enterprise Act 2002 do not apply in Scotland the Scottish Executive issued a report in November 2003 ("Personal Bankruptcy Reform in Scotland: A Modern Approach")[132] recommending reforms along broadly similar lines. Moreover in 2004 a new debts arrangement scheme, somewhat similar to the English county court administration order model, was introduced under the provisions of the Debts Arrangement and Attachment (Scotland) Act 2002.[133] As far as Northern Ireland was concerned it operated an antique system

---

[128] Witness the July 2004 Department of Constitutional Affairs Consultative Document on Over-Indebtedness.

[129] See G. Weisgard [1999] Ins Law 9.

[130] See W. McBryde, Chapter 8 in H. Rajak (ed.), *Insolvency Law: Theory and Practice* (1993).

[131] Scotland Act 1998 ss. 29 and 30. On the potential impact of Enterprise Act-type reforms in Scotland see D. McKenzie-Skene [2004] JBL 171 and H. Patrick [2003] 16 Ins Intell 65.

[132] For comment on this document see R. Grant [2004] Recov (Spring) 32.

[133] Discussed by D.W. McKenzie-Skene in [2002] Ins Law 212 . See also The Debt Arrangements Scheme (Scotland) Regulations 2004 (SI 2004/468).

of bankruptcy until 1991 when the reforms introduced into English law some five years previously were accepted by that jurisdiction via the coming into force of the Insolvency (Northern Ireland) Order 1989. In substance the law in Northern Ireland now mirrors English law though there are terminological differences (the Official Receiver is termed the Official Assignee[134] in Northern Ireland) and there are substantial points of departure on debt enforcement.[135] Looking further afield in the British Isles, the Isle of Man and the jurisdictions within the Channel Islands[136] have their own distinctive regimes of bankruptcy. These regional variations can cause jurisdictional problems in cases of cross border insolvency and may also create other operating difficulties for practitioners.

---

[134] This term is derived from the 1869 Act. The critical 1883 Act was not extended to Ireland for political reasons. Thus the official assignee is used also in the Republic of Ireland where the system of bankruptcy still bears many similarities to the UK 1914 model in spite of significant reforms in the 1980s. See M. Sanfey and G. Holohan, *Bankruptcy Law and Practice in Ireland* (1991).

[135] There is for example an Office for the Enforcement of Judgments – see the case of *Hallmark Furniture Co Ltd v Collins* [1998] 1 NI 4 for judicial discussion of this novelty. See generally Capper (op cit footnote 71).

[136] For discussion of the *en d'esastre* procedure (which is now embodied in a 1990 Jersey statute of that name) see *Re A Debtor, Viscount of the Royal Court of Jersey v The Debtor* [1980] Ch 758 and M. Wilkins (1989) 5 IL&P 98.

Chapter 2

Legality and Personal Insolvency Procedures

Bankruptcy as a Procedural Regime

Bankruptcy is an institution comprising of many facets. It is an economic criterion, a continuing legal status, a sanction,[1] a safe haven, but most important of all it is a *legal procedure* (or, more accurately, a bundle of procedures) designed to deal with the consequences of debt. It has an ambivalent aspect in that the debtor who activates it will be looking to expunge debt, whereas a petitioning creditor will view it as a means of debt recovery. It is this Janus-like feature that distinguishes bankruptcy from many of the other debt enforcement procedures, such as charging orders or garnishee proceedings, which are purely hostile processes. The realisation that bankruptcy is not simply a partisan debt collection procedure is reflected by the fact that it is well settled that the court may declare an individual bankrupt even if at the date of the adjudication there is no prospect of the creditors receiving a dividend.[2] The collective nature of the procedure also undermines any suggestion that bankruptcy is a mere private debt collection tool. Moreover, the legal characteristic that it is a regime that can only be invoked through the aid of the court marks it out as different from self-help remedies such as distress. It is the fact that the court is in charge of the procedure (see s. 363 of the Insolvency Act 1986 for indisputable evidence of that fact) that makes it a *collective* regime. It can thus be denied to a creditor who is seeking to make use of it for improper motives[3] and if a petitioning creditor is paid off by the debtor in order to forestall the proceedings, the creditor may not be allowed to retain the payment if the debtor is declared bankrupt at the instance of other creditors. Such a debt settlement can be avoided because the petition

---

[1]   It is justifiable to view it in these terms when one considers the power of an IVA supervisor under s. 276 to petition for bankruptcy if the debtor fails to live up to his or her promises under the arrangement or if the arrangement is failing.

[2]   See *Leonard v Legal Services Commission* [2002] BPIR 994. One reason for this apparent curiosity is that assets might be uncovered during the course of investigations – *Re Field* [1978] 1 Ch 371. Having said that, the court retains discretion to dismiss the petition if it considers it to be oppressive; a conclusion it may arrive at if the creditor appears to be acting purely vindictively rather than in an effort to recover debt – see *Re Emma Somers, ex parte Union Credit Bank Ltd* (1897) 4 Mans 227.

[3]   *McGinn v Beagan* [1962] IR 364.

has already been presented, albeit by the payee, and therefore the collective interest has crystallised.[4]

It is misguided to talk about bankruptcy as a unitary procedure; rather it is a collection of interlocking procedures. These procedures provide for the initiation of bankruptcy, the management of the regime and ultimately the discharge of the bankrupt. What is more, these procedures are not necessarily replicated for all bankrupts. For example, recidivist bankrupts have always been treated more severely – see now Insolvency Act 1986 Sched 4A para 2(3) (previous bankruptcy relevant factor when considering a BRO). At the other end of the scale a streamlined regime known as "summary administration" was for a number of years made available by s. 275 of the Insolvency Act 1986 for bankrupts with debts of less than £20K. Where this procedure was invoked, there was no mandatory investigation by the Official Receiver and automatic discharge was available after two years (s. 279(2)). It is not clear how regularly this procedure was used but in recent years many bankruptcies have been initiated by consumer debtors for relatively small amounts. In any case, this "light touch" procedure was made redundant by the Enterprise Act 2002 with discharge in all cases being available after a maximum of one year and the requirement for an official investigation in all cases being removed. Accordingly, s. 269 and Sched 3 of the Enterprise Act 2002 have decreed that summary administration has ceased to be available after 1 April 2004 . However, even after this abolition the two-tier nature of the bankruptcy regime reasserted itself with the move towards discretionary investigations by the Official Receiver and with the advent of the bankruptcy restrictions mechanism.

The courts are frequently called upon to adjudicate upon bankruptcy procedures. On a superficial level such rulings appear to be little more than technical exercises of statutory interpretation. This impression is fortified as these cases often appear to be preoccupied with the minutiae of the Insolvency Rules 1986 (SI 1986/1925). Nevertheless, on closer analysis[5] powerful forces can be detected as factors affecting the outcome of such procedural jousting. The courts are ever alert to the possibility that bankruptcy procedures may be misused by both debtor and creditor. For example, a debtor may exploit procedural technicalities to postpone the evil day of the bankruptcy hearing.[6] On the other hand, there is a general willingness not to allow mere technicalities to defeat substantive justice. This latter concessionary philosophy is apparent in both the primary and secondary legislative structures (see for example s. 376 and Insolvency Rule 1986 r. 7.55).[7] This change in the law, which reflects the

---

[4]   Insolvency Act 1986 s. 284. It was the risk of this happening that induced the creditor to refuse an 11th hour offer in *Smith v Ian Simpson & Co* [2000] BPIR 667. On the other hand, a payment made by the debtor in response to the threat of a bankruptcy petition being presented by the creditor is unlikely to be set aside by the court as a preference because there is no influential desire to prefer – see Chapter 3 post.

[5]   For a review see D. Milman [1994] Conv 289.

[6]   On this possibility and judicial reaction see the comments of Hart J in *Strongmaster Ltd v Kaye* [2003] EWHC 2696 (Ch), [2004] BPIR 335.

[7]   The courts are less inclined to allow procedural arguments to rule the day where no injustice has been caused – see the recent corporate case of *Re Buildlead Ltd* [2004] EWHC 2443 (Ch), [2004] BPIR 1139 where Insolvency Rule 7.55 was invoked in circumstances where preference proceedings had been initiated

diminished stigma associated with bankruptcy, was recommended by the Cork Committee (para 1026). The traditional approach formerly favoured by the courts was to pounce on any technical flaws by the creditor to nullify proceedings. This stance was adopted in view of the penal nature of bankruptcy and mirrored judicial attitudes to flaws in criminal prosecution procedures.[8] As the new insolvency regime introduced in the wake of the Cork Report (Cm 8558) was more favourably inclined towards debtors, judicial attitudes towards procedural irregularity on the part of creditors with undisputed claims mollified for the simple reason that the courts did not feel that debtors were being condemned to such a draconian regime. Indeed, Cork favoured a less pernickety approach to procedural matters (para 118). The new judicial perspective was announced by the Court of Appeal in *Re A Debtor (No. 1 of 1987)*,[9] where the Court of Appeal stressed the significance of the break with the old law. Errors in statutory demands are not fatal unless the debtor can show that prejudice has been caused by the errors. In spite of the latitude dispensed by the Court of Appeal, Nicholls LJ sounded a warning at the conclusion of his judgment:

> The new statutory code affords the court a desirable degree of flexibility when confronted with an application to set aside a statutory demand containing one or more defects. But this is not to be taken by banks or others as a charter for the slipshod preparation of statutory demands. The making of a bankruptcy order remains a serious step so far as a debtor is concerned, and the prescribed preliminaries are intended to afford protection to him.

This philosophy was applied in *Cartwright v Staffs and Moorlands DC*[10] where a statutory demand produced on the wrong form was allowed to stand because it was not misleading. A similar relaxed approach towards errors by the creditor (in the sense of a failure to comply with IR r. 6.8) was apparent in *Re Blackman*.[11] In *Barclays Bank v Mogg*[12] the error made by the petitioner was potentially more serious. Here a creditor with security by oversight had failed to disclose the security and indeed had provided an affidavit confirming the absence of security. This was an innocent error and indeed the statutory demand had included the necessary reference to security. At first instance the district judge held that there had been non-compliance with the requirements of s. 269 and the petition would have to be dismissed. On appeal David Richards J, whilst acknowledging the importance of s. 269, ruled that not every case of non-compliance with its terms would produce the consequence of automatic dismissal of the petition. Here there had been a genuine error and the debtor, although fully aware of this mistake, had not sought to take advantage of it until the day of

---

by the wrong type of application. Note also the comments of Hart J in *Re McKay (a Bankrupt) (No. 1)* [2002] EWHC 2825 (Ch), [2004] BPIR 1272. However, r. 7.55 is not available to cure defects in execution processes – *Re A Debtor (No. 340 of 1992)*, The Times July 19 1993.

[8]   *Re A Debtor (No. 21 of 1950)* [1951] 1 Ch 313 (incorrect court identified in bankruptcy notice). This criminal law heritage undoubtedly led the courts to restrict the scope of acts of bankruptcy by introducing a mens rea requirement in *Fowler v Padget* (1798) 7 Term Rep 509.

[9]   [1989] 1 WLR 271.

[10]   [1998] BPIR 328. See also *Morley v IRC* [1996] BPIR 452 (amount of debt overstated) and *Khan v Breezevale* [1996] BPIR 190.

[11]   [1999] BCC 446.

[12]   [2003] EWHC 2645 (Ch), [2004] BPIR 259.

hearing. There was authority[13] under the 1914 Act to reserve a discretion to amend the petition and those precedents could be applied to the present case. The latest authority on the subject, *Coulter v Chief Constable of Dorset*,[14] is consistent with this relaxed view, with the Court of Appeal holding that a demand which misdescribed the creditor need not be set aside as no injustice had been done to the debtor. A more generous approach towards procedural matters is also reflected in cases dealing with the amendment of the title to proceedings[15] and with flaws in execution processes.[16] The further liberalisation of the bankruptcy regime by the Enterprise Act 2002 may also reinforce judicial willingness to overlook procedural shortcomings on the part of the petitioning creditor, though a point must be reached where some respect for procedural compliance will have to be reasserted.

These cases where *creditors* have not been penalised for procedural laxity are to be contrasted with *Ariyo v Sovereign Leasing*[17] where the Court of Appeal took a censorious view of a *debtor* seeking to set aside a statutory demand by the use of an informal letter sent to the court out of time but prior to the relevant hearing. This conclusion may be explained by virtue of the fact that several years had elapsed before the case had come before the Court of Appeal with the result that there would have been much greater difficulty in unravelling matters. Moreover, the bankrupt did not appear to have availed himself of the opportunity to attend the bankruptcy hearing when his arguments could have been properly aired. This strict attitude is likely to persist with the impression that too many debtors are overkeen on using bankruptcy to expunge debt.

Bankruptcy is a civil law regime and as such it has been significantly affected by the perturbations in this field caused by the Woolf Report[18] and the ensuing Civil Procedure Rules 1998.[19] The formal position here is that the CPR do not apply, though comparable principles have been incorporated by the introduction of a new Insolvency Rule 7.51.[20] There is no doubt that in practice the change of philosophy as underpinning the CPR will have a profound effect upon bankruptcy procedures. What is that philosophy? The basic driving force appears to be the desire to speed up legal proceedings particularly through the device of robust case management and thereby to reduce the cost burden on the state. This utilitarian philosophy is however tempered by a reassertion of the overriding objective of securing a just determination (see CPR r.1.1).

---

[13] *Re Small* [1934] Ch 541, *Re A Debtor (No. 39 of 1974)* [1977] 1 WLR 1308.
[14] The Times October 22 2004. [2004] EWCA Civ 1259, [2005] BPIR 62.
[15] See *Michael Yee Fun Chu v Price* [2003] EWCA Civ 1744, [2004] BPIR 603 and *Hocking v Canyon Holdings* [2004] EWHC 1966 (Ch), [2005] BPIR 136.
[16] See *Skarzynski v Chelford Property Ltd* [2001] BPIR 673.
[17] [1998] BPIR 177.
[18] Access to Justice: Final Report (1996) (HMSO).
[19] SI 1998/3132 (L.17). The CPR have been frequently updated since 1998.
[20] See Insolvency (Amendment No. 2) Rules 1999 (SI 1999/1022). For discussion see G. Davis [2000] Ins Law 33 and V.S. Dennis (2000) 16 IL & P 83.

Initiating Bankruptcy

The procedure for initiating bankruptcy was fundamentally changed by the 1985–86 reforms.[21] Gone was the old complicated troika of acts of bankruptcy,[22] followed by receiving orders and then adjudications. This complex multi-stage procedure was not mirrored by the more straightforward model adopted in Scotland. In its place was introduced a simplified system based upon the *exclusive* route of the statutory demand which can be served upon a debtor by a creditor[23] without the assistance of the court.[24] Statutory demands (unlike the old bankruptcy notices) can be used to enforce any undisputed debts and not merely judgment debts.[25] Having said that, the debt must be enforceable. Thus if the debt is time-barred a demand cannot be served.[26] If the demand was not satisfied within the specified period or set aside by the court, the creditor could then proceed to petition for bankruptcy. In cases of real emergency, petitions can be brought before the court more promptly under the terms of s. 270, though this route can only be used if the statutory demand has been served.[27] There is a power to adjourn bankruptcy petitions but in *Judd v Williams*[28] Lloyd J was at pains to emphasise that the courts are suspicious about the motives of the debtor seeking an adjournment in such cases. Where proceedings have been commenced by one creditor the court has power under Insolvency Rules 1986 rule 6.31 to order a change of carriage in favour of another creditor.[29] Once again this reflects the collective nature of bankruptcy proceedings.

---

[21] One must, however, be careful not to overestimate the change. The most common act of bankruptcy was the failure to meet a bankruptcy notice. Thus the new procedure, based exclusively upon the statutory demand, may not in practice involve such a great transformation.

[22] For an illuminating account of this concept see M. Servian (1988) 4 IL&P 117. See also *Re Dennis* [1992] 3 WLR 204. The Cork Committee recommended that acts of bankruptcy be discarded (see para 529). Ireland retained acts of bankruptcy in spite of pressure to reform when the Bankruptcy Act 1988 was enacted. Australia has also stuck to the idea of acts of bankruptcy – see Bankruptcy Act 1966 s. 40. The same is true of Canada – Bankruptcy and Insolvency Act s. 42 and New Zealand where acts of bankruptcy are to be retained under the 2005 Bill.

[23] Creditor here includes an assignee of the original creditor – on this issue see *Coulter v Chief Constable of Dorset* [2004] EWCA Civ 1259, [2005] BPIR 62.

[24] The fact that statutory demands cannot be characterised as issuing from the court was stressed in *Re A Debtor (No. 88 of 1991)* [1993] Ch 286 – statutory demand not an "action" for the purposes of s. 69 of the Solicitors Act 1974 therefore the moratorium of one month on a solicitor chasing up bills presented to clients did not apply. Equally as the presentation of a demand does not involve the court there is no power to stay under s. 9 of the Arbitration Act 1996 – *Shalson v DF Keane* [2003] EWHC 599 (Ch), [2003] BPIR 1045. Similar reasoning underpins *Practice Note (Bankruptcy: Service Abroad)* [1988] 1 WLR 461. For a comparison between statutory demands as employed in bankruptcy law and those in cases of corporate insolvency see *Re A Debtor (No. 544/SD/98)* [2000] 1 BCLC 103.

[25] See *Schooler v Customs and Excise* [1995] 2 BCLC 610, *Mills v Grove Securities Ltd* [1997] BPIR 243. The debt might arise out of an obligation to meet legal costs – *Galloppa v Galloppa* [1999] BPIR 352.

[26] The courts are reluctant to conclude that an otherwise enforceable debt is time-barred – see *Times Newspapers v Chohan* [2001] EWCA Civ 964, [2001] BPIR 943 and *West Bromwich Building Society v Crammer* [2002] EWHC 2618 (Ch), [2003] BPIR 783. Compare *Re A Debtor (No. 647 SD of 1999)*, The Times April 10 2000 (reported sub nomine *Bruton v CIR* in [2000] BPIR 946).

[27] *Wehmeyer v Wehmeyer* [2001] BPIR 548.

In hearing the petition the court enjoys complete discretion as to whether to grant the bankruptcy order. Indeed in *Re Ross (No. 2)*[30] the Court of Appeal reminded judges of their broad discretionary power under section 266(3) to dismiss inappropriate petitions and they should not shrink from using that power. The breadth of the power enjoyed by the bankruptcy court is exemplified by the fact that it has the exceptional power of looking behind an earlier judgment upon which the bankruptcy debt may have been based.[31] The reasoning here is the fact that bankruptcy is such a major step that the interests of justice prevail over those of finality in litigation.

Serving the Demand

A statutory demand must be properly served and the law needs to maintain a careful balance between protecting a debtor who may be genuinely unaware of the demand and facilitating a creditor in enforcing a lawful debt. The requirements on service are detailed in the Insolvency Rules 1986. Substituted service is possible (e.g. by use of a newspaper advert).[32] Service outside the jurisdiction may be required and the relevant procedures here have been set forth.[33] The acid test in all cases of service is whether the creditor has done all that could be reasonably expected to bring the demand to the attention of the debtor. Thus, in *Regional Collection Services v Heald*[34] the Court of Appeal refused to interfere with the first instance finding that the creditor had not taken reasonable steps to bring the petition to the debtor; the creditor here had omitted either to visit the debtor's business premises or even to send communications there, preferring instead to try to effect service at a home address. We have noted a liberal approach on the part of the court towards defects in the statutory demand. That flexible attitude does not extend to failures on the question of service. As was stressed by Judge Boggis in *Re Awad*[35] the court insists upon strict compliance with procedures here and the general power of waiver as set forth in Insolvency Rule 7.55 is not applicable. In this particular case failure to present an affidavit to the court pursuant to the requirement in IR 1986 r. 6.14(2) was fatal. The reason for this strict approach is that bankruptcy should not be imposed upon an ignorant party.

---

[28] [1998] BPIR 88. See also *Neely v IRC* [1996] BPIR 632.

[29] *Re Purvis* [1998] BPIR 153.

[30] [2000] BPIR 636. Compare the approach taken in *Oxted Financial Services v Gordon* [1998] BPIR 231. On s. 266(3) see also *Re Micklethwaite* [2002] EWHC 1123 (Ch), [2003] BPIR 101.

[31] *Eberhardt & Co Ltd v Mair* [1996] BPIR 142, *McCourt and Siequien v Baron Meats Ltd* [1997] BPIR 114. Where the demand is based upon a judgment, the courts are loath to go behind that judgment and will only do so in exceptional cases – see *Dawodu v American Express* [2001] BPIR 983, *Re Thorogood* [2003] EWHC 997 (Ch), [2003] BPIR 1468. This respect for earlier judgments is part of the policy of promoting finality in litigation – see *Atherton v Ogunlende* [2003] BPIR 21, *Balendran v The Law Society* [2004] EWHC 859 (Ch), [2004] BPIR 859 and *Chauhan v Commissioners of Inland Revenue* [2004] EWHC 1304 (Ch), [2004] BPIR 862 for recent manifestations of that policy at work in bankruptcy cases. The fact that the debtor may have been unsuccessful in a set aside application is no guarantee that the petition will be granted – *Royal Bank of Scotland v Farley* [1996] BPIR 638.

[32] *Lilly v Davison* [1999] BPIR 81 – the question is whether on the balance of probabilities it is reasonably likely that the demand has been seen by the debtor.

[33] *Practice Note: Service Abroad* [1988] 1 WLR 461.

[34] [2000] BPIR 661 reported sub nomine *Re H (a Debtor No. 38 SD of 1997)*, The Times May 10 2000.

[35] [2000] BPIR 241.

Procedural Irregularities in IVA Cases

Different considerations come to the fore in this alternative form of insolvency procedure. As the IVA regime was novel in 1985 there was no body of precedent here with which an illuminating contrast could be drawn. Where procedural irregularities occur in the IVA environment it will usually be the debtor (or the chair of the creditors' meeting) who has transgressed. The courts tend to be fairly strict on procedural lapses here. The reason for this is that a voluntary arrangement deprives a creditor of traditional enforcement rights and in particular the right to petition for bankruptcy. Thus, the courts have set aside voluntary arrangements, or at least have nullified their effect against a particular creditor, where procedures have not been followed. In *Mytre Investments v Reynolds (No. 2)*[36] Blackburne J has gone to the lengths of denying that a doctrine of "substantial compliance" operates in this context; instead stressing that absolute fidelity to the prescribed statutory procedures is required:

> In my view it would introduce all manner of uncertainties into what I conceive is intended to be a simple and easily implementable code if the clear requirements of the procedure, at all events where matters of notice are concerned, can be disregarded in favour of "substantial compliance" in pursuit of a purposive approach to the provisions.

Other members of the judiciary may adopt a more relaxed stance. For instance, in *IRC v Duce*[37] the court was prepared to overlook breaches of formality in terms of setting up an IVA, where to adopt a draconian view might injure the interests of innocent creditors. The balance between respect for formality and utilitarian outcomes is notoriously difficult to draw and it is hardly surprising to find a lack of unanimity reflected in the case law. The most recent cases on the subject shows that the court's patience is limited. In *Inland Revenue Commissioners v Bland and Sargent*[38] the court found that the original proposal did not fall within the ambit of the IVA regime as it contained no element of quid pro quo. Moreover, a belated attempt to save it by introducing some element of exchange came far too late in the day. Similarities may be drawn with the approach of the court in *Tanner v Everitt*.[39] Here a suggestion that an IVA had been effectively modified and a new supervisor correctly substituted was rejected by Mann J after a close examination of the facts.

The onus is on the debtor to ensure that creditors receive proper notice of the meeting at which the arrangement is to be voted upon. Failure to ensure this used to leave creditors outside the binding effect of the arrangement. There are clear procedures for giving notice and the law will protect a creditor who can show that those procedures have not been complied with.[40] The parallel with the courts' approach to service of statutory demands is obvious. The problems of unnotified creditors have been addressed by the Insolvency Act 2000[41] so that failure to notify a creditor may not

---

[36] [1996] BPIR 464.
[37] [1999] BPIR 189.
[38] [2003] BPIR 1247.
[39] [2004] BPIR 1026. For a detailed review of the case see S. Brown (2004) 20 IL&P 235.
[40] *Skipton Building Society v Collins* [1998] BPIR 267 (notices correctly sent by post but did not arrive).

prove damaging to the scheme by leaving that creditor on the outside and in a position to wreck the arrangement. Creditors bound by this statutory mechanism in these circumstances do have available protection from the court.[42]

Another serious defect that could not be cured was illustrated by *Vlieland-Boddy v Dexter Ltd*[43] where a creditors' meeting had gone ahead in spite of the fact that there had been no direction from the court to convene such a meeting. The IVA regime was thus not engaged and therefore there was no possibility of the nominee to have recourse to s. 262 to seek relief from any potential liability arising out of the irregular meeting. One of the most common irregularities encountered is the treatment of voting rights – it is well settled that it is an irregularity to fail to take into account the votes of a genuine undisputed creditor who has lodged a proof. But what if the debt is disputed or the amount of the debt is unascertained? In *Emery v UCB Corporate Services Ltd*[44] the correct procedure was outlined. This involves taking the creditor's votes into account but marking them as "objected to". In *Doorbar v Alltime Securities (No. 2)*[45] the court was at pains to facilitate the task of a chairman in managing these difficult cases by refusing to impose on him an obligation to negotiate to put a value on disputed claims. Instead the exercise of professional discretion is all that is required subject to a review procedure.

What are the consequences of procedural irregularity in the setting up of an IVA? Essentially there are effects both for the arrangement and for the individuals involved. As far as the arrangement is concerned a procedural irregularity may result in it being set aside. Challenges can be made to the chair's decision to admit or reject a vote by using the appeal procedure outlined in Insolvency Rule 5.22(3). The power to set aside arrangements on procedural grounds is often triggered by a petition pursuant to s. 262 of the Insolvency Act 1986. One of the grounds for such a petition is "material irregularity". This has been defined in a sensible way so as to refer only to significant errors that might have affected the outcome of the vote.[46] In so interpreting this provision the courts have to some extent neutralised the possibility of promising IVAs being frustrated on specious grounds. Certainly, errors in the preliminary proposal documentation fall within the scope of purview. A failure to accord voting rights to a creditor entitled to vote would also constitute a material irregularity.[47]

A significant procedural irregularity arose in *Fletcher v Vooght*[48] where an arrangement had been entered into with debtors and indeed had operated successfully for a number of years when it came to light that no interim order had actually been obtained! Lloyd J felt compelled to hold that this was not a valid IVA and that the court had no power to grant the interim order retrospectively. This case illustrates that judicial tolerance has its limitations. The effect of this case was neutralised by s.

---

[41] Insolvency Act 2000 s. 3 and Sched. 3 inserting s. 260(2)(b) into the 1986 Act.
[42] Ibid inserting s. 262(2)(b)(ii).
[43] [2003] EWHC 2592 (Ch), [2004] BPIR 234. In *Re Plummer* [2004] BPIR 767 the debtor had not agreed to the modification.
[44] [1999] BPIR 480.
[45] [1995] BCC 1149.
[46] *Doorbar v Alltime Securities* [1996] 1 WLR 456 and *Re Tack* [2000] BPIR 164.
[47] *Roberts v Pinnacle Entertainment Ltd* [2003] EWHC 2394 (Ch), [2004] BPIR 207.

3 and Sched. 3 (para 7) of the Insolvency Act 2000 which introduced the possibility of IVAs without the necessity for an interim order, though this change did not have retrospective effect. Another serious flaw was found to have occurred in *IRC v Bland and Sargent*.[49] The error here was more substantive than procedural in that the initial proposal did not fall within the range of possibilities anticipated by the voluntary arrangement regime. In these circumstances the court concluded that the subsequent procedure was tainted irreparably and could not be salvaged by a late modification of the original proposal. A lesser option in such cases would be to allow the IVA to stand but to permit a creditor who would otherwise be bound by it to stand outside. This is undesirable because that individual may then be able to initiate a parallel bankruptcy. Apart from creating complications in the management of the IVA it may bring the arrangement to an end if that is specified as a terminating event by the provisions of the arrangement.

Individuals other than the debtor may suffer the consequences of procedural irregularity. For example, the chair of the creditors' meeting may be held liable for the attendant costs of abortive proceedings. Thus, in *Re A Debtor (No. 222 of 1990) ex parte Bank of Ireland (No. 2)*[50] the unfortunate insolvency practitioner was ordered by Harman J to pay half of the applicant's costs on a s. 262 application as this was felt to be a thoroughly exceptional case. Again, in *Re N (A Debtor)*[51] the court made a nominee responsible for costs where the meeting had been convened at a time and place different to that notified to the court in the application for an interim order.

Judicial Intervention

We have already emphasised that the court is in charge of the bankruptcy procedure. It is exclusively responsible for its initiation and can issue controlling orders at any time during the continuance of the bankruptcy (s. 363). The new case management system introduced by the Civil Procedure Rules merely serves to reinforce that control, a fact exemplified by the comments of Neuberger J in *Re Debtors (Nos. 13 and 14/ MISC/2000)*.[52] When the court is exercising its jurisdiction in bankruptcy matters it adheres to the basic principle favouring open justice. This much is apparent from the *Practice Direction: Insolvency Proceedings*.[53] There are exceptions to this rule of practice. For example it does have the power under a *Beddoe* application[54] to examine evidence on a confidential basis which has been supplied by one party to the exclusion of another.[55]

---

[48] [2000] BPIR 435.
[49] [2003] EWHC 1068 (Ch). A similar irredeemable flaw was exposed in *Vlieland-Boddy v Dexter Ltd* [2004] BPIR 235.
[50] [1993] BCLC 233. See also *Fender v IRC* [2003] BPIR 1304 where financial liability for the consequences of the irregularity was split 65/35 between nominee and debtor respectively. This costs threat for the chair of the meeting does not exist in the case of appeals under IR 1986 r. 5.22 – see r. 5.22(7).
[51] [2002] BPIR 1024.
[52] The Times April 10 2000.
[53] [2000] BCC 92 para 9.1 and 9.3.
[54] So named after *Re Beddoe* [1893] 1 Ch 547.
[55] See *Official Receiver v Davis* [1998] BPIR 771 at 781. For a review of this matter in insolvency law see *Craig v Humberclyde Industrial Finance Ltd* [1999] BPIR 53.

Bankruptcy proceedings can be smothered at birth if the court exercises its jurisdiction to set aside a statutory demand.[56] This well-used jurisdiction is detailed in r. 6.5 of the Insolvency Rules 1986. However, it is an all or nothing outcome; there is no such thing as a conditional setting aside of a statutory demand.[57] This provision lays down specific grounds for the setting aside of a demand; for example, existence of a counterclaim by the debtor,[58] or a set off or cross demand, a concept that was widely interpreted by the Court of Appeal in its pragmatic judgment in *Popely v Popely*.[59] Another commonly cited ground justifying a set aside is the existence of a dispute over the debt.[60] This latter ground is becoming increasingly important as more and more debtors are seeking to dispute the underlying debt. Such a dispute may prove fatal to the bankruptcy process as Sir Donald Nicholls VC explained in *Re a Debtor (Nos 49 and 50 of 1992)*:

> The scheme of the bankruptcy legislation is that substantial disputes about indebtedness are not matters to be resolved by the bankruptcy courts as part and parcel of the bankruptcy process. The bankruptcy courts are not intended to be the forum for resolving such disputes. Where such a dispute exists, the creditor should pursue his claim in the ordinary way outside the bankruptcy courts.[61]

Another specified justification for set aside is failure by a creditor with security to comply with procedures, and this ground is then followed by a general power to act "if the court is satisfied on other grounds that the demand ought to be set aside". This latter ground is to be kept as wide as possible.[62] The leading authority is *Re A Debtor (No. 1 of 1987), ex parte Lancaster*[63] where the Court of Appeal refused to set aside a statutory demand that was admittedly confusing because no real injustice had been done to the debtor. An important point was made in *Garrow v Lloyds*,[64] namely that if there was any doubt about the validity of the statutory demand it should be set aside; failure to do this would give the creditor an unfair advantage by prematurely triggering time periods for transactional avoidance when the resulting petition is forthcoming.

Clearly the court plays a critical role in deciding whether a bankruptcy order should be granted. This discretion is however subjected to certain regulatory constraints imposed by s. 271. Thus the order should not be granted unless the court is satisfied

---

[56] See *Practice Note (Bankruptcy: Statutory Demand: Setting Aside)* [1987] 1 WLR 119.

[57] *Re A Debtor (No. 32/SD/1991) (No. 2)*, The Times May 3 1994.

[58] The claim must be bona fide, substantial and genuine – see *Gustavi v Moore* [2003] EWHC 3101 (Ch), [2004] BPIR 268. An element of mutuality between claims is also required – *Hurst v Bennett* [2001] EWCA Civ 182, [2001] BPIR 287. Any such cross claims should be raised at this early stage of the procedure to prevent the need for later consideration and potentially wasted costs – *Turner v Royal Bank of Scotland* [2000] BPIR 683. For the relevant principles see *Re A Debtor (No. 87 of 1999)* [2000] BPIR 589.

[59] [2004] EWCA Civ 463, [2004] BPIR 778.

[60] See *Krajczynski v General Guarantee Finance Ltd* [2002] BPIR 324, *Re Bleach* [2002] BPIR 890.

[61] [1994] 3 WLR 847 at 851.

[62] *City Electrical Factors v Hardingham* [1996] BPIR 541.

[63] [1989] 1 WLR 271. See also *Khan v Breezevale SARL* [1996] BPIR 190.

[64] [1999] BPIR 885 at 892.

that the debt forming the demand is immediately payable. It can also exercise discretion to reject the petition if the debtor has made a reasonable offer to pay or offer security and the creditor has unreasonably rejected such offer. In determining the latter issue the courts are most reluctant to find that a creditor has acted unreasonably in rejecting the debtor's offer.[65] For example, in *John Lewis plc v Pearson Burton*[66] Pumfrey J indicated that it would not be unreasonable for a creditor to reject an offer to pay where payment would take some seven years to complete. This stance may be attributed to impatience on the part of the court in that it looks unfavourably upon debtors who wait until this late stage before making such an offer. It may ultimately reflect a contractarian approach on the part of the court based upon principles of *laisser faire* and free bargaining. The court enjoys jurisdiction under s. 266(3) to stay or dismiss petitions and we can remind ourselves that the Court of Appeal urged in *Re Ross (No. 2)*[67] fellow judges to make use of this power in appropriate cases. The court can still make a bankruptcy order even if the underlying debt claim is the subject of an appeal. In such circumstances the court will naturally take into account the prospects of such an appeal being successful.[68] What the court will not permit, however, is for issues that had been determined on the set aside application to be revisited on the hearing of the petition. As the Court of Appeal stressed in *Turner v Royal Bank of Scotland*[69] such a "second bite of the cherry" will only be permitted in exceptional cases where there has subsequently been a real change of circumstances, rendering the matter apt for reconsideration. Equally, as was made clear in *Adams v Mason Bullock*[70] the court will not look kindly upon a debtor who had the opportunity to pursue matters on the hearing of the set aside application but who decided to hold fire until the hearing of the petition. Both cases reflect appropriate concerns with regard to case management.

A dramatic aspect of intervention may come in the form of an annulment order. Annulment has the advantage that the fact of bankruptcy is scrubbed out with the assets being returned to the debtor; however, the liability for debts will be reactivated. This annulment jurisdiction is now governed by s. 282 of the Act.[71] Under this provision the court may annul the order if it should not have been made or if the debts have been fully paid since the order was granted. The former ground is for obvious reasons more frequently relied upon. Although the court clearly enjoys considerable discretion[72] within the parameters of s. 282 it does not possess an inherent and

---

[65]   *Re Gilmartin* [1989] 1 WLR 513, *Re A Debtor (No. 32 of 1993)* [1994] 1 WLR 899, *Re A Debtor (No. 415/SD/1993)* [1994] 1 WLR 917, *Inland Revenue v A Debtor* [1995] BCC 971, *IRC v The Debtor* [1996] BPIR 271, *Maple Division Ltd v Wilson* [1999] BPIR 102, *O'Brien v IRC* [2000] BPIR 306, *Customs and Excise v Dougall* [2001] BPIR 269.
[66]   [2004] BPIR 70.
[67]   [2000] BPIR 636.
[68]   *Westminster CC v Parkin* [2001] BPIR 1156.
[69]   [2000] BPIR 683.
[70]   The Times January 6 2005.
[71]   The power to annul originated in the inherent jurisdiction of the court – *Ex parte Ashworth* (1874) LR 18 Eq 705. See N. Briggs and H. Sims [2002] Ins Law 2.
[72]   As annulment involves the exercise of discretion, an appellate court will be reluctant to upset the conclusion of a trial judge – *Owo-Samson v Barclays Bank (No. 3)* [2003] EWHC 2900 (Ch), [2004] BPIR

unlimited power to annul, a limitation which was acknowledged by Harman J in *Royal Bank of Scotland v The Debtor.*[73] The criteria that the court might see as relevant in cases governed by s. 282(1)(b) were outlined by Deputy Registrar Barnett in *Harper v Buchler.*[74] Firstly the overriding discretion of the court in all cases of annulment was stressed. In exercising this discretion all circumstances of the case are relevant. The duration[75] between the bankruptcy order and annulment application would be relevant to the question of whether statutory interest on debts should be charged – it was not a requirement of every annulment that statutory interest be paid. The source of funding from which bankruptcy debts (and also possibly statutory interest) would be paid might also be a pertinent consideration.

Although the usual applicant for annulment will be the bankrupt, it seems that any interested party may bring this matter to the attention of the court. Thus the wife of a bankrupt has successfully invoked the facility where the aim of the husband in bankrupting himself was to defeat a claim for matrimonial provision.[76] The power to annul is a judicial power and should be exercised with discretion; the mere fact that the petitioning creditor supports the annulment is no guarantee that annulment will be granted because once again the court needs to take account of the principle of collectivity.[77] The court is careful to restrict the effects of this interventionist power. This caution is well reflected by *Choudhury v IRC*[78] where the Court of Appeal was at pains to emphasise that a successful s. 282 application leads only to the bankruptcy order being annulled; the underlying petition remains extant. Indeed, the power will not be exercised at all if the applicant is merely seeking to reopen issues determined at an earlier unsuccessful set aside hearing.[79]

The position with regard to annulment has been modified as a result of changes introduced via the Enterprise Act 2002 particularly with regard to post-bankruptcy IVAs. Debtors may conclude that such an IVA carries with it more benefits than a quick fire bankruptcy followed by discharge.

A potentially much broader review jurisdiction is created by s. 375(1). This enables the court to review any order made in connection with bankruptcy proceedings.[80] The fact that the order in question is being appealed does not exclude the review jurisdiction.[81] It is a jurisdiction, which because of its potential width, requires careful

---

303. The court is under no obligation to annul simply because the terms of s. 282 are met – *Askew v Peter Dominic Ltd* [1997] BPIR 163. On this discretion and disputed debts see *Guinan III v Caldwell Associates* [2004] BPIR 531.

73　[1996] BPIR 478.

74　[2004] BPIR 724.

75　Protracted delay could of course preclude annulment on purely pragmatic grounds – *Gill v Quinn* [2004] EWHC 883 (Ch), [2005] BPIR 129.

76　See *F v F* [1994] 1 FLR 359, *Couvaras v Wolf* [2000] 2 FLR 107 and the comments of Balcombe LJ in *Woodley v Woodley (No. 2)* [1994] 1 WLR 1167 at 1176. See also the discussion in Chapter 6 post.

77　*Housiaux v Customs and Excise* [2003] EWCA Civ 257, [2003] BPIR 858. See also *Leicester v Plumtree Farms* [2004] BPIR 296.

78　[2000] BPIR 246.

79　*Atherton v Ogunlende* [2003] BPIR 21.

80　See D. Milman [1994] 12 Ins Law 5.

81　*Re Northlands Cafe Inc* [1999] BPIR 747 (Queen's Bench of Alberta) following *ex parte Keighley* (1874) LR 9 Ch 667.

handling. In *Re A Debtor (No 32 of 1991)(No.2)*[82] Vinelott J explained the position on the review jurisdiction thus:

> The court's power under s. 375(1) is an exceptional power, not to be found in any other jurisdiction. The reason for conferring this exceptional power on the court in exercising bankruptcy jurisdiction must, I think, lie in the fact that bankruptcy results in a serious restriction on the debtor's freedom of action and on his reputation. It should not be resorted to in place of the ordinary process of appeal, save in cases where the court is satisfied that there has been something amounting to a miscarriage of justice which cannot be corrected by the ordinary process of appeal.

Thus it is clear that s. 375 will not be allowed as an avenue for late appeals[83] or to undermine the principle of *res judicata*.[84] On the latter point repeated and unmeritorious applications under s. 375 might result in the applicant being subjected to a civil restraint order.[85] An illuminating illustration of the review jurisdiction at work is to be found in *Fitch v Official Receiver*.[86] Here the Court of Appeal considered the circumstances under which it might be appropriate to rescind a bankruptcy order because the creditors had changed their mind about the wisdom of initiating a state of bankruptcy. A number of factors were identified as relevant to this determination. The relationship between the annulment and review jurisdictions was discussed by the High Court in *IRC v Robinson*.[87] The conclusion arrived at was that the general power of review must not be used to destroy by a sidewind the specific criteria for annulment as laid down in s. 282. One issue that often arises in cases of review is whether the court is merely exercising a true power of review or is considering the case *de novo*. The outcome of this question is germane both to the administration of justice but also the effective management of litigation. The courts have ruled that where a case is being reviewed the higher court can reach its own conclusion on the facts and can hear fresh evidence.[88] This compares with the position on straightforward or true appeals where the role of the court is more circumscribed, being limited to seeing whether there was an error of law or a serious procedural irregularity at first instance.[89]

We have already seen that the court enjoys a specific power of intervention in IVA cases where material irregularity can be established. It can also effectively negate a supposed IVA by recharacterising it in such a way as to bring it outside the statutory scheme, thereby removing its binding nature on all creditors. No further comment on these matters is required at this stage.

---

[82]   [1994] BCC 524 at 528.
[83]   *Re Debtors (Nos VA7 and VA8) ex parte Stevens* [1996] BPIR 101. A similar philosophy is manifest in *Hurst v Bennett (No. 2)* [2001] EWCA Civ 1398, [2002] BPIR 102 where the court refused to allow a s. 375 application to be used to circumvent the 12-month time limit imposed by s. 255.
[84]   *Brillouet v Hachette Magazines* [1996] BPIR 518. See also *Egleton v IRC* [2003] EWHC 3226 (Ch), [2004] BPIR 476.
[85]   *Hurst v Bennett* [2004] EWCA Civ 230, [2004] BPIR 732.
[86]   [1996] 1 WLR 242.
[87]   [1999] BPIR 329.
[88]   *Re A Debtor (No. 32/SD/1991)* [1993] 1 WLR 314.
[89]   See *Fender v IRC* [2003] BPIR 1304 and *Maloney v St George* [2004] EWHC 1724 (Ch), [2005] BPIR 189.

Temporal Factors

The general approach to time limits is once again more relaxed than it used to be. Thus, under s. 376 the court has the power to ignore specified limits. This explicit statutory provision thus enables the court to ignore other sections in the Act. The court recognised this fact in *Tager v Westpac Banking Corporation*,[90] a case dealing with a contested IVA. Here Judge Weeks had to grapple with the apparent tension between the 28-day time limit for appeals specified in s. 262(3) and the general power of extension expressed in s. 376. The judge explained the problem thus:

> The problem is that there is an inherent conflict between s. 262 standing alone, which seeks to achieve finality and certainty, and s. 376, which introduces an element of flexibility and discretion. In the field of bankruptcy both aims are understandable and desirable, and there may be an inherent tension between the interests of the debtor and the interests of the creditors as well as the age-old conflict between certainty and justice.[91]

Judge Weeks resolved this particular conflict in favour of justice over certainty. In so deciding he drew comfort from an authority under the old bankruptcy regime and concluded:[92]

> If Parliament had intended in 1986 that time limits in respect of decisions at a creditors' meeting on a proposed individual voluntary arrangement should be inviolable then the course to adopt was not to continue to use negative wording and to introduce positive wording for other time limits, but to strengthen the negative wording by making it clear that the power to extend did not apply.

Having said that, time limits are important considerations to be treated with respect because legitimate expectations may be founded upon them. Unravelling actions based upon an understanding of the correct legal position which is then overturned by the court is inherently unattractive. This matter was revisited by HHJ Norris QC in *Warley Continental Services v Johal*[93] where the conclusion was arrived at that it was not appropriate to extend the time for challenging here. Although this refusal to extend time might impact negatively upon the applicant who had much merit in his case there had been no explanation for the delay. The judge noted the policy behind the imposition of such a tight time limit and did not feel that the circumstances of the case justified lifting the deadline. One way around this particular time limit imposed for the challenge of IVAs is to launch a more fundamental attack on the proposal so as to render it incapable of falling under the statutory scheme.[94]

There is, according to s. 268, supposed to be a three-week time limit between the service of the statutory demand and the presentation of the winding up petition. This represents one final chance for the debtor to pay up or to take professional advice.

---

[90] [1998] BCC 73. See also *Re A Debtor (No. 488 IO of 1996)* [1999] 2 BCLC 571.
[91] Ibid at 76.
[92] Ibid at 77. The 1914 Act authority cited was *Re Vanbergen* [1955] 1 WLR 20.
[93] [2004] BPIR 353 – see M. Mulligan and J. Tribe (2002) 18 IL&P 190.
[94] *Re Plummer* [2004] BPIR 767.

That said, this interval may be misused by the debtor who may be tempted to dispose of assets to frustrate the creditor. Although such disposals are vulnerable to challenge that vulnerability is crucially dependent upon the hazards of avoidance litigation. Thus s. 270 permits the presentation of an expedited petition and this facility may be taken advantage of in an appropriate case, even though there is an extant set aside application. There may in other cases be a time limit for lodging an appeal, though such a limit will always be subject to the inherent power of the court to override it.[95] Time limits assume particular significance in situations where transaction avoidance may be a possibility. Thus, under s. 341 a fixed period of six months prior to the bankruptcy commencing is specified for challenging preferences. Transactions at an undervalue are vulnerable for a five-year period and preferences in favour of connected persons can be impugned within an extended two-year period. As these limits may be critical to establishing substantive rights it is a fair bet that they cannot be overridden by judicial whim.[96] In considering whether to adjourn bankruptcy petitions the question of time limits for avoidance purposes looms large.[97] Temporal issues can arise in many other bankruptcy episodes.[98]

Fresh Evidence

An issue that frequently crops up in bankruptcy cases is whether on an appeal or review of a prior judicial decision fresh evidence can be admitted. The traditional rule here as expressed in *Ladd v Marshall*[99] was that fresh evidence should not be admitted where there had been a trial on the merits. This rule of civil procedure is designed to produce finality in litigation and also reflects the view that a party should not enter a courtroom with a case that has not be fully prepared. In the event of a case not being ready the appropriate course is to seek an adjournment. The rule in *Ladd v Marshall*[100] is a product of the common law. Has it been affected by the advent of the Civil Procedure Rules? This question was raised in *Lombard Nat West Factors v Arbis*[101] and the conclusion of Hart J was that the rule was very much alive. This conclusion is hardly surprising in an era where case management is to the fore. The modern expression of this principle is to

---

[95] *Re A Debtor (no. 799 of 1994) ex parte Cobbs Property Services* [1996] BPIR 575 (appealing against a bankruptcy order).
[96] For the critical importance of time limits see *Clarkson v Clarkson* [1994] BCC 921. Although Parliament has introduced some flexibility through the medium of s. 423 of the Insolvency Act 1986, this provision is difficult to invoke successfully, particularly as the waters get muddier the further away from the date of the commencement of the bankruptcy the disputed transaction occurred – see here *Re Brabon* [2000] BPIR 537.
[97] *Neely v IRC* [1996] BPIR 632.
[98] For example, the relative rights of creditors and the bankrupt's family towards the family home change after one year of bankruptcy, with the rights of the creditor becoming paramount after that period – see s. 335A. The three-year "use it or lose it" rule introduced with regard to the sale of the family home by Enterprise Act 2002 s. 261 (inserting s. 283A into the 1986 Act) should also be noted. Even in cases where no fixed time limit is breached, unreasonable delay could create problems in securing a remedy (e.g. with respect to annulment) – *Gill v Quinn* [2004] EWHC 883 (Ch), [2005] BPIR 129.
[99] [1954] 1 WLR 1489.
[100] *Supra.*
[101] [2000] BPIR 79.

be found in Civil Procedure Rules r. 52.11(2) which adopts a slightly different formulation namely that fresh evidence should not be admitted unless it is necessary to ensure that the overriding objective of securing civil justice is achieved. It is doubtful if this represents any significant change in practice and at the end of the day the court will look at why the evidence was not adduced earlier and the potential impact on each of the parties in admitting the evidence at this later stage.[102] To what extent does this rule operate in bankruptcy cases? Firstly, set aside applications do not involve a determination of the case on its merits and therefore the rule in *Ladd v Marshall*[103] does not apply, with the result that fresh evidence may be admitted on an appeal against a set aside decision.[104] The CPR would not appear to change the position here. A decision on a hearing of a bankruptcy petition is clearly a trial on the merits and the exclusionary rule (as restated in modified form in the CPR) does indeed operate.[105]

Costs

The general rule on costs is that the loser pays both the costs of itself and the successful party. Thus a debtor who has been bankrupted must foot the bill out of the estate for the bankruptcy proceedings.[106] These costs are dealt with specifically by Insolvency Rules 1986 r. 6.224(1)(h) which places an appropriate priority on this item. If bankruptcy is averted by the debtor making a last minute settlement with creditors, he would normally be expected to meet the costs of the petitioner, unless there are special circumstances present.[107] Conversely, an unsuccessful petitioner would normally have to find the costs of the successful debtor[108] unless the conduct of the debtor was such as to render that debtor responsible for the initiation of the proceedings.[109] The court retains the power under s. 51 of the Supreme Court Act 1981 to impose a liability for costs on a third party, though the scope for this in bankruptcy cases is more restricted than one finds in winding up cases.[110] Having said that, solicitors may also be subjected to a wasted costs order if they have acted in such a way as to encourage or prolong unnecessary litigation.[111]

---

[102] *Sadrolashrafi v Marvel International Food Logistics Ltd* [2004] EWHC 777 (Ch), [2004] BPIR 834.
[103] [1954] 1 WLR 1489.
[104] *Royal Bank of Scotland v Binnell* [1996] BPIR 352, *Norman Laurier v United Overseas Bank* [1996] BPIR 635, *AIB Finance Ltd v Alsop* [1998] BCC 780, *Salvidge v Hussein* [1999] BPIR 410, *Heavy Duty Parts Ltd v Anelay* [2004] EWHC 960 (Ch), [2004] BPIR 729. Compare *Neely v IRC* [1996] BPIR 473.
[105] See also *Purvis v Customs and Excise* [1999] BPIR 396 – appeal against a review decision made in bankruptcy proceedings where fresh evidence was admitted.
[106] Unless costs have been increased by errors appearing in the creditor's petition.
[107] *Fitzgerald and Law v Ralph* [1998] BPIR 49, *Oben v Blackman* [2000] BPIR 302.
[108] See *Re A Debtor (No. 620 of 1997)*, The Times June 18 1998 where the petitioner withdrew the petition in order to get the disputed debt resolved at trial; the court ruled that the petitioner must pay the debtor's costs on the petition.
[109] In *Re Ross (No. 3)* [2002] BPIR 185 the debtor was successful in resisting the petition but was only awarded 75% of his costs. For further proceedings in this case on the costs issue see *Ross v Stonewood Securities Ltd* [2004] EWHC 2235 (Ch), [2005] BPIR 196.
[110] See here *Re Mordant* [1996] BPIR 302, *Vickery v Modern Security Systems* [1998] BPIR 164 and *Re Ross (No. 3)* (supra).
[111] See Courts and Legal Services Act 1990 s. 4 and the useful discussion in H. Evans (2001) 64 MLR 51.

Overview

Looking at this mass of authorities one trend is apparent. That is the willingness of the courts to view liberally procedural flaws by the creditor whilst at the same time cracking down hard on lapses by the debtor. This pattern has already been identified in the context of statutory demands, but it is much more pervasive than that. It really reflects a swing in sympathy away from debtors at a time when the official policy of the legislature is to liberalise personal insolvency law.

Chapter 3

The Bankrupt's Estate[1]

Why is the Estate Critical?

The bankrupt's "estate" is the central functional concept underpinning the operation of bankruptcy law. Securing and realising the estate is, after all, the main rationale of the bankruptcy regime. How that estate is first defined, then protected and finally realised will affect not only the prospects of the creditors recovering their debts, but also the future rehabilitation of the bankrupt and the wellbeing of the bankrupt's family. The relative effectiveness of the estate rules will also impact significantly upon the perceived status of the bankruptcy institution as a whole. In *Re Rae*[2] Warner J provided a clear summary of the rationale for the estate rules:

> Bankruptcy, putting it in the simplest terms, is a process whereby on the one hand all a debtor's property, with certain specific exceptions, is vested in his trustee in bankruptcy for realisation and distribution of the proceeds among his creditors and, on the other hand, he is forever relieved of personal liability to those creditors.

We are told by s. 306 of the Insolvency Act 1986 that the estate vests *automatically* in the trustee on bankruptcy once the appointment is made. This, of course, begs the question as to what that estate comprises. The legislation does offer some assistance in this regard but there is no gainsaying the fact courts have played a critical role in mapping out the parameters of the bankruptcy estate. Judicial creativity has not been stifled by the dead hand of legislation. On the contrary, certain judicial decisions have in some cases frustrated current legislative policy.

Parameters of the Estate

The central statutory provision governing the composition of the estate is s. 283.

---

[1]   For analysis see S. Elwes (2004) 20 IL&P 5. The concept of the estate has not been a problematical feature of IVA law in that where a debtor seeks to have a voluntary arrangement approved by creditors he may agree to pool assets to provide a managed fund to produce income or realisations. The existence and parameters of that fund, however, are essentially matters of contract. Having said that, issues of "estate" definition can crop up in IVA cases – *Welburn v Dibb Lupton Broomhead* [2002] EWCA Civ 1601, [2003] BPIR 768. What is clear is that an IVA backed by assets has a much greater chance of success – see Chapter 7.

[2]   [1995] BCC 102 at 111.

This provides that the estate comprises all property belonging to or vested in the bankrupt at the commencement of the bankruptcy, together with property that is deemed by the remainder of Part IX to be so included. Section 436 offers a broad interpretation of "property" for these purposes:

> Property includes money, goods, things in action, land and every description of property wherever situated and also obligations and every description of interest, whether present or future or vested or contingent, arising out of, or incidental to, property.

The estate thus comprises both legal and beneficial interests vested absolutely in the bankrupt.[3] Intangible assets such as goodwill, intellectual property rights or secret processes are also encompassed.[4] There are no territorial limits on what may be included in the estate, though actual realisation may be affected by practical constraints.[5] A good indication of the breadth of the bankruptcy estate is provided by *Dear v Reeves*[6] where the Court of Appeal held, eschewing a precedent from conveyancing law,[7] that a right of pre-emption (i.e. a right of first refusal on property to be sold) was capable of falling within the definition of property and therefore fell within the estate for bankruptcy purposes.

> A distinguishing feature of a right of property, in contrast to a purely personal right, is that it is transferable: it may be enforced by someone other than the particular person in whom the right was initially vested. This right of pre-emption has that feature.

In response to a claim that such a right had no commercial value Mummery LJ retorted with irrefutable logic that if that were so there would be no need for the present contested litigation!

The inclusion of a wide range of pension benefits (an issue discussed below) within the estate is typical of modern judicial attitudes. When deciding whether an asset falls within the estate the courts are aware of the social policy implications but these will not be allowed to force the day. In *Cork v Rawlins*[8] Chadwick LJ made this clear:

> It is plainly in the general public interest that persons should be encouraged to make provision against the possibility that they will be unable to meet their commitments as a result of misfortune for which they are not responsible. But if public policy requires that they should be encouraged to do so by permitting them to shelter that provision from the claims of their

---

[3]   *St Thomas' Hospital v Richardson* [1901] 1 KB 21, *Rooney v Cardona* [1999] BPIR 291 (bankrupt was the beneficiary of a life policy held on trust and the fact that he was also trustee does not exclude the policy from the estate). See also the useful discussion by the Federal Court of Australia in *Re Silverstein* [1999] BPIR 813. This wide statutory definition of the estate is mirrored in other jurisdictions e.g. s. 541 of US Bankruptcy Code.

[4]   *Re Keene* [1922] 2 Ch 475.

[5]   *Singh v Official Receiver* [1997] BPIR 530, *Pollard v Ashurst* [2000] BPIR 347. These realisation difficulties have eased somewhat for assets located in EU member states as the EC Regulation on Insolvency Proceedings (1346/2000) will promote recognition of the status of UK insolvency practitioners in EU jurisdictions.

[6]   [2001] BPIR 577.

[7]   *Pritchard v Briggs* [1980] Ch 338.

[8]   [2001] BPIR 222 at 233.

creditors, then it is for Parliament to say so. It is not, in my view, for the courts to distort the bankruptcy code in order to achieve that result.

It has never been the case that all assets in the possession of the bankrupt form part of the estate for bankruptcy purposes; under the 1705 Act (4 Anne, c.17) a bankrupt was permitted to retain 5% of his assets. Again returning to *Re Rae*[9] Warner J provides an explanation for these exceptions:

The specific exceptions exist either because the property is not appropriate for distribution among the bankrupt's creditors, such as property of which he is only a trustee, or because, unlike an insolvent company, the bankrupt is a human being whose life must continue during and after insolvency.

Bearing this general observation in mind we see why trust assets have always been excluded[10] and so are other items which have been appropriated in favour of some third party.[11] However, mortgaged property is included, subject to the rights of the secured creditor (see s. 283(5)). Increasingly, a range of personal possessions have been put outwith the trustee's grasp.[12] "Tools of the trade" are excluded from vesting in the estate by virtue of s. 283(2)(a) of the Act. This category includes tools, books, vehicles and items of equipment necessary for use in the bankrupt's employment, business or vocation. The thinking here, as explained by the Cork Committee (para 1096), is that the bankrupt may need these to remain productive and thereby to be rehabilitated. A recent illustration of this concession at work is found in the case of *Pike v Cork Gully*[13] where the Court of Appeal viewed a horse box as falling within the concept of the tools of the trade of a bankrupt in the circumstances of this particular bankruptcy. This "personal possession" category has been modified in recent years. On the one hand, the general exemption has been extended to remove a wider range of personal items from the estate.[14] This strategy has been compensated to some extent in the case of so-called luxury items; under a procedure outlined in s. 308 of the Insolvency Act 1986 (and IR 1986 rr. 6.187-6.188) these can be sold by the trustee and the bankrupt given a cheaper version with the estate pocketing the difference. Where this approach is adopted, the purchase of the replacement takes priority over other financial claims on the estate as Michael Hart QC explained in *Re*

---

[9]   [1995] BCC 102 at 111.

[10]   See now s. 283(3)(a) and the Northern Irish case of *Re McKeown* [1974] NI 226. IVA trusts are effective in the event of the debtor subsequently being adjudicated bankrupt – *Re Coath* [2000] BPIR 981. The costs incurred in unravelling trust assets from the estate may be treated as a bankruptcy expense – *Re Sobey* [1999] BPIR 1009.

[11]   If the debtor has paid a sum of money into court prior to bankruptcy that money no longer forms part of his estate – *Re Ford* [1900] 2 QB 211. See also *Re Mordant* [1996] BPIR 302.

[12]   These exemptions (e.g. for bedding and clothing) mirror the old exemptions from the bailiff's power of distraint – see County Courts Act 1959 s. 129.

[13]   [1997] BPIR 723.

[14]   For discussion see D. Milman (1989) 4 IL& P 71. This pattern of exclusions from the estate is replicated in a number of jurisdictions – Ireland (Bankruptcy Act 1988 s. 45(1)); Australia (Bankruptcy Act 1966 s. 116(2)); Canada (Bankruptcy and Insolvency Act s. 67(1)(b)).

Rayatt.[15] There is no empirical evidence[16] to indicate how regularly this power is resorted to and there is a suspicion that it may be a cosmetic provision for public relations purposes rather than a significant contribution to asset maximisation. Certainly, the courts are ambivalent about its usage and have indicated that trustees may in some cases be exploiting it simply as a way of "talking tough" with the bankrupt rather than as a genuine tool to maximise asset values. Student loans held by a bankrupt are specifically excluded from the estate.[17] This reflects a policy of protecting the interest of the state as creditor and maintaining public confidence in the student loan system. It is a policy concern that is by no means unique to the UK. We shall return to this issue when considering the consequences of discharge in Chapter 7. A further statutory exclusion has been introduced through the enactment of the Proceeds of Crime Act 2002. This legislation deals with procedures to recover assets from individuals convicted of crime (for example drug trafficking). If a recovery procedure under criminal legislation is already afoot by the time the bankruptcy commences then that recovery process can run its course.[18] If, however, bankruptcy commences before a recovery process is started, then the recovery of assets is subordinated to bankruptcy principles.[19] In other words, we have adopted a familiar legal solution of the first in time prevailing.

A novel addition to the "personal possessions" exemption was encountered in the celebrated case of *Haig v Aitken.*[20] Here Rattee J held that certain private papers belonging to the imprisoned former Cabinet Minister Jonathan Aitken could not be seized by his trustee in bankruptcy. These papers admittedly had a commercial value and prima facie fell within the concept of property as defined by s. 436, but Rattee J opined that Parliament could not have intended that private documents be expropriated in this way.

> In my judgment it is inconceivable that Parliament really envisaged, by passing the Insolvency Act, that the effect of bankruptcy should be that a bankrupt's personal correspondence should be available for publication to the world at large by sale at the behest of the trustee in bankruptcy. In my opinion, the concept of such a gross invasion of privacy is repugnant.

---

[15]   [1998] BPIR 495.

[16]   For another rare case of section 308 being utilised see *Pike v Cork Gully* (supra).

[17]   Higher Education Act 2004 s. 42 and reg 5 of the Education (Student Support) (No. 2) Regulations 2002 (Amendment No. 3) Regulations 2004 (SI 2004/2041) – these provisions amend s. 22 of the Teaching and Higher Education Act 1998 and reg 39 of the Education (Student Support) (No. 2) Regulations 2002 (SI 2002/3200) with 1 September 2004 being specified as the cut-off date for the new regime. For student loans made under earlier regimes, e.g. the Education (Student Loans) Act 1990 Schedule 2 para 5(1) transitional provisions apply. Note that such an exclusion by other legislation is anticipated by s. 283(6) of the Insolvency Act 1986.

[18]   Proceeds of Crime Act 2002 s. 417(2)(a). Note also Insolvency Act 1986 s. 306A–C which provide for the revesting in the estate of the property once the restraint order, etc., is discharged.

[19]   Proceeds of Crime Act 2002 s. 418. For discussion of the interface between recovery remedies and bankruptcy see K. Rees (1996) 12 IL&P 120.

[20]   [2000] BPIR 462. An entertaining account of the background to the case is to be found in the autobiographical *Pride and Perjury* (2000) (Harper Collins) at 363.

In so ruling Rattee J referred to s. 311 of the Act, which he believed related only to financial documents. If necessary, Rattee J would also have been prepared to support the bankrupt's case on the basis of the right to privacy conferred by Art. 8 of the European Convention on Human Rights (now incorporated into English law by virtue of the Human Rights Act 1998). It will be interesting to see whether this supposed exception is supported by other judges in future cases. One can certainly foresee difficulties in determining what is private correspondence, particularly in an era where many public figures have few qualms about converting so-called private correspondence into profitable autobiographies. In reality the accumulation of such documentation by a public figure is often viewed as providing the basis for an additional "pension". If so, it should be treated on a comparable basis to pensions.

The general norm is that the trustee can assert no better claim to property than could the bankrupt himself.[21] From 1623 it used to be the case that assets in the possession of the bankrupt of which he *appeared* to be the *reputed owner* would be treated as estate assets (see s. 38(2)(c) of the Bankruptcy Act 1914 for a statutory exposition of that principle). That much-criticised[22] doctrine of reputed ownership, which owed much to a fear of fraud where ownership and possession were separated,[23] was increasingly marginalised[24] during the 20th century with the growth of hire purchase and other social changes relating to personal credit and it was eventually abolished in 1985 in the wake of a strong recommendation from the Cork Committee (para 1093). The estate can, however, encompass assets vesting in the bankrupt after the date of the adjudication. Under the old law such items automatically vested in the trustee without requiring any action on the part of the trustee.[25] This was perceived to cause practical difficulties particularly in the case of worthless items which would then have to be disclaimed and now such property will only be brought into the estate pool if positively claimed by the trustee exercising powers under s. 307 (as supplemented by IR 1986 rr 6.200-6.202).[26] Such items might include bequests, lottery winnings,[27] tax rebates,[28] insurance payouts,[29] and other windfalls.[30] In line with general reforms

---

[21] *McEntire v Crossley* [1895] AC 459.

[22] See Parke B in *Belcher v Bellamy* (1848) 2 Exch 303.

[23] See E. Jenks, *A Short History of English Law* (1912) at 236–237.

[24] The Cork Committee (Cmnd 8558 para 1086) identified *Re Fox* [1948] Ch 407 as the last case where the concept was successfully invoked by a trustee. Here building materials in a builder's yard were held to be in the reputed ownership of the bankrupt builder even though they belonged to a supplier. The opposite conclusion was arrived at with regard to materials on site.

[25] *Re Pascoe* [1944] Ch 219.

[26] See *Re X* [1996] BPIR 494 and *Hardy v Buchler* [1997] BPIR 643.

[27] On the assumption of course that the winnings do belong to the bankrupt – *Abrahams v Trustee in Bankruptcy of Abrahams* [1999] BPIR 637.

[28] However, this is only true if the rebate relates to pre-bankruptcy earnings – *Re Wagner* (1980) 117 DLR (3d) 414. See the illuminating discussion by the Canadian Supreme Court in *re Marzetti* [1998] BPIR 732.

[29] *Cork v Rawlins* [2001] BPIR 222 – but the insurance money cannot be claimed by the estate if it represents compensation for pain and suffering.

[30] See *Trustee of FC Jones v Jones* [1996] BPIR 644 (need to avoid unjust enrichment). Compare *Abrahams v Trustee of the Property of Abrahams* [1999] BPIR 637 where the lottery ticket was bought by the wife of the bankrupt and the court found a resulting trust in her favour. An unusual windfall arising as

noted above student loans are excepted. This change in the law thus reflects a desire to maximise the freedom of manoeuvre enjoyed by trustees in bankruptcy when managing the estate and its constituent parts. Having said that, the court stressed in *Solomons v Williams*[31] that the trustee must strictly observe deadlines when making a claim under s. 307. This is necessary in order to promote certainty. When reviewing this category it should be noted that assets coming to the bankrupt for the first time after discharge (where no right existed before discharge) cannot be claimed by the trustee.[32]

The boundaries of the estate have thus changed over time. The range of exempt assets has grown. However, empirical evidence from the US finds no evidence that this pattern of change has had a detrimental effect on creditors at large. In the US the position on exempt assets is quite complex and involves an interaction between federal law and state law.[33] The same is true to some extent of Canada.[34]

The Family Home

The most significant asset held by any bankrupt will normally be a private residence. With property price inflation that significance has become more skewed. This property may be the sole family home. It may be jointly owned by a spouse (or unmarried partner) or at least occupied by a spouse, partner or children. Under English bankruptcy law the starting point is that the house is included in the estate: there is no "homestead" exception unlike the concession found in a number of jurisdictions in North America.[35] Clearly the realisation of this "jewel in the crown" of the bankrupt's estate is a top priority for any trustee in bankruptcy. However, the law increasingly places limitations upon the realisation process. As these limitations relate to the interests of non-debtors and involve delicate issues as to the balancing of competing social interests, we will consider them later in Chapter 6. The Enterprise Act 2002 has made significant changes in this area.[36] Although it did not implement the idea of a "homestead" exception it placed restrictions on the right of the trustee to delay action on realising the family home by introducing a requirement that action must be taken within three years or the estate would lose the benefit of the family home asset.[37] Moreover, certain "low

---

a result of a trustee's disclaimer of a lease (which turned out to have value when it was sold) was encountered in *Lee v Lee* [1999] BPIR 926. On the other hand, a mere *spes* that materialises after the commencement of the bankruptcy could not be claimed in *Re A Bankrupt (No. 145 of 1995)* [1996] BPIR 238, but probably because the compensation payment belatedly received related to personal injury.

[31] [2001] BPIR 1123.

[32] *Re Stockwell* (Evans-Lombe J, unreported) New Law Online 25 June 1999.

[33] See W.D. Warren and D.J. Bussel, *Bankruptcy* (2002) at 40 et seq.

[34] See J. Ziegel, *Comparative Consumer Insolvency Regimes: A Canadian Perspective* (2003) at 21-25.

[35] In a number of US states (e.g. Texas and Florida) and Canadian Provinces the homestead is excluded from the estate. It has been suggested that the idea emanates ultimately from Spanish law – see "A Fresh Start" at paras 4.1–4.18, 8.1–8.8 and the later White Paper, "A Second Chance" at para 1.5 where the homestead idea was not pursued further.

[36] See S. Frieze [2004] 17 Ins Intell 106.

[37] Enterprise Act 2002 s. 261 inserting s. 313A and s. 283A into the Insolvency Act 1986. See C. Hiley [2003] Recov (Summer) 18. For an abortive attempt to give the three-year time limit retrospective effect see *Vidyarthi v Clifford* [2004] EWHC 2084 (Ch), [2005] BPIR 232.

value" properties were entirely excluded from the estate.[38] Modifications were made to the s. 313 charging system to further protect the interests of the bankrupt.[39]

Income

It is apparent from s. 307(5) that the continuing income of the bankrupt does not form part of the estate unless specifically attached by an income payments order made under s. 310 of the Insolvency Act 1986. This exclusion was clearly articulated by judges under the former regime where the point was made that to deprive a bankrupt of his income would be to reduce him to the status of a slave of the trustee.[40] Having acknowledged that clear-cut point, the relationship between income and capital is a difficult legal distinction to grasp, as the experience in a number of areas of English law attests. In *Supperstone v Lloyds Names Association*[41] Evans-Lombe J explained that a sum of money may still be characterised as income notwithstanding it emanates from an irregular or one-off payment; each case turns on its own facts. In *Dennison v Krasner* [42] Chadwick LJ confirmed that income produced from preexisting rights at the date of bankruptcy formed part of the estate and did not require to be appropriated by an income payments order. Only genuinely "new" income fell within the ambit of s. 310. Another instructive authority here is provided by the Canadian Supreme Court in *Re Marzetti*[43] where it was held that an income tax refund was to be viewed as wages for the purposes of s. 68 of the Canadian Bankruptcy and Insolvency Act and therefore this statutory mechanism prevailed over the wide ambit given to the estate by s. 67. Notwithstanding this general rule special principles apply to share dividends. The position here is that on the bankruptcy of a shareholder the trustee in bankruptcy does not automatically become a member.[44] Dividends therefore remain payable to the bankrupt but should then be handed over to the trustee. The position with regard to income payments orders (and income payments agreements) will be reviewed in Chapter 7.

Causes of Action

One of the most vexed issues in bankruptcy law concerns the fate of causes of action vested in the bankrupt prior to the date of bankruptcy. A prior cause of action, which is a thing in action within the meaning of s. 436, will in general be viewed as an asset

---

[38] Ibid s. 261.   As to what constitutes a low value property see SI 2004/547.
[39] Ibid s. 313.
[40] See *Re Wilson, ex parte Vine* (1887) 8 Ch D 364 at 366 per James LJ and *Affleck v Hammond* [1912] 3 KB 162.
[41] [1999] BPIR 832.
[42] [2000] BPIR 410.
[43] [1998] BPIR 732.
[44] *Morgan v Gray* [1953] 1 Ch 83.

properly belonging to the estate.[45] Causes of action have commercial value in that they may be successfully pursued, settled or assigned.[46] So far so good. These conclusions are perfectly consistent with the inclusive embrace of s. 436. In *Ord v Upton*[47] Aldous LJ entered the following note of caution:

> Section 436 is not in truth a definition of the word "property". It only sets out what is included. As will appear later from the cases that have been decided over many years, actions which relate to a bankrupt's personal reputation or body have not been considered to be property and therefore do not vest in anybody other than the bankrupt.

Thus, certain personal claims (such as defamation actions or claims in respect of personal injury) do not fall within this inclusive category and therefore remain the property of the bankrupt.[48] Where the claim is mixed or "hybrid"– such as a claim for compensation against a tortfeasor where the plaintiff is claiming damages both for personal injury and loss of earnings – the possibility of apportionment between the bankrupt and the estate is present as the Court of Appeal indicated in *Ord v Upton*.[49] The methodology was explained as follows by Aldous LJ:

---

[45] *Heath v Tang* [1993] 1 WLR 1421. See also *Hunt v Peasegood* [2001] BPIR 76, *Francis v National Mutual Life Association* [2001] BPIR 480, *Qayoumi v Qayoumi* [2003] EWHC 2961 (Ch), [2004] BPIR 620, *Simmons v Mole Valley DC* [2004] EWHC 475 (Ch), [2004] BPIR 1022. A bankrupt is also deprived of any right of appeal which also vests in the estate – *Boyd and Hutchinson (A Firm) v Foenander* [2003] EWCA Civ 1516, [2004] BPIR 20. Compare *Cummings v Claremont Petroleum* [1998] BPIR 187.

[46] The 1603 Act (1 Jac I, c. 15) provides an early recognition of this fact by permitting the Commissioners to assign debts due to a bankrupt. The power to assign is implicit in Schedule 5 para 3 – for examples of its usage see *Weddell v Pearce (JA) & Major* [1988] Ch 26, *Re Cirillo* [1997] BPIR 166, *Official Receiver v Davis* [1998] BPIR 771. The assignment may be back to the bankrupt personally but this is a delicate matter requiring caution – *Re Papaloizu* [1999] BPIR 106. On the dangers of assignment to a third party without first giving the defendant an opportunity to buy the claim see the comments of Lightman J in *Hopkins v TL Dallas Group Ltd* [2004] EWHC 1379 (Ch) at [105].

[47] [2000] 2 WLR 755 at 760.

[48] *Beckham v Drake* (1849) 2 HLCas 579 (general exclusionary principle discussed), *Re Wilson, Ex parte Vine* (1887) 8 Ch D 364 (damages for slander), *Rose v Buckett* [1901] 2 KB 449 (trespass to goods claim but main element related to distress), *Bailey v Thurston & Co Ltd* [1903] 1 KB 137 (wrongful dismissal claim), *Wilson v United Counties Bank* [1920] 1 AC 102 (damage to reputation), *Collins v Official Receiver* [1996] BPIR 553 (personal injuries damages), *Re A Bankrupt (No. 145 of 1995)* [1996] BPIR 238 (criminal injuries compensation), *Nelson v Nelson* [1997] 1 WLR 233 at 236 per Peter Gibson LJ (restatement of general principle). For comparable Canadian authority see *Re Ritenburg* (1961) 33 DLR 498, *Re Holley* (1986) 26 DLR (4th) 230, *Lang v McKenna* [1996] BPIR 553 and *Rahall v McLennan* [2000] DLR 1. A claim for matrimonial relief by a bankrupt spouse would also not pass to the trustee – see by analogy *D(J) v D(S)* [1973] 1 All ER 349.

[49] [2000] 2 WLR 755 – discussed by R.S. Sharpe [2001] Ins Law 182. A personal injury claim that features a loss of earnings element is hybrid – *Re Bell* [1998] BPIR 27. If the trustee in bankruptcy refuses to pursue such a mixed claim the bankrupt (as a beneficiary of part of the claim) could arguably commence proceedings in his own name and join the trustee as a defendant. See also *Haq v Singh* [2001] BPIR 1002 where the purported assignment of the claim to the bankrupt was frustrated by limitation. If this strategy produces a successful result the trustee may claim the benefit of the hybrid element – *Davis v Trustee of Estate of Davis* [1998] BPIR 578.

I believe that when there is but one cause of action which includes a head of damage relating to property, then the cause of action vests in the trustee as it does not fall within an exception to the general rule. If so, the right to recover the damages which are personal and any damages which are recovered are held on constructive trust for the bankrupt by the trustee.[50]

This is a neat solution but three recent cases illustrate the real problems that may be encountered in trying to apply these rules in practice. In *Grady v Prison Service*[51] a former prison officer made a number of employment-related claims against her former employer. The Court of Appeal, having decided that this was not a case of hybrid claims but rather three distinct claims, ruled, somewhat unexpectedly, that a claim for unfair dismissal was personal to the bankrupt as a theoretical remedy was reinstatement. The claim therefore fell outside the estate. Having thus concluded, ironically the Court of Appeal added that the proceeds of a successful claim might be captured by the estate (presumably by virtue of the after-acquired property rules). An even more extreme example of the problem is provided by *Mulkerrins v PricewaterhouseCoopers*,[52] a case which provoked the ire of Lord Millett when it eventually reached the House of Lords (see the passage quoted above at page 5). The case concerned a right of action to sue a firm of insolvency practitioners for failure to process an IVA proposal with the result that the claimant was unnecessarily adjudged bankrupt. This cause of action was found not to vest in the trustee because the complaint did not crystallise until the bankruptcy commenced. Notwithstanding this curious reasoning the House of Lords ruled that it was improper for the insolvency practitioners (who had not been parties to the original ruling) to seek to relitigate the point. The complexities in this area of law have been added to by the ruling of the Court of Appeal in *Khan v Trident Safeguards Ltd.*[53] Here the Court of Appeal by a majority decision (Arden and Buxton LJJ, Wall LJ dissenting) indicated that a claim alleging race discrimination would not necessarily be viewed as "hybrid" within the terms of *Ord v Upton*[54] if the remedy sought was limited to a declaration and compensation for injured feelings (which would clearly be viewed as a personal claim). In reaching this conclusion public policy came to the fore in the minds of the majority and in particular the need to ensure that claims alleging discrimination were not stifled by the technicalities of bankruptcy law. Buxton LJ argued:

> I do not think that it would be right to shut him out just because he is a bankrupt whose trustee has no interest in pursuing claims that Mr Khan does not now make.

Buxton LJ also hinted that for a legal system to obstruct such a claim simply because the complainant was bankrupt might be a disproportionate response and so breach the terms of Art 6 ECHR. Therefore in this particular instance the applicant was

---

[50]   [2000] 2 WLR 755 at 769-770.
[51]   [2003] EWCA Civ 527, [2003] BPIR 823.
[52]   [2003] UKHL 41, [2003] 1 WLR 1937. For comment see D. Capper [2003] Ins Law 234.
[53]   [2004] EWCA Civ 624, [2004] BPIR 881. See D. Preston, S. Morgan and A. Brown [2004] 17 Ins Intell 142.
[54]   Supra.

permitted to amend the claim to restrict the remedies sought. Quite frankly, this is a curious decision. Clearly the courts, mindful of the fact that they are operating in a pluralistic society, are anxious not to be seen to be stifling such claims by letting technicalities of bankruptcy law dominate the day. However, they have produced an uncertain brew. Far better to have stuck to the *Ord v Upton*[55] guidelines and to have pushed for the promulgation of professional guidelines to advise trustees on the exploitation of such sensitive claims.

Contractual Rights

The trustee may inherit the rights of a bankrupt under a contract as the contract itself would be regarded as "property" because these rights would be akin to a cause of action.[56] Rights of appeal arising under a contract may also vest in the trustee in bankruptcy.[57] Having said that, personal contracts, such as contracts for the performance of personal services, would not normally be so regarded.[58] This exception can probably be explained by reference to the attendant difficulties in enforcement.

Social Benefits

By definition a bankrupt will be short of cash. He or she may be receiving social benefits from the state. To what extent can the trustee lay claim to these? Income related benefits do not, according to the decision of the House of Lords in *Mulvey v Secretary of State for Social Security*,[59] fall within the estate; instead they form part of a reserved income for the bankrupt and therefore can be subject to a right to recoupment exercised by the social security authorities. The English courts came to the same conclusion in *R v Secretary of State for Social Security ex parte Taylor*[60] where it was held by Keene J that, notwithstanding the protection offered by s. 285 against actions hostile to the estate, the authorities could still make deductions from benefits to ensure that social fund loans were recouped. Apart from protecting the needs of the exchequer these cases are consistent with the general rule that income is not comprised in the estate.

---

[55]	Supra.
[56]	*Beckham v Drake* (1849) 2 HL Cas 579, *Morris v Morgan* [1998] BPIR 764.
[57]	*Morris v Morgan* (supra).
[58]	*Lucas v Moncrieff* (1905) 21 TLR 683. Unless executed and producing income as a result – *Bailey v Thurston & Co Ltd* [1903] 1 KB 137 at 145–6 per Cozens-Hardy LJ, *Royal Bank of Canada and Burlingham Associates Inc v Chetty* [1997] BPIR 137 (executed conditional fee agreement) and *Performing Right Society v Rowland* [1998] BPIR 128 (royalties formed part of estate).
[59]	[1997] BPIR 696.
[60]	[1997] BPIR 505.

Pensions

The interface between the inclusive demands of bankruptcy law and the priorities of social policy in an ageing population has been tested to the limit in the area of pension rights. For many years the law was settled and in practice trustees left alone pension rights. Normally under the terms of a pension scheme the entry of a pension holder into bankruptcy would lead to a forfeiture of rights under the scheme.[61] By using the device of a protective trust to prevent the estate creditors claiming the benefits of the fund, the trustees would retain discretion to disburse the pension as they thought fit – e.g. to a spouse. The calm was shattered by the ruling of Ferris J in *Re Landau*[62] where the benefits arising under a personal pension were held to vest in the estate. Such benefits could not be construed either as after-acquired property or income and so they were automatically appropriated to the estate. This controversial decision (which caused panic for many self-employed persons) was mirrored in a number of other subsequent decisions both in the UK[63] and in comparable foreign jurisdictions.[64]

This matter was revisited by the Court of Appeal in *Dennison* v *Krasner (Lesser v Lawrence)*.[65] In spite of predictions that a different approach might have been taken the Court of Appeal upheld the views expressed by Ferris J., concluding that retirement annuities and personal pension policies automatically vested in the trustee pursuant to s. 306 without the need for the making of an income payments order under s. 310. On the argument that the terms of the pension arrangement prevented such vesting Chadwick LJ stated:

> It is to my mind, unarguable that a mere restriction against alienation in an annuity contract, or in a pensions scheme, can prevent the benefits under that contract, or under that scheme, from vesting in a trustee in bankruptcy.

Parliament could subvert that rule but had chosen not to do so in the area of personal pensions until the enactment of the 1999 Act which was not relevant to this bankruptcy. Dealing with the argument that the automatic vesting of personal pension rights infringed Art 1 of the First Protocol of ECHR Chadwick LJ declared that rights under Art 1 were not absolute but could be reduced in the public interest and in deciding what was in the public interest, Parliament was in the best position to decide:

---

[61] Absolute interests in possession could not be forfeited but normally pension schemes were drafted in such a way as to make the right a future and contingent right which may therefore be forfeited. Much depended on the terms of the individual pension scheme – compare *Caboche v Ramsay* [1997] BPIR 377 and *Re The Trusts of The Scientific Investment Pension Plan* [1998] BPIR 410.
[62] [1998] Ch 223. For comment see S.A. Frieze [1999] 12 Ins Intell 76, M. Thomas [1998] 62 Conv 317 and [1998] 2 CFILR 268.
[63] *Re Stapleford* (High Court, unreported, April 1 1998) (noted in [1998] 11 Ins Intell 63 (benefits under an occupational pension scheme).
[64] *Re Sykes* [1998] BPIR 516 (Supreme Court of British Columbia).
[65] [2000] BPIR 410.

This, then, cannot be said to be an area in which Parliament has been inactive over the past 25 years. Clearly, Parliament has been responding to a perception of what the public interest requires in this field. It has done so against a background of judicial decisions, over very many years, that the public interest requires, generally, that a bankrupt's property should be available to answer the claims of his creditors.

Another authority on the subject is *Rowe v Sanders*[66] where once again the Court of Appeal was adamant that pension benefits vested automatically within the estate. In so doing there was no breach of non-alienation provisions in the pension trust deed. The court also concluded that this vesting did not infringe any property expectations arising under Art 1 of the First Protocol ECHR. In his judgment Jonathan Parker LJ expressed support for the views of Chadwick LJ quoted above.

A further cause for concern was the enactment of provisions in the Pensions Act 1995 (characterised as ss. 342A-342C of the Insolvency Act 1986) which allowed a trustee to claw back excessive payments by an individual into a pension scheme prior to bankruptcy. There was concern that pensions were being used to shield assets from the legitimate demands of a debtor's creditors. Inexplicably, these provisions were never put into force.[67] These legal developments took on a marked significance in an era when it was government policy to encourage individuals to make provision for their retirement. If such provision could be frustrated by the intervention of bankruptcy law many potential investors in pension policies might be deterred. At the same time there was a clear trend in making the bankruptcy estate as inclusive as possible. Something had to give and at this stage of the drama the bankruptcy lobby prevailed over the pensions protagonists. The equilibrium was restored by the Welfare and Pensions Reform Act 1999. For the purposes of our study three key reforms were effected by this legislation with these changes applying to bankruptcies commenced after 29 May 2000.[68] First and foremost, s. 11 of the 1999 Act reverses *Re Landau*[69] by excluding personal pensions from the estate. The rules on forfeiture were changed by s. 14 so as to prevent pensions being forfeited on bankruptcy. The third significant reform in the 1999 Act was the remodelling through s. 15 of the clawback provisions originally enacted in the 1995 Act. This latter provision only applies to bankruptcies commenced by a bankruptcy order granted after 6 April 2002.

The position today therefore is one of a new and complex balance between maximising the estate and maintaining the credibility of pension provisions. Bankrupts will be allowed to keep their pension benefits but there may be clawback in cases

---

[66] [2002] EWCA Civ 242, [2002] BPIR 847. See also *Patel v Jones* [2001] EWCA Civ 779, [2001] BPIR 919 (occupational pensions).

[67] See I. Greenstreet (1995) 11 IL&P 168, (1997) 13 IL& P 101 and M. Simmons (1997) 13 IL&P 98.

[68] See D. Grant [1999] Recov (Sept) 24, S.A. Frieze [1999] 12 Ins Intell 76, A. Deacock and A. Martin (2000) 16 IL&P 127, I. Greenstreet (2001) 17 IL&P 43, D. Hosford [2002] Recov (June) 28 and C. Stanley [2002] 15 Ins Intell 68. These provisions were not retrospective and did not come into effect until April 2001.

[69] This reversal only operates prospectively – i.e. for bankruptcies commencing after 29 May 2000. Thus the rules laid down in *Re Landau* (supra) and *Dennison v Krasner* (supra) will continue to be significant for several years to come.

where the building up of the pension was carried out at the expense of creditors. Presumably if pension benefits are excluded from the estate they may be available to fund an income payments order (or agreement). There is little evidence on how these new rules are panning out in practice. It should be stressed that this new regime only applies in respect of bankruptcies commencing after 29 May 2000. For older bankruptcies the former law applies and for the self employed with private pensions this is a much more draconian regime. This differential was unsuccessfully challenged by a bankrupt in *Malcolm v Benedict Mackenzie*[70] on various grounds including the suggestion that it constituted a breach of Art 14 ECHR. This argument was rejected by Lloyd J on the grounds that the differential regime had been deliberately introduced by Parliament and it was a necessary result of a reform measure coming into force on a specified date. This ruling was subject to an appeal on the Art 14 point but when that appeal was heard it was dismissed and attempts to challenge the inclusion of pension rights within the estate received short shrift from the Court of Appeal.

Personal Rights

Such rights may be derived from a variety of sources, including legislation. If these have an economic value they are capable of vesting in the trustee. An example of such a right is found in *Re Rae*[71] where an expectation to renew a sea fishing licence (which had a real market value) was held by Warner J to form part of the estate. This expectation could fall within the s. 436 catchment as it was best viewed as an interest incidental to property (i.e. the fishing vessels). The fact that the bankrupt could nominate a third party to hold the licence may have influenced the court. A similar conclusion was taken by the court in *De Rothschild v Bell*[72] and the reasoning is consistent with what has been said above. Here the question was whether a continuation tenancy under Part I of the Landlord and Tenant Act 1954 was capable of forming part of the estate. The Court of Appeal reasoned that it was because it was a right that could be assigned. The acid test therefore seems to be whether the right is assignable; if so it is capable of being brought within the boundaries of the estate.

Protecting the Estate

Having defined the estate it is vital to protect it from diminution at the hands of self-interested parties. Applying the principle that prevention is better than cure the protective strategy kicks in at an early stage in the procedure. In some senses this

---

[70] [2004] EWHC 339 (Ch), [2004] BPIR 747 (Lloyd J); [2004] EWCA Civ 1748, [2005] BPIR 175 (Court of Appeal).
[71] [1995] BCC 102. A waste management licence for example is capable of being transferred and therefore "property" – *Re Celtic Extraction Ltd* [1999] 4 All ER 684.
[72] [1999] 2 All ER 722. For criticism see M. Davey [2000] Ins Law 46. See also *Sutton v Dorf* [1932] 2 KB 304. Compare *Griffiths v CAA* [1997] BPIR 50 (Federal Court of Australia holds that a non-assignable pilot's licence did not form part of estate).

harks back to the old "relation back" doctrine which existed under the former law in conjunction with acts of bankruptcy and allowed the trustee to assert title to property owned by the bankrupt at the time of the act of bankruptcy notwithstanding its disposal thereafter.[73] The protective strategy manifests itself in a variety of ways. General civil law principles may place disabilities on the debtor.[74] Judicial discretion may be exercised to prevent one creditor stealing a march over others.[75] The criminal law may be brought to bear to ensure full disclosure.[76] One common law principle which has been resurrected in recent times is the rule that any arrangement that provides for the divestiture of assets on bankruptcy is contrary to public policy and therefore void.[77] Having said that, this rule can be circumvented if the arrangement when properly construed does not constitute a divestiture of an asset vested absolutely in the future bankrupt but rather is correctly viewed as the mere grant of a conditional interest in favour of the person who later becomes bankrupt.[78] Fine distinctions are drawn here.[79] Having noted this common law principle our focus however in the forthcoming survey will be on dedicated statutory protective mechanisms.

Under s. 284 of the Insolvency Act 1986 this protection predates the making of the bankruptcy order in that dispositions made by the debtor after the presentation of the bankruptcy petition are void unless the consent of the court has been obtained (at the time of the disposition or subsequently).[80] The concept of a "disposition" is wide and certainly encompasses payments and transfers of property. This provision applies to property that might not have been included in the estate on bankruptcy unless it was trust property (see subs (6)). Note that the court has the power to lift the restrictive effect of this provision. Thus in *Rio Properties v Al Midani*[81] HHJ Maddocks was

---

[73]   See Fletcher Moulton LJ in *Ponsford Baker & Co v Union of London and Smiths Bank* [1906] 2 Ch 444 at 452. The "relation back" doctrine was originally of common law origin but was put into statutory form by the 1869 Act. For its last statutory formulation see Bankruptcy Act 1914 s. 37 and the illuminating discussion by Millett LJ in *Re Dennis* [1996] BPIR 106. For commentary on this latter case see L. Tee [1996] 55 CLJ 21. Note also *Re Gunsbourg* [1920] 2 KB 426. Australia affords an example of a jurisdiction that has retained the twin concepts of acts of bankruptcy and "relation back" (see Bankruptcy Act 1966 ss 40 and 115 respectively). The two concepts are not however mutually dependant – in Ireland the 1988 Bankruptcy Act retained acts of bankruptcy but abolished the relation back principle and New Zealand appears to be heading in this direction.

[74]   Thus there is a rule that precludes the bankrupt from raising estoppels against a trustee wishing to realise his estate – see *Smith v Lock* [1998] BPIR 786 and *Fryer v Brook* [1998] BPIR 687.

[75]   Thus a charging order nisi will not be made absolute once bankruptcy intervenes – *Roberts Petroleum v Bernard Kenny Ltd* [1983] 2 AC 192. The same is true of a third party debt order – *Fraser v Oystertec and Yorkshire Bank* [2004] EWHC 1582 (Ch).

[76]   Concealment of assets by a bankrupt is a criminal offence and it will almost certainly result in imprisonment – *R v Mungroo* [1998] BPIR 784.

[77]   See *Higinbotham v Holme* (1811) 19 Ves Jun 88, *Re Jeavons, ex parte MacKay* (1873) 8 Ch App 643, *Re Harrison, ex parte Jay* (1880) LR 14 Ch D 19 at 26 per Cotton LJ, *Money Markets International Stockbrokers v LSE* [2001] BPIR 1044, *Fraser v Oystertec plc* [2003] EWHC 2787 (Ch), [2004] BCC 233.

[78]   See Neuberger J's second rule as laid out in *Money Markets International Stockbrokers v LSE* (supra).

[79]   A perusal of Neuberger J's judgment in *Money Markets International Stockbrokers v LSE* (supra) will attest to the real difficulties experienced in applying the law.

[80]   The courts have been most generous in permitting retrospective leave nunc pro tunc – *Re Saunders* [1997] Ch 60 and *Re Melinek* [1997] BPIR 358.

[81]   [2003] BPIR 128.

minded so to act to permit a debtor who was facing bankruptcy to release funds to pay for legal representation. Equally by virtue of s. 285 hostile actions by creditors against the estate are impeded once the procedure leading to bankruptcy has been commenced through presentation of a petition. The protection offered by s. 285 is not absolute. It only extends to actions, executions[82] or other legal process against the property or person of the debtor. Actions to enforce security are specifically exempted by s. 285(4) and a landlord retains a right to forfeit a lease.[83] A spouse can maintain legal proceedings to enforce a lump sum payment as such a payment cannot be enforced through normal bankruptcy procedures.[84] We have seen that deductions can be made from social security benefits being received by the bankrupt. Fines (which are regarded as non-provable debts) can be enforced against a bankrupt.[85] These conservative provisions are reinforced by the possibility of an expedited hearing under s. 270 or by the appointment of an interim receiver[86] pursuant to s. 286.

Once the bankruptcy order is made the estate is well protected as a general rule. Any interference with the trustee would be a contempt of court for the simple reason that the trustee is an officer of the court. Executions against estate assets are prohibited by ss. 346 and 347 unless the execution is completed before bankruptcy commences. However, distress by a landlord can proceed but only in order to recover six months rent arrears. This preferential treatment of landlords in insolvency situations is sadly characteristic of English law. The exercise of liens over the bankrupt's papers and records is also prohibited by s. 349. The estate can also be protected from wastage by permitting the trustee to disclaim continuing obligations. More of this later in Chapter 4.

Maximising the Estate

The law recognises that the estate in the hands of the bankrupt at the date of his bankruptcy may in fact be less than the creditors might reasonably have anticipated. Such a shortfall can occur for many reasons, including the possibility that the debtor has deliberately reduced the estate prior to the bankruptcy for selfish reasons. There may have been an attempt to favour certain creditors by repaying them whilst their fellows are left to whistle for their money. Alternatively, assets may have been

---

[82] In *Industrial Diseases Compensation Ltd v Marrons* [2001] BPIR 600 a garnishee order nisi granted after presentation of a bankruptcy petition was set aside under the general jurisdiction of the court on the grounds that it should never have been made.
[83] *Razzaq v Pala* [1998] BCC 66. This concession is curious and made more so because an amendment contained in the Insolvency Act 2000 s. 3 changed the position for landlords wishing to forfeit leases where the tenant/debtor was undergoing an individual voluntary arrangement. See P. McCartney [2000] 13 Ins Intell 73 and also D. Milman and M. Davey [1996] JBL 541 for strong arguments favouring such a reform.
[84] *Re X* [1996] BPIR 494.
[85] Note here the IVA case of *R v Barnet JJ ex parte Phillippou* [1997] BPIR 134.
[86] On interim receivers see *Re Baars* [2002] EWHC 2159 (Ch), [2003] BPIR 523. An interim receiver need not necessarily be the Official Receiver – *Gibson Dunn & Crutcher v Rio Properties Inc* [2004] EWCA Civ 1043, [2004] 1 WLR 2702.

transferred simply to escape the clutches of the trustee. The common law was averse to the unravelling of transactions simply because one party had become bankrupt.[87] In taking this view there was evidence that concerns about the uncertainty caused to commerce had swung the day. The legislature has, however, felt fewer inhibitions. The Cork Committee (in Chapter 28 of its Report) favoured upgrading the avoidance provisions.

Section 340 allows for the recovery of preferences given within six months of the presentation of the bankruptcy petition.[88] In order to satisfy the requirements of s. 340 the person giving the preference must have been *influenced by a desire* to do so. In other words the mere fact that a preference may have *resulted* from the conduct of the bankrupt is not in itself sufficient. This point was emphasised in *Re Ledingham Smith*.[89] Thus there is no "effects test" operating in English law. This markedly affects the utility of the English law of preferences and compares unfavourably with the position found in a number of other jurisdictions (e.g. Scotland and Australia). The Cork Committee, after considerable debate, favoured the status quo largely because it did not want to radically change the rule that a debtor should be allowed to pay off debts in the order he pleases (see paras 1217-1218). Another prerequisite which is not expressly included in s. 340 is that the creditor must be preferred in fact; the mere intention to prefer on the part of the debtor is insufficient to bring the statutory mechanism into play. In *Lewis v Hyde*[90] the Privy Council concluded that this fundamental rule laid down by Lord Mansfield in the early preference cases (mentioned above at page 23) had survived statutory consolidation. A review of recent preference actions[91] reveals a picture of mixed success and no clear pattern emerges.

Transactions at an undervalue entered into by the bankrupt[92] and taking place within five years of the presentation of the bankruptcy petition may be set aside under s. 339. A good illustration of this avoidance mechanism at work is offered by *Re Kumar*[93] where a transfer of an interest in the family home by a debtor to his wife was subsequently set aside on the grounds of the inadequacy of the consideration provided by the wife. One loophole with the s. 339 avoidance mechanism is that it only comes into play if the estate has lost value as a result of the transaction. In *Re MC Bacon Ltd*[94] Millett J ruled that there is no loss of value simply because the

---

[87] See *Merry v Pownall* [1898] 1 Ch 306, *Aitchison and Tuivati v NZI Life* [1996] BPIR 215.

[88] If the beneficiary is a connected person this period is extended to two years.

[89] [1993] BCLC 635 – discussed by S. Frieze and S. Stone [1992] 5 Ins Intell 65. For the difficulties of proving the requisite intention see *Rooney v Das* [1998] BPIR 404. This requirement of a voluntary act uninfluenced by pressure can be traced back to comments of Lord Ellenborough in *De Tastet v Carroll* (1813) 1 Stark 88.

[90] [1998] 1 WLR 94. For comment see M. Hemsworth (2000) 16 IL & P 54.

[91] Compare *Doyle v Saville and Hardwick* [2002] BPIR 947 (unsuccessful claim) with *Re Thoars (dec'd) (Reid v Ramlort Ltd)* [2003] EWHC 1999 (Ch), [2003] BPIR 1444 – for subsequent proceedings in the latter case see [2004] EWCA Civ 800, [2004] BPIR 985.

[92] See *Re Brabon* [2000] BPIR 537.

[93] [1993] 1 WLR 224. See also *Simms v Oakes* [2002] EWCA Civ 08, [2002] BPIR 1244 and *Hocking v Canyon Holdings Ltd* [2004] EWHC 1966 (Ch), [2005] BPIR 136.

[94] [1990] BCLC 324.

debtor has created security over its assets. This point was developed further in *Re Brabon*[95] where it was held by Jonathan Parker J that in the case of a property subject to a mortgage where there is a negative equity scenario the transfer of such property cannot fall under s. 339 because there is no loss of value to the estate. These decisions, although exemplifying high levels of intellectual achievement, would fall foul of any test based upon common sense. An asset in reality does lose value if security is created over it. With fluctuating and unpredictable property prices what is negative equity today may be a real asset tomorrow. Furthermore, it is respectfully submitted that this reasoning is inconsistent with the precautionary thinking embodied in s. 284(6) of the Insolvency Act 1986. A more realistic view of valuation was taken in *Pozzuto v Iacovides*[96] where the court took into account the fact that a debtor (and no one else) was able to buy an asset at a discount; this fact was then factored into the valuation process when evaluating differentials in consideration.

We have also noted that there is a time limit constraining the operation of the s. 339 provision. Accordingly, the trustee (or indeed any creditor) who is out of time may prefer to exploit the avoiding effect of s. 423 of the Insolvency Act 1986.[97] Section 423 has a long pedigree which can be traced back via s. 172 of the Law of Property Act 1925 ultimately to the Statute of Fraudulent Conveyances in 1571 (13 Eliz I, c. 5). The current formulation, which in spite of its statutory location is not confined to insolvency situations, enables transactions carried out by a debtor at any time to be set aside if they were carried out in order to defeat creditors. This latter requirement has been refined by the courts to mean that the intention must have been a substantial purpose but not necessarily the dominant reason.[98] The issue of mixed motives was revisited (and hopefully settled) by the Court of Appeal in *Hashmi v IRC*[99] where Arden LJ stated:

> Accordingly, in my judgment, the section does not require the inquiry to be made whether the purpose was a dominant purpose. It is sufficient if the statutory purpose can properly be described as a purpose and not merely as a consequence, rather than something which was indeed positively intended.

Arden LJ further elaborated:

> ... for something to be a purpose it must be a real substantial purpose; it is not sufficient to quote something which is a by-product of the transaction under consideration, or to show that it was simply a result of it.

The utility of s. 423 was revealed in *Moon v Franklin*[100] where intra family property disposals entered into by a debtor who was facing damaging litigation were set aside.

---

[95] [2000] BPIR 537.
[96] [2003] EWHC 431 (Ch), [2003] BPIR 999.
[97] For general discussion of s. 423 see G. Miller [1998] 62 Conv 362 and S. Elwes (2001) 17 IL & P 10.
[98] See *Royscot Spa Leasing Ltd v Lovett* [1995] BCC 502 and *Re Brabon* [2000] BPIR 537.
[99] [2002] EWCA Civ 981, [2002] BPIR 974.
[100] [1996] BPIR 196.

Likewise, in *Midland Bank v Wyatt*[101] a transfer of a property to family members by an individual about to embark upon a hazardous business speculation was set aside under s. 423. In *National Westminster Bank v Jones*[102] the Court of Appeal also adopted a robust approach when considering the potential application of s. 423. In this particular case a highly artificial agricultural tenancy arrangement had been set up apparently in order to defeat the rights of a mortgagee. In viewing this arrangement as a transaction at an undervalue, the court concluded that although it was not a sham it involved a transfer of consideration where there was a sufficiently significant differential so as to engage s. 423. The common law doctrine of shams was thus bolstered by this statutory avoidance tool. This expansive view of s. 423 is mirrored in other recent decisions; for example, when the courts have been asked to consider what constitutes participation in a transaction at an undervalue.[103] Although these cases represent examples of the potential utility of s. 423 as an avoidance tool it has to be said that the difficulties facing a trustee are not to be underestimated. The case of *Re Brabon*[104] provides a salutary lesson in this respect. Here a trustee in bankruptcy sought inter alia to set aside various property transfers which had taken place over several years between a bankrupt, his father and his wife. The claims were all dismissed by Jonathan Parker J because the trustee was unable to establish either that there had been an undervalue or that the transactions had been carried out with the substantial purpose of defeating creditors. Within a family there may be many reasons why property rights are transferred (e.g. for reasons of affection or for the more efficient running of the family unit or for the maximisation of its investments) and to establish an improper purpose is not easy. The burden of proof under s. 423 has been lightened by the courts permitting applicants to have access to privileged legal correspondence between the debtor and his advisers where there is prima facie evidence of malpractice by the debtor.[105] Where a s. 423 case is established the court enjoys wide powers under s. 425 to unravel the transaction.[106]

There is one other avoidance mechanism worthy of note. Section 344 of the Act states that a general assignment of book debts owed to a debtor engaged in business is void against the trustee with respect to debts which had not been collected at the date of the bankruptcy petition. This provision, which offers an interesting differential between consumer and trader debtors, has attracted minimal judicial comment over the years but it was the subject of discussion in *Hill v Alex Lawrie Factors (Re Burfoot).*[107] Here the point was made that this provision only avoids a general assignment; the assignment of certain specified debts is not affected.

---

[101] [1996] BPIR 288. See also *Re Schuppan* [1997] BPIR 271, *Habib Bank Ltd v Ahmed* [2003] EWCA Civ 1697, [2004] BPIR 35, *Hocking v Canyon Holdings Ltd* [2004] EWHC 1966 (Ch), [2005] BPIR 136 and *Gil v Baygreen Properties Ltd* [2004] EWHC 1732 (Ch), [2005] BPIR 95 for other examples of s. 423 being successfully invoked.

[102] [2001] EWCA Civ 1541, [2002] BPIR 361 – discussed by I. Dawson [2002] Ins Law 61. On the general problem of challenging artificial farm tenancy schemes see A. Ibrahim and S. Barton (2004) 20 IL&P 163. See also *Trowbridge v Trowbridge* [2003] BPIR 258.

[103] See *DEFRA v Feakins*, The Times December 29 2004.

[104] [2000] BPIR 537.

[105] *Barclays Bank v Eustice* [1996] BPIR 1.

[106] See *Moon v Franklin* (supra).

[107] [2000] BPIR 1038.

In all cases of avoidance limitation considerations may thwart the possibility of producing benefits for the estate.[108] Furthermore, even if an action is instituted within the limitation period it must be prosecuted with reasonable despatch or risk being dismissed by the court for want of prosecution.[109] Another problem with the avoidance mechanisms is that they rely upon the trustee having funds in hand to pursue the necessary action in the courts.[110] Where no such funds existed there were problems. Legal aid is a non-starter. Until recently attempts by trustees to secure external finance to fund litigation were fraught with difficulty. A funding creditor ran the risk of a third party costs order made pursuant to s. 51 of the Supreme Court Act 1981 if the action failed.[111] Certain funding transactions might fall foul of the bar on champerty. In *Ramsey v Hartley*[112] it was decided that certain general causes of action (such as a negligence claim) could be sold outright by the trustee, but it appears from subsequent case law that this latitude does not extend to those claims vested exclusively in the trustee. Particular problems arise when a trustee tries to realise the fruits of an action. In *Grovewood Holdings plc v James Capel & Co Ltd*[113] Lightman J indicated that an office holder could not dispose of the fruits of an action in return for finance whilst retaining the cause of action itself. A problem of indivisibility was perceived to exist. The Court of Appeal treated this inconvenient conclusion with some scepticism in *Re Oasis Merchandising Services Ltd.*[114] The matter was revisited by the Court of Appeal in *ANC Ltd v Clark Goldring and Page Ltd*[115] where certain propositions put forward by counsel were approved in obiter dicta including the view that an equitable assignment of the fruits of an action which did not involve the assignee intermeddling[116] in the action was valid. More recently in *Farmer v Moseley Holdings Ltd*[117] Neuberger J expressed his dissent from the view of Lightman J that the fruits of an action could not be separately realised. This issue is therefore still open to debate. The picture generally with regard to financing avoidance litigation on insolvency has changed considerably in recent years. Conditional fees, under which solicitors bear a proportion of the risk of litigation, were introduced in 1995 and efforts have been made to

---

[108] It appears that the limitation period is 12 years – by analogy with *Re Priory Garage (Walthamstow) Ltd* [2001] BPIR 144 (a case on corporate insolvency dealing with ss. 238 and 239 of the Insolvency Act 1986) where it was held that the limitation period is governed by ss. 8, 9 and 23 of the Limitation Act 1980.

[109] See *Hamblin v Field* [2000] BPIR 621.

[110] One way round this problem is to create procedures whereby certain transactions are presumed to be voidable and can therefore be set aside by the trustee serving a notice on the party who now has possession of property formerly belonging to the debtor. The onus then switches to that party to establish that the transaction was unimpeachable. Such a reversal of the burden of proof applies in Australia under s. 139ZQ of the Bankruptcy Act 1966.

[111] This, however, is a remote possibility if the case of *Eastglen v Grafton Ltd* [1996] 2 BCLC 279 is any guide.

[112] [1977] 1 WLR 686. Note the county court decision in *Talling v Lawrence* [1999] BPIR 414 where a breach of contract claim was assigned back to the bankrupt in return for 49% of the proceeds. The court held that the trustee could not be required to post security for costs.

[113] [1995] Ch 80.

[114] [1998] Ch 170. See the guarded comments of Peter Gibson LJ at 179-180 in particular.

[115] [2001] BCC 479.

[116] This point seems to have been accepted long ago in *Glegg v Bromley* [1912] 3 KB 374.

[117] [2001] 2 BCLC 572, [2002] BPIR 473 at 479.

encourage their usage.[118] They are now controlled by s. 27 of the Access to Justice Act 1999 and regulations passed thereunder. The ancient bar on champerty, much diminished in recent years,[119] was swept away by s. 28 of the Access to Justice Act 1999, which authorised litigation funding agreements. Trustees in bankruptcy who pursue certain specified recovery actions are now reassured that the costs of the proceedings will be treated as a bankruptcy expense.[120] However this status will only operate if the action has been properly authorised.[121] What is lacking in English law is some public funding for the support of avoidance litigation. If avoidance is seen not merely as a tool to enhance the recoveries of creditors but rather a device to promote proper conduct by insolvents then there is a good argument for the state to get involved. A possible model exists in Australia under the auspices of s. 305 of the Bankruptcy Act 1966. Under s. 305 the trustee or Official Receiver can apply to the State for public financial support for litigation where there are insufficient funds within the estate. The Minister can offer support on a conditional basis if appropriate. Published figures suggest a modest but steady recourse to this facility; certainly the cost to the public exchequer is not great and, when weighed against the public interest often served by such litigation, that expenditure may represent value for money.

---

[118] The Insolvency Lawyers Association has produced a model conditional fee agreement – see (1996) 17 Ins Law 24. The relevant statutory rules are to be found in the Conditional Fee Agreements Regulations 2000 (SI 2000/692) and the Conditional Fee Agreements Order 2000 (SI 2000/823) as amended by SI 2003/2344.

[119] The House of Lords did much to undermine the concept of champerty in *Giles v Thompson* [1994] 1 AC 142. For discussion of champerty see A. Walters (1996) 112 LQR 560.

[120] Insolvency Rules 1986 r. 6.224 which was amended to this effect from 1 January 2003 by the Insolvency Amendment (No 2) Rules 2002 (SI 2002/2712).

[121] See Enterprise Act 2002 s 262 inserting a new para 2A into Schedule 5 of the Insolvency Act 1986.

Chapter 4

The Institution of Stewardship in Personal Insolvency Law

The Trustee in Bankruptcy

English law does not permit debtors who have become subject to the bankruptcy process to retain control of their assets; in other words there is no "debtor in possession" syndrome operating in this jurisdiction. The orthodox wisdom states that to permit this phenomenon might open up avenues for abuse by recalcitrant debtors. Conversely, we do not allow creditors (at least if they are unsecured) to take control of the debtor's estate through the bankruptcy process. The latest experiment to permit this type of regime in the years between 1869 and 1883 ended in failure.[1] Rather the law requires that in bankruptcy cases some independent person[2] of proven professional ability undertake this task having been appointed so to act by the court. That person is the "trustee in bankruptcy". Terminologically this is an interesting choice of phrase by immediately conjuring up fiduciary connotations. Section 305(2) of the Insolvency Act 1986 amplifies by describing the functions of the trustee as follows:

> The function of the trustee is to get in, realise and distribute the bankrupt's estate in accordance with the following provisions of this Chapter; and in carrying out that function and in the management of the bankrupt's estate the trustee is entitled, subject to those provisions, to use his own discretion.

This provision is reinforced by s. 306, which, as we have seen, automatically vests the estate in the trustee without requiring the trustee to positively claim assets. Having said that, it is important to note that it is the *responsibility* of the trustee to take control of the estate; there is no question of choice. This point is emphasised by s. 311. The existence of this obligation may explain cases where the trustee might appear to be acting in a rapacious manner.

---

[1]   See Chapter 1 and also the lucid account by V.M. Lester, *Victorian Insolvency* (1995). Creditors' assignees were given a stewardship role by the 1732 Act but subject to the supervision of the Commissioners. The 1869 model of absolute creditor control was a direct response to the failure of the 1861 option which overplayed the role of the State and lead to a large increase in cost. Creditor apathy and the disappearance of the investigation function meant that the 1869 deregulated scheme had to be replaced if public confidence was to be maintained. The 1883 scheme was essentially a compromise that has stood the test of time.

[2]   As we shall see this independence is underpinned in a variety of ways. For example a trustee must not tout for office (Insolvency Rules 1986 r. 6.148) or be a hired gun acting for one creditor (*Re Ng* [1997] BCC 507).

In chronological terms it is the Official Receiver who takes immediate responsibility for the estate on the making of the bankruptcy order. It is only when the creditors have appointed a trustee at the meeting called by the Official Receiver pursuant to s. 293 that the transfer of stewardship occurs. Since the introduction of mandatory licence holding in 1985 the trustee will be a private practitioner holding an insolvency practitioner licence. The trustee is subordinate to the Official Receiver (who retains a residual role) under the express terms of IR 1986 r. 6.149. In cases where no private practitioner can be found to act (often because the estate is insufficient enough even to fund professional fees) or where the creditors are unable to make an appointment, s. 295 makes it clear that the state will provide the trustee in the guise of the Official Receiver. Formerly, the Official Receiver also fulfilled this role in cases of summary administration where the estate was expected to be minimal (s. 297), but this is no longer the case as summary administration was abolished in the wake of the liberalisation of bankruptcy law effected by the Enterprise Act 2002.[3] If the estate includes assets requiring skilful management (such as a going business concern) the court enjoys the power under s. 370 to appoint a special manager. This power is rarely used these days because most potential trustees in bankruptcy themselves (or managers within their firm) have broad commercial expertise. A special manager appointed under s. 370 must not be confused with an interim receiver appointed pending the hearing of the petition.[4]

The stewardship of the trustee survives discharge.[5] This has become a more noticeable phenomenon since the Enterprise Act 2002, which was designed to reduce substantially the period before a bankrupt becomes eligible for discharge, came into force in April 2004. Truncated periods of bankruptcy will leave more loose ends to be tied up. With the best will in the world many estates will require more than 12 months to be fully realised; this is particularly true if litigation is required.

Trustees in Bankruptcy: Ethical Standards

As the Cork Committee recognised (para 781) trustees in bankruptcy occupy a fiduciary position vis-à-vis the estate. This obligation of stewardship is a common facet of English law where one person has been selected to oversee the assets of another. Clearly one consequence of this status is that trustees should not profit from handling the estate assets over and above their agreed remuneration. Thus it would be improper for a trustee to sell estate assets to himself or to a connected party for a knock-down price. Explicit statutory provision now covers such malpractice (see Insolvency Rules 1986 r. 6.147).

As the court is responsible for the appointment of trustees in bankruptcy this additionally renders them officers of the court. As such they become subject to the

---

[3]	Enterprise Act 2002 s. 269 and Sched. 23.

[4]	Insolvency Act 1986 s. 286. The role here is similar to that carried out by a provisional liquidator in relation to an insolvent company. See *Re Baars* [2002] EWHC 2159 (Ch), [2003] BPIR 523.

[5]	*Re A Debtor (No. 6 of 1934)* [1941] 3 All ER 289.

duty to act honourably as laid down by the court in *Ex parte James.*[6] The principle was stated thus by James LJ (no relation):

> I am of the opinion that a trustee in bankruptcy is an officer of the court. He has inquisitorial powers given to him by the Court and the Court regards him as its officer and he is to hold money in his hands upon trust for its equitable distribution among the creditors. The Court, then finding that he has in his hands money which in equity belongs to someone else, ought to set example to the world by paying it to the person really entitled to it. In my opinion the Court of Bankruptcy ought to be as honest as other people.[7]

This rule was applied in *Re Cornish*[8] where an attempt by a trustee to refuse to pay a dividend on the grounds that it had become time-barred was rejected; such opportunism was not acceptable on the part of a court officer. A further analysis of the principle is to found in *Re Clark* [9] where Walton J set out *four* preconditions. Firstly, the estate must actually be enriched. The second condition is that the claimant must not be in a position to submit an ordinary proof of debt. Thirdly, the circumstances should be such that an honest man would admit that it was not fair to retain any advantage gained. Finally, if the rule applies it can only do so to the extent of nullifying any advantage gained but not to the extent of providing a windfall for the claimant. Although the principle of honourable conduct is well established in the courts there are a number of recorded instances where it has been ruled inapplicable to the circumstances of the case.[10] Thus, in *Re Byfield*[11] payments made after the commencement of bankruptcy by a bank from the bankrupt's account to the mother of the bankrupt, which served to benefit the estate because some of this money was used to pay off creditors, did not trigger an equity enforceable against the trustee because the trustee had not asked the bank to make such payment. Goulding J held that the fact that the creditors had gained an unexpected windfall could not be used to justify the imposition of obligations on the trustee. In *Walker v Hocking*[12] Harman J, in a typically robust assertion, indicated that there was no authority to the effect that to adhere to one's commercial rights might contravene obligations of honour. Equally, in *Re Ouvaroff*[13] the court indicated that a trustee could make use of privileged documents which had been mistakenly disclosed to him without fear of an accusation of dishonourable conduct being upheld. More significantly, in *Boorer v Trustee in Bankruptcy of Boorer*[14] Jacob J held that the duty of the trustee to secure the best deal for the estate prevailed over any supposed duty to act honourably:

---

[6]   (1874) LR 9 Ch App 609. For Canadian illustrations see *Re McDonald* (1971) 23 DLR (3d) 147 and *Re Appleby Estates Ltd* (1984) 12 DLR (4th) 435. This concept is reviewed by I. Dawson in [1996] JBL 437.

[7]   Ibid at 614.

[8]   [1891] 1 QB 99. See also *Re Thellusson* [1919] 2 KB 735, *Re Wigzell* [1921] 2 KB 835.

[9]   [1975] 1 WLR 559.

[10] See for example *Re Gozzett* [1936] 1 All ER 79.

[11] [1982] 2 WLR 613.

[12] [1998] BPIR 789.

[13] [1997] BPIR 712.

[14] [2002] BPIR 21. For a Scottish authority of similar ilk see the House of Lords ruling in *Burnett's Trustee v Grainger* [2004] UKHL 8, [2004] SLT 513 (trustee entitled to exploit failure by disponee to register property interest sold by debtor).

But here it is manifest that the trustee changed his mind when he realised that there was actually equity in the property. It is not his duty to give away property which he has.

Another recent analysis of this duty of honour undertaken by the English courts is to be found in *Green v Satsangi*.[15] Here as a result of a quirk in the tax system a trustee received income but the associated liability to tax fell on the bankrupt. Rimer J concluded that the estate had not been unjustly enriched and there was no moral obligation to hand over the income to the bankrupt. Although it is clear that the tide is running against this particular obligation, it cannot be dismissed entirely as an irrelevance in modern conditions. For instance, it seems to have provided a basis for the subsidiary conclusion in *Patel v Jones*[16] by denying the estate the benefit of certain payments made by the bankrupt who was acting under a misapprehension as to his position with regard to his pension. Questions continue to be asked as to whether this rule has any significance today, particularly in the light of the imposition of professional codes of conduct by self-regulatory bodies. The burgeoning case law on unjust enrichment would also appear to cut much of the ground from beneath the feet of this curious rule. Matters have been made more difficult by a recognition of the fact that there is a duty imposed on insolvency practitioners to maximise the estate; a trustee who acts honourably may fall foul of this common law obligation. In spite of these reservations it is submitted that it may still have a residual role. One situation where it might come into play is where the trustee uses a strong bargaining position to place undue pressure on a contracting party. Thus, if a trustee is prepared to block a property development by holding onto a "ransom strip" of land or is prepared to see a manufacturer of products lose valuable production unless it pays an extortionate price for essential products which can only be supplied by the bankrupt, this might attract the application of this rule of ethics.[17] The Australian courts have also indicated that it would also be dishonourable for a trustee to sell a worthless cause of action to a gullible purchaser.[18]

The court takes a dim view of trustees in bankruptcy who allow their position to be compromised by aligning themselves too closely with a particular creditor. This point was emphasised by Lightman J in *Re Ng*:[19]

> A trustee in bankruptcy is not vested with the powers and privileges of his office so as to enable himself to accept engagement as a hired gun.

Legislation can also serve to promote improved ethical standards. For example Insolvency Rule 1986 r. 6.147 allows the court to set aside self-dealing transactions

---

[15] [1998] BPIR 55. For comparable Canadian authority see *Re Treacy* [1998] BPIR 528.

[16] [2001] EWCA Civ 779, [2001] BPIR 919. See also the observations of Rimer J in *Upton v Taylor* [1999] BPIR 168 at 182 (use of the rule to control remuneration of trustee).

[17] Compare *Ford AG-Werke AG v Transtec Automotive (Campsie) Ltd* [2001] BCC 403 where administrative receivers of a company (who are not officers of the court) were permitted by Jacob J to engage in what might be characterised as "commercial blackmail" in order to maximise realisations. But see the comments of Judge Norris in *Land Rover v UPF UK Ltd* [2003] 2 BCLC 222.

[18] *Re (Bankrupt Estate of) Cirillo* [1997] BPIR 166 at 176 per Branson J.

[19] [1997] BCC 507 at 509. See also *Trustee in Bankruptcy of Bukhari v Bukhari* [1999] BPIR 157 per Robert Walker LJ at 160. Having said that it may be appropriate in some cases in the interests of economy for a trustee to engage the solicitors acting for one of the creditors – *Re Schuppan* [1996] BPIR 486.

involving estate assets which the trustee may have entered into with associates. Rule 6.148 prohibits touting for office on pain of loss of remuneration. Additional ethical standards may be imposed by virtue of their position as members of a recognised profession of insolvency practitioner. Statements of Insolvency Practice are particularly relevant in this context. For example, there are SIPs dealing with handling receipts (SIP 7), remuneration (SIP 9) and informing creditors (SIP 15). In addition in January 2004 the ICAEW issued a revised statement of professional ethics insofar as they affect insolvency practice.[20] These standards are rigorously enforced through a system of spot checks carried out by JIMU and the use of disciplinary procedures (see above at page 21).

Standards of Competence

A lay person would naturally assume that a trustee in bankruptcy, like many a professional person, should be subject to a duty to take reasonable care whilst carrying out his functions. Matters are not so simple. We have seen that a trustee as an officer of the court is subjected to additional ethical obligations. There is no quid pro quo however in the form of immunity from liability in negligence for private trustees notwithstanding their status as court officers.[21] However, there is still no formal statutory duty of care, a fact lamented by the Cork Committtee (paras 777–778) which recommended the introduction of such a duty but with limited enforcement options (para 708). By way of contrast the duties of the Official Receiver were limited by the Court of Appeal in *Mond v Hyde*.[22] Here it was held that negligent misstatements made to a trustee in bankruptcy by an Official Receiver could not form an enforceable cause of action because it was contrary to public policy to expose such an official to this possibility. This decision has been criticised[23] and certainly does little to promote accountability. Notwithstanding these criticisms an application to the European Court of Human Rights suggesting that there had been an infringement of the civil rights of the trustee in barring the claim against the Official Receiver was unsuccessful.[24] Although Art 6 was engaged its guarantees were not infringed because the grant of immunity from suit to the Official Receiver was justified as it was a proportionate measure to enable this public official to discharge his duties without fear of disruptive litigation. This is a surprising conclusion, but is in line with human rights jurisprudence insofar as it impacts upon bankruptcy practice.

The position is rendered more anomalous once the Court of Appeal judgment in

---

[20]   See *ICAEW Guide to Professional Ethics* (1.202) available on *www.icaew.co.uk*. Apart from outlining general principles this Guide covers questions of self interest/conflict of interest by identifying situations where a conflict may arise.

[21]   *IRC v Hoogstraten* [1984] 3 WLR 93.

[22]   [1998] 3 All ER 833. Compare *IRC v Hamilton* [2003] EWHC 3198 (Ch), [2004] BPIR 334 where the Official Receiver was held liable in negligence for prematurely advertising a bankruptcy order in contravention of a direction from the court not to do so before a specified date fixed in order to allow the bankrupt an opportunity to seek an annulment.

[23]   See J. Murphy [1999] Ins Law 206.

[24]   [2003] BPIR 1347.

Medforth v Blake[25] is added to the equation. This case is concerned with the responsibilities of a company receiver but its conclusions are relevant to all insolvency practitioners. Here a receiver had continued to manage a pig farming business owned by the mortgagor. Unfortunately realisation proceeds were depressed because the receiver had not been aware of special discounts available on the purchase of bulk pig food. Expenditure was therefore higher than it should have been. Although the Court of Appeal was at pains to stress that the duty of a receiver in such circumstances was fixed in equity, that did not exclude a requirement to take reasonable care when managing the debtor's assets. Of course, this case dealt with the position of a private practitioner acting for profit rather than a public official discharging statutory responsibilities. Nevertheless, the lack of formal statutory responsibilities is odd. Particularly so when compared with the regime for administrators governed by Schedule B1 where there is a clear statutory duty to conduct the process with despatch (see para 4).

Broader Responsibilities?

To what extent does a trustee in bankruptcy owe duties beyond those previously considered? Specific duties are found in the Insolvency Act 1986, Insolvency Rules 1986,[26] the Insolvency Regulations 1994 (SI 1994/2507) (as amended)[27] and also by the Insolvency Practitioner Regulations 2005 (SI 2005/524).[28] An important obligation is the duty to pay funds into the Insolvency Services Account. The fact that this is a matter of duty not choice was stressed by the Court of Appeal in *Re Walker*[29] and was subsequently confirmed by legislation (see Insolvency Act 1986 s. 406). The interest earned on this Account has traditionally funded the running costs of the Insolvency Service. The Insolvency Act 2000 s. 13 offers much greater flexibility to trustees as to the investment of estate moneys and the Enterprise Act 2002 ss. 270–272 will impact upon this area of law by further increasing flexibility, reducing cross subsidies between estates, eliminating windfalls to the Consolidated Fund and offering investment benefits to insolvent estates through increased returns by interest on balances in the ISA. These recent statutory modifications were long overdue and represent a considerable financial sacrifice by the State for the benefit of insolvent estates.

Mechanisms for Accountability

It is one thing to impose theoretical duties upon trustees in bankruptcy. Experience has taught us that such obligations are unlikely to have much impact unless supported

---

[25] [1999] 3 WLR 922. Applied by Jacob J in *Ford AG-Werke AG v Transtec Automotive (Campsie) Ltd* [2001] BCC 403. For discussion of *Medforth v Blake* (supra) see S. Frisby (2000) 63 MLR 413.
[26] See SI 1986 No. 1925, especially Part 6 Ch 10.
[27] See SI 2005/512.
[28] The 2005 Regulations replace the 1990 model.
[29] [1974] 1 Ch 193. The Cork Committee (para 861) called for the statutory reversal of this authority.

by efficient enforcement procedures. The stewardship of the trustee is not unsupervised. A creditors' committee appointed under s. 301 may be in existence, but such a committee is purely optional and generally the rights of creditors are not extensive.[30] Gone are the days when the bankrupt was a mere thrall of vengeful creditors. Members of the creditors' committee are, according to *Re Bulmer*,[31] in a fiduciary position vis-à-vis the estate and this general obligation is reinforced by specific prohibitions set forth in Insolvency Rules 1986 r. 6.165 on self-dealing with the estate assets.[32] As a corollary to these duties the creditors' meeting has the power under s. 298 to remove a trustee.

If a party to the bankruptcy feels that the trustee is in breach of obligations, the most obvious avenue to have recourse to is s. 303 of the Insolvency Act 1986. The facility of making an application under s. 303 extends only to "dissatisfied persons" but the courts have been adept in extending the categories of persons who might be so regarded.[33] This statutory grievance procedure dates back to the 19th century but historically the courts have displayed a marked reluctance to interfere with the administration of a bankrupt's estate. Traces of this diffident attitude can be detected in the days when that administration was vested in the Commissioners of Bankruptcy.[34] It came as no surprise therefore that when undertaking their review of the subject the Cork Committee could find no recorded instances of the statutory predecessor of s. 303 being successfully used (see para 779). A typical example of this reluctance to interfere with stewardship (which is not unique to cases of bankruptcy) is to be found in *Re A Debtor (No. 400 of 1940)*[35] where Harman J dismissed an attempt to question the actions of the trustee who had experienced real difficulty in realising assets due to difficult wartime conditions. According to Harman J, provided there was no bad faith on the part of the trustee, the court would not be receptive to complaints about errors of professional judgment; indeed the judge commented that the "plight" that the now discharged bankrupt found himself in was considerably more comfortable than residing in the Fleet Prison for debtors! The Cork Committee did make recommendations for reform (see para 779) but the consequences have not produced a dramatic change on the ground. Thus in *Osborn v Cole*[36] the court, after indicating that the 1914 Act authorities were still relevant, stressed that a test along the lines of the well-known *Wednesbury*[37] public law standard would be applied to any attempt to challenge the actions of a trustee. The question therefore is not whether the trustee is acting unreasonably but whether he is acting in a way that no reasonable trustee would act.

---

[30] Generally creditors have no direct right of access to documents relating to the bankrupt's affairs – on a related point see *Plant v Plant* [1998] BPIR 243.

[31] [1937] Ch 499.

[32] This principle is deemed to be sufficiently important in Australia as to be included in primary legislation – Bankruptcy Act 1966 s. 72.

[33] See *Re Cook* [1999] BPIR 881. Note that a bankrupt who has been discharged can use s. 303 – *Osborn v Cole* [1999] BPIR 251.

[34] The classic manifestation of this policy of non-intervention is provided by the *Ex parte King* saga (1805) 11 Ves Jun 417, (1806) 13 Ves Jun 181 and (1808) 15 Ves Jun 127 – see Chapter 1 ante.

[35] [1949] Ch 236.

[36] [1999] BPIR 251. See also *Re Cook* [1999] BPIR 881.

[37] *Associated Provincial Picture Houses v Wednesbury Corporation* [1948] 1 KB 223.

This is well known to be a difficult legal burden to discharge. Furthermore there is a hidden limitation in the ambit of s. 303. It only applies to review the private law powers of the trustee. It does not bring within its purview the exercise of public law functions by the Official Receiver, a point made forcefully in *Hardy v Focus Insurance Co.*[38] The court did suggest a way of addressing this lacuna; s. 303 could be used to get the court to direct the trustee to approach the Official Receiver about the exercise of public law functions. The prospects of this stratagem meeting with success are minimal. A rare example of s. 303 being exploited by a dissatisfied person is afforded by *Re Cook*[39] where a solicitor, who had been sent a letter by a trustee directing him to cooperate with a Serious Fraud Office investigation, even to the extent of disclosing privileged information, applied to the court and got the letter withdrawn.

This provision must be read in concert with s. 304 which renders trustees liable for breach of trust or other duty. The author is not aware of any reported instance of this provision being used successfully.[40] The relationship between ss. 303 and 304 was reviewed by Hart J in the significant authority of *Brown v Beat*[41] where the judge reviewed the law governing leave applications under s. 304(2) in a case where the bankrupt was already the subject of a *Grepe v Loam*[42] order. The relationship between s. 303 and s. 363 in turn was revisited in *Engel v Peri*[43] where Ferris J stated:

> Accordingly although I am doubtful whether s. 303 is strictly relevant to the fixing of remuneration, because it seems to me that no act, omission or decision of the trustee is involved, I find that jurisdiction exists by virtue of s. 363. The fact that the application has invoked the wrong section is, in my view, something which clearly can and should be cured by amendment.

Litigating trustees are also subject to the discipline of the courts which can order them to pay the costs of proceedings which they have instituted (or defended) without success.[44]

One advantage of the requirement that all trustees hold an IP licence is that other options for the enforcement of duties become available. Self-regulation is very much the theme with the profession doing much to clarify practical questions and to discipline those who fail to live up to such standards. Professional sanctions are unlikely to be of much help to a particular complainant but they can help to eradicate bad practices. For example, professional inquiries have highlighted deficiencies with regard to handling estate funds. In view of the perceived importance of professional sanctions the move in the Insolvency Act 2000 (s. 4) to permit non-qualified persons to manage IVAs is surprising, to say the least. The policy goal of promoting competition in the provision of insolvency-related services (where admittedly there is limited consumer

---

[38]　[1997] BPIR 77.
[39]　[1999] BPIR 881.
[40]　For an illustration of unsuccessful usage see *Green v Satsangi* [1998] BPIR 55.
[41]　[2002] BPIR 421.
[42]　(1887) 37 Ch D 168.
[43]　[2002] EWHC 799 (Ch), [2002] BPIR 961.
[44]　*Watson v Holliday* (1882) 20 Ch D 780, *Borneman v Wilson* (1884) 28 Ch D 53, *Hill v Cooke-Hill* [1916] WN 62. Compare *Talling v Lawrence* [1999] BPIR 414. Furthermore if a trustee delays unreasonably in prosecuting a civil action it may be struck out with costs – *Hamblin v Field* [2000] BPIR 621.

choice) lies behind this curious move. In English law the further regulatory device of an Insolvency Ombudsman, in spite of a recommendation from the Cork Committee (para 1772) in favour of that idea, has not been introduced.[45] Having said that, as we saw in Chapter 1, there is now an opportunity to make complaints about the operation of the Insolvency Service. This complaints procedure involves the use of an independent Adjudicator.

Powers of Trustees

Moving away from responsibilities imposed on trustees in bankruptcy it is important to consider the range of powers with which they are invested. Although a trustee has wide powers it may be necessary on occasions to obtain the guidance of the court. Section 303(2) thus offers a facility for directions to be sought. Trustees face a common dilemma here. In an age of increased litigiousness the seeking of directions is a sensible policy in cases of difficulty. But such a strategy is guaranteed to increase realisation costs. A careful line therefore needs to be drawn and the courts can do much here by offering clear guidelines in test cases. The courts treat applications with sensitivity. In *Re Omar*[46] Jacob J stressed that in offering advice to trustees it will assume that the question raised is a matter falling within the bankruptcy and therefore requiring clarification. What is the purpose of the powers given to a trustee? First and foremost, they are intended to facilitate the realisation of the assets to the maximum benefit of creditors. Secondly, powers are given to ensure that the public interest is properly protected. Attaining this second goal may require the exercise of investigatory powers. The use of avoidance powers serves both functions.

The powers of a trustee are diverse. The starting point is s. 314 which immediately directs us to Schedule 5. Some powers listed in Parts II and III can be exercised at the discretion of the trustee. Others require the approval of creditors (see Part I). The Enterprise Act 2002 makes a significant change by requiring trustees to obtain prior approval before instituting specified recovery actions.[47] This regulatory constraint is a quid pro quo for the change in the Insolvency Rules permitting costs of recovery actions to be treated as a bankruptcy expense.[48] In determining the scope of the powers of a trustee in bankruptcy the courts have invariably sought to maximise their latitude. In *Stein v Blake*[49] the House of Lords held that a trustee could assign a cause of action back to a bankrupt with the result that a net balance could be assigned and the claim could be pursued with the benefit of legal aid. In response to the defendant's complaint that this was unfair Lord Hoffmann argued:

[45]   Australia does make use of an Ombudsman in its system.
[46]   [1999] BPIR 1001.
[47]   See Enterprise Act 2002 s. 262 inserting a new para 2A into Sched. 5 of the 1986 Act.
[48]   Insolvency Rules 1986 r. 6. 224 inserted by Insolvency Amendment (No. 2) Rules 2002 SI 2002/2712.
[49]   [1995] 2 WLR 710.

I mention these questions because they were alluded to by [counsel for defendant] as a policy reason for why the courts should be restrictive of the right of bankruptcy trustees or liquidators to assign claims. But the problems can be said to arise not so much from the law of insolvency as from the insoluble difficulties of operating a system of legal aid and costs which is fair both to plaintiffs and defendants.

Similar attitudes have come to the fore when the trustee has reached a decision to assign a cause of action; only in rare instances will the court intervene.[50] This area of the law was revisited by the Court of Appeal in *Faryab v Smith*[51] where a trustee was directed to assign the claim back to the bankrupt as his offer to purchase represented the only reasonable possibility of securing some benefit to the estate.

The most distinctive power enjoyed by a trustee is the power of disclaimer of onerous property and unprofitable contracts.[52] This power, originally introduced in 1849 but now found in s. 315 (supplemented by IR 1986 rr. 6.178–6.186), is a fascinating mechanism whereby the estate can rid itself of crippling ongoing obligations. It involves a clear erosion of the contract/property rights of individuals by compelling them to prove as unsecured creditors for their loss and thereby to receive but a fraction of their anticipated income.[53] This infringement of property rights can only be justified by the utilitarian desire to protect the collective good. The power of a trustee in bankruptcy to disclaim has never required the leave of the court.[54] On a disclaimer the court enjoys considerable discretionary powers particularly with regard to the vesting of a disclaimed lease. The ownership of the discarded lease may be vested in any party. In *Lee v Lee*[55] the lease which had been disclaimed ironically produced a surplus on sale. In such circumstances the Court of Appeal confirmed that it was appropriate that the surplus proceeds should be handed back to the trustee as a windfall for the benefit of the estate.

The powers of a trustee survive discharge and persist until the conclusion of the bankruptcy.[56] In order to escape the exposure to these powers former bankrupts are keen to investigate the option of annulment.

Concluding the Bankruptcy

The trustee's powers vis-à-vis the estate continue until the trustee is of the opinion that the assets have been fully realised. The final task of the trustee is to use the

---

[50]   See *Weddell v Pearce (JA) and Major* [1988] 1 Ch 26, *Official Receiver v Davis* [1998] BPIR 771 and *Re (Bankrupt Estate of) Cirillo* [1997] BPIR 166. Compare *Re Papaloizu* [1999] BPIR 106. In *Phelps v Spon Smith & Co (a firm)* [2001] BPIR 326 the court concluded that no such assignment had taken place.

[51]   [2001] BPIR 246. Compare *Re Shettar* [2003] BPIR 1055 where to order a reassignment might expose the trustee to liability in costs.

[52]   As to what is an unprofitable contract see *Re SSSL Realisations Ltd* [2004] EWHC 1760 (Ch), [2004] BPIR 1334.

[53]   However, a landlord is under no duty to mitigate his loss – *Bhogal v Mohinder Singh Cheema* [1999] BPIR 13.

[54]   Liquidators who were only given this power much later used to have to seek court leave. This requirement was dropped in 1985.

[55]   [1999] BPIR 926.

realised assets to repay creditors according to the specified priorities. The priority order is mapped out by s. 328. In satisfying debts in the established priority certain principles must be borne in mind. Distributions can only be made in respect of provable bankruptcy debts.[57] The rules on proof of debts are partly based upon common law principles (for example the rule against double proof). There are also technical provisions contained in the Insolvency Rules 1986. Of particular interest is the right of set off as created by s. 323.[58] There is a related rule at common law (the hotchpot rule) which precludes a creditor from participating in the fund without first making good any dues (or remittances in respect of the debt received from other sources) to that pool.[59] In effecting a distribution the trustee has the power under the Act to make distributions in specie (s. 326). This may be a useful tactic to minimise realisation costs and also to tackle the thorny problem of family heirlooms. A trustee may also pay interim dividends (s. 324), a particularly important facility where the bankruptcy is likely to be a protracted affair. Final distributions are governed by the terms of s. 330. Sadly much of the empirical evidence points to there being minimal returns for unsecured creditors. Thus, Michael Green in his impressive report on IVAs and personal insolvency regimes generally suggests that of some 23,000 bankruptcies in 2000 a nil dividend was the result in some 80% of the cases.[60]

Stewardship in IVAs

Insolvency practitioners engaged in promoting IVA activity are subject to a different range of responsibilities. Some of these are indicated in the legislation, whereas others depend upon case law or on professional guidance (for example SIP 3).

When receiving the initial proposal from the debtor nominees must convince themselves that it is viable[61] and not simply a delaying tactic offering them the opportunity of some short-term income. Indeed, this requirement was formalised under the Insolvency Act 2000 (s. 3 and Sched. 3) by requiring nominees to state in their report to the court whether they regard the proposal as having a reasonable prospect of being approved and implemented. This requirement is now found in s. 256(1)(a) of the 1986 Act. This issue was considered in *Prosser v Castle Sanderson*[62] where the court laid great emphasis on the need to distinguish between the various roles that may be played by an insolvency practitioner in the IVA context. The

---

[56]   *Official Receiver v Schultz* (1990) 170 CLR 306.
[57]   The common law adopted a wide definition of provable debts – see James LJ in *Re Hide* (1871) 7 Ch App 28 at 31. However, unliquidated tort claims were not regarded as provable. The position today is determined by the Insolvency Rules 1986 r. 13.12 which allows proof of such a claim.
[58]   One of the many anomalies in insolvency law is that this right is found in primary legislation in bankruptcy law but is relegated to secondary legislation (IR 1986 r. 4.90) in liquidation law.
[59]   This is the rule in *Cherry v Boultbee* (1839) 4 My & Cr 442 which certainly applies in insolvency cases – *Canada (AG) v Standard Trust* (1995) 128 DLR (4th) 747.
[60]   Michael Green, *Individual Voluntary Arrangements: Over-indebtedness and the Insolvency Regime* (November 2002) (Short Form Report available on Insolvency Service website) at 22.
[61]   For the questions a nominee should ask himself see *Greystoke v Hamilton-Smith* [1997] BPIR 24.
[62]   [2002] EWCA Civ 1140, [2003] BCC 440.

insolvency practitioner may start off as an adviser owing duties of professional competence and then will become a nominee and finally supervisor; these latter roles have duties prescribed by legislation. Again in *Fender v IRC*[63] Judge Norris reviewed the duties of nominees. The point was made that there is a duty to exercise independent professional judgment when considering the debtor's proposal. Although a nominee can place reliance on the figures supplied by the debtor, where inconsistencies appear they should be clarified. Thus we have manifested the traditional expectation of an auditor to act as a watchdog and not a bloodhound! In *Tanner v Everitt*[64] the issue was revisited by Mann J. Here we had IVAs that had failed to deliver as expected. A second supervisor had been appointed but the breakdown in relations with the debtors got worse. Questions arose as to whether the initial IVAs were valid, whether later modifications were binding and whether the replacement of the first supervisor was in accordance with the law. It was held that the original IVAs were binding; the debtors had signed up to them and there was no requirement that they receive independent advice. Moreover, an attempt to challenge the validity of the IVAs some 13 years after the event was doomed to failure. However, the later modifications and replacement of the supervisor were not effective as there was no power to do this in the original proposals. This procedural mess was resolved by Mann J making an appointment of a supervisor (the insolvency practitioner who happened to be the supervisor whose earlier appointment was found to be irregular!).

Clearly it is the function of the nominee to facilitate creditor approval for the proposal. If a nominee breaches his duty in getting an arrangement approved (for example by allowing material irregularities to creep into the vital creditors' meeting) he may be held liable for the resulting costs if matters become unstuck.[65] Even if there is a breach of duty (for example by unreasonably delaying in seeking creditor approval) that breach will only trigger compensation if it can be shown that there was a reasonable prospect that the creditors would have approved the proposal.[66] But the nominee is not under a duty of care to creditors to underwrite its success. This conclusion appears to follow from *Heritage Joinery v Krasner.*[67] Whether the proposal for arrangement is accepted is ultimately the responsibility of the creditors.

The question of the standard of competence expected of a nominee and supervisor was the central issue in *Pitt v Mond*[68] where a voluntary arrangement had produced disappointing results for the debtors concerned. Although the court had some reservations about the original proposals, the real difficulty was caused by changing macro-economic conditions that were not foreseeable when the proposal was put to creditors. HHJ Roger Cooke was at pains to point out that an IVA supervisor could not be expected to play the sort of creative role played by a company doctor – this was primarily because of public law obligations that had to be fulfilled. The judge summarised the duty of care position with regard to nominees/supervisors in the following terms:

---

[63]   [2003] BPIR 1304.
[64]   [2004] EWHC 1130 (Ch), [2004] BPIR 1026.
[65]   See here *Harmony Carpets v Chaffin-Laird* [2000] BPIR 61.
[66]   *Hurst v Kroll Buchler Phillips* [2002] EWHC 2885 (Ch), [2003] BPIR 872.
[67]   [1999] BPIR 683.
[68]   [2001] BPIR 624.

There must be a duty to the debtor at least up to the point when the proposal is accepted... However once the scheme is approved in the ordinary way his duties to the debtor would cease as he then becomes the supervisor of the arrangement. As such his duties can only be his public duties to the creditors with which any private duty to the debtor would be inconsistent. No private law liability attaches at this stage ... and any attack on his activities has to be done by way of an application to the court under the statutory procedure.

The duties of a supervisor when managing the IVA are limited, though once again they were extended by the Insolvency Act 2000 to include more rigorous reporting requirements.[69] This reform was designed to weed out those instances of abusive recourse to the IVA procedure.

An IVA supervisor is, according to passing comments in *King v Anthony*,[70] apparently an officer of the court, and therefore subject to the obligation to act honourably. This throwaway conclusion is open to question; the supervisor is surely appointed by the creditors and not the court. Moreover, there is a clear weight of authority set against extending the anomaly of the rule in *Ex parte James*.[71] Indeed as there are a number of ways in which alleged breaches of statutory duty can be enforced, there is no scope for admitting a private law action for breach of statutory duty.

It is important that supervisors respond professionally to an arrangement that is clearly failing. The preservation of doomed IVAs damages both the IVA system as a whole and the reputation of particular practitioners. This latter point is important; there is a strong self-interest factor pointing to the need to be ruthless because the ability of a practitioner to sell a future IVA to sceptical creditors may be profoundly damaged if word gets out that he or she is a "soft touch". Supervisors are obliged by virtue of s. 276 to petition for bankruptcy in such circumstances. The express terms of the arrangement may impose additional responsibilities. The supervisor in *Vadher v Weisgard*[72] responded in the appropriate manner in circumstances where the continuance of the arrangement would result in continuing supervision fees but little or no return to creditors. Drastic intervention by a supervisor may be appropriate even in cases where the debtor has rectified the position before the case has come to court.[73] Where a supervisor fails to act on his own initiative the court is prepared to step in and give the necessary directions for corrective action.[74] In *Harris v Gross*[75] the court confirmed that the power of the supervisor to intervene may even continue beyond the lifespan of the arrangement. The courts will set their face against provisions in an IVA which seek to curb the statutory power of the supervisor to petition for bankruptcy.[76]

---

[69]   See Insolvency Act 2000 s.3, sched. 3 para 12 which inserts a new s. 262B into the 1986 Act.
[70]   [1999] BPIR 73 per Brooke LJ at 78.
[71]   (1874) LR 9 Ch App 609.
[72]   [1998] BPIR 295.
[73]   See the discussion in *Carter-Knight v Peat* [2000] BPIR 968.
[74]   *Ing Lease (UK) Ltd v Griswold* [1998] BCC 905.
[75]   [2001] BPIR 586. See also *Stanley v Phillips* [2003] EWHC 720 (Ch) [2004] BPIR 632.
[76]   This is apparent in the comments of Peter Gibson LJ in *Re Gallagher (NT) & Sons Ltd* [2002] EWCA Civ 404, [2002] 1 WLR 2380 at para [20].

IVA supervisors quite naturally enjoy less extensive powers than trustees in bankruptcy. They are not involved in asset realisation, have no power of disclaimer and do not distribute assets according to the priority regimes laid down by Parliament. Essentially their role is to collect the income from the arrangement and to disburse it according to the terms of the IVA.

It will be interesting to see how Official Receivers adapt to their new role as supervisors of post-bankruptcy IVAs. This fast-track scheme, which is designed to be cheap and cheerful, was introduced by the Enterprise Act 2002. Early indications suggest that it is not being widely used. That is hardly surprising in view of the relative attraction of a standard bankruptcy offering discharge after a maximum of one year. Moreover, a debtor having something to offer by way of IVA may well have avoided bankruptcy in the first place and therefore would fall outside this new scheme.

Changing Patterns of Stewardship

One constant trend in bankruptcy law over the past 500 years has been the progressive relaxation by the State and its agents of control over the management of the estate. The earliest ad hoc models had the King's Council taking control of a bankrupt's assets. That evolved into a system in which the Lord Chancellor, acting through Bankruptcy Commissioners, held sway. Creditors' assignees were then permitted to act under the watchful eyes of the Commissioners. The next turn of the wheel had creditors' assignees in total control in the years 1869–1883. The State reasserted supervisory jurisdiction with a more balanced model in the 1883 Act. Finally, there was the move towards debtor in possession via the IVA model in 1985. Under this model the debtor's retention of control is supervised by a qualified insolvency practitioner. If the provisions of s. 4 of the Insolvency Act 2000 come to fruition (in the sense of the Secretary of State exercising delegated powers under the newly inserted s. 389A in the 1986 Act) that supervision may be vested in the hands of unqualified practitioners commonly characterised as "turnaround specialists". This move away from control by licensed insolvency practitioners carries with it dangers but may help to drive down costs and in so doing may cut the ground from under those unlicensed debt advisers who in practice operate in an entirely unregulated fashion. Indeed, when reviewing this aspect of stewardship it must be borne in mind that the day-to-day management of a bankrupt's estate is often in the hands of employees working for the firm in which the licence holder is a partner.[77]

---

[77]   See *Re Alt Landscapes Ltd* [1999] BPIR 459.

Chapter 5

Fundamental Rights in
Bankruptcy Law

Consequences of Bankruptcy: Stigma

There is no doubt that most developed legal systems have moved towards a more
enlightened view of the bankrupt. This change (which is a trend that can be traced
back to the 18th century[1]) is linked to a realisation that enterprise is essential to the
wellbeing of capitalist society and that those who lose out in the game of commercial
risk should not be treated with excessive severity. Economists would also argue that
the consumer debtor (who is usually not engaged in enterprise) plays a vital role in
oiling the cogs of capitalism by consuming its products and for that reason deserves
sympathetic treatment where personal expenditure gets out of control.[2] However, in
spite of the progressive liberalisation of the law, bankruptcy is not a state of affairs to
be welcomed. Adam Smith, writing in the 18th century, described bankruptcy as the
greatest humiliation that could befall an honest man.[3] Although undoubtedly traumatic
and life shaping,[4] few would go that far these days, but even fewer would wish that
status on themselves.[5] The former Cabinet Minister Jonathan Aitken described his
feelings thus:

---

[1]   Daniel Defoe (himself an entrepreneur and bankrupt) commented upon this development in *The
Complete English Tradesman* (1726) in the chapter entitled "Tradesmen in Distress" – for discussion see
R. West, *The Life and Strange Surprising Adventures of Daniel Defoe* (1998) at 395–6.

[2]   See J.K. Galbraith, *The New Industrial State* (1967).

[3]   *The Wealth of Nations* (1776) Vol I, p. 363. The courts have recognised that there is a stigma attached
to bankruptcy and are prepared to compensate a person who has wrongly been declared bankrupt – see *Rey
v Graham & Oldham* [2000] BPIR 354 at 370 per MacKinnon J. Where a person appears incorrectly on a
public register as a debtor there may also be a cause of action in negligence if a lack of care can be
established against the defendant on the balance of probabilities – see here *Du Bey v Lord Chancellor's
Department* (Gray J, June 9, 2000, unreported but noted in Current Law Week, November 3 2000).

[4]   Bankruptcy, or the mere prospect of it, has shaped literary careers and the lives of the famous/infamous
– examples being provided by Daniel Defoe (attested by his obsession with discovering untold wealth as
reflected in *Robinson Crusoe* (1719)), Sir Walter Scott (who eschewed bankruptcy and wrote to pay off his
debts) and Mark Twain (who undertook international speaking tours to settle business debts). For the
contemporary social impact upon Defoe see R. West, *The Life and Strange Surprising Adventures of Daniel
Defoe* (1998) at 219. It is argued that the radicalism of the 17th century thinker Gerrard Winstanley (the
leading protagonist in the radical agrarian reform group labelled "The Diggers") was profoundly affected
by his entry into bankruptcy in 1643 – for discussion see J. D. Alsop (1989) 28 Jo of Brit Stud 97. The
financial troubles of John Bellingham may have been the spark that led to his assassination of Prime
Minister Spenser Perceval in 1812. On a more prosaic level William Addis is reputed to have invented the
toothbrush in 1780 whilst residing in a debtor's prison!

Bankruptcy was an outcome I was desperately anxious to avoid. Quite apart from the further disgrace, it seemed the equivalent of having to serve a three year financial prison sentence during which I could not earn an adequate living.[6]

The fact that bankruptcy is still seen as a damaging status is reflected by the fact that a malicious initiation of bankruptcy is actionable,[7] as is a failure by a solicitor or insolvency adviser to take reasonable steps to prevent a client from being bankrupted.[8]

In *Re Stern*,[9] Lawton LJ, while recognising the need to give honest debtors a fresh start, expressed the following view:

> It was recognised, however, that not all debtors were the victims of misfortune. Some were rogues, some were fools and some were willing to risk other people's money when trying to make their own fortunes. For over 100 years the law has required the Bankruptcy Court to consider whether the conduct of the bankrupt has been such that the public ought to be protected against his further operations for a period of time or even permanently.

These comments are as relevant today in shaping policy and the law. A perusal of the Insolvency Service April 2000 Consultative Document "Bankruptcy: a Fresh Start" is ample proof of that. This perception was reinforced by the subsequent White Paper, "Insolvency: A Second Chance" (Cm 5234) and produced significant liberalising reforms in Part 10 of the Enterprise Act 2002. The 2002 Act heralds a much more benign view of the honest bankrupt whilst introducing a more draconian regime for those perceived to be guilty of misconduct. More of this later.

Real Consequences

Bankrupts will have their estates seized and sold with the proceeds divided amongst creditors. A statutory obligation to hand over assets is imposed on the bankrupt by the Insolvency Act 1986 (s. 312) and there is a continuing duty to make oneself available to assist the trustee.[10] The duty to be forthcoming, which is imposed by

---

[5]   The associated disabilities, etc., might suggest that a person would desire to end this status as soon as possible. Unfortunately the statistics prior to the discharge reforms in the 1976 Act show that the vast majority of undischarged bankrupts could not be bothered to take the initiative to seek their own discharge – see Civil Judicial Statistics for 1974 (Cmnd 6361). It is unclear whether this reflects apathy or an ability on the part of bankrupts to accept a new *modus vivendi*.

[6]   J. Aitken, *Pride and Perjury* (2000) (Harper Collins) at 349. This sense of humiliation was reinforced by early incidents in the bankruptcy – see ibid p. 363.

[7]   For the issue of abusive petitions in the corporate insolvency context see the articles by R. Gregory [1997–98] 3 RALQ 137 and A. Keay [2001] Ins Law 136.

[8]   See the discussion in *Fraser v Gaskell* [2004] EWHC 894 (QB), [2004] PNLR 32.

[9]   [1982] 1 WLR 860 at 866. Bankruptcy can also be used to gain tactical legal advantages provided the bankrupt is genuinely insolvent – *Collins v Official Receiver* [1996] BPIR 552.

[10]   See *Fryer v Brook* [1998] BPIR 687 where the duty to assist (formerly imposed by section 22(3) of the Bankruptcy Act 1914) was deemed to preclude the raising of an estoppel which might obstruct realisation of the estate. Failure to cooperate could lead to imprisonment for contempt – *Official Receiver v Cummings-John* [2000] BPIR 320 (sentence of 20 months imprisonment imposed). This sanction can also be applied to third parties, see *Bird v Hadkinson* [1999] BPIR 653. For discussion of the duty to cooperate see S. Baister [2000] Recov (Nov) 16.

s. 333, is one which the court will support by the issue of injunctions.[11] Intrusive investigations may be conducted by the Official Receiver and trustee, though this is likely to be a less common experience in view of changes introduced by the Enterprise Act 2002.[12] The possibility of arrest under the terms of s. 364 of the Act for a bankrupt who is deemed likely to abscond, conceal assets or avoid examination cannot be discounted. The courts can be quite severe in punishing bankruptcy offences and have indicated that any attempt to conceal property from the trustee is likely to result in a sentence of imprisonment.[13] In *R v Daniel*[14] the courts have indicated that the offence of concealing debts created by s. 354 is perfectly consistent with modern concepts of criminality. This was reinforced in *R v Kearns*[15] where an attempt to challenge the bankruptcy offence in s. 354 by invoking expectations generated by Art 6 ECHR met with no support from the Court of Appeal. The provisions on bankruptcy offences are complex and often create various types of burden of proof which the bankrupt must discharge if the prosecution can establish certain facts. As a general rule these may be ECHR compliant but as always each case has to be scrutinised carefully. In *Attorney General's Reference No. 1 of 2004*[16] the Court of Appeal held that if section 357(1) when read with s. 352 is deemed to create a reverse legal burden of proof then it does infringe Art 6 ECHR. If these provisions are read only to create a reverse evidential burden of proof then there is no contravention, and this indeed was the favoured interpretation of these sections. With regard to the reverse burden created by the interaction between ss. 352 and 353(1) this would not breach Art 6 even if read so as to create a reverse legal burden of proof. The potential for a bankrupt to be stigmatised as a criminal has been reduced by changes introduced in the Enterprise Act 2002 under which those contentious offences such as incurring losses through gambling and failing to keep proper records of account have been abolished.[17]

During the period of bankruptcy an undischarged[18] bankrupt is restricted in the pursuit of further credit to the value of £250 or more and cannot carry on business using another name (s. 360). The House of Lords limited the scope of the first element in this offence in *Fisher v Raven*[19] by restricting what was meant by "obtaining credit" by excluding the demand for the receipt of advance payment for goods and services to be supplied. Reading between the lines of their judgment, their Lordships appear to have been influenced in arriving at their conclusion by the interpretation of the crucial phrase by the courts when dealing with the Debtors Act 1869. This judgment was clearly inconsistent with notions of modern commercial credit and was reversed

11 See *Morris v Murjani* [1996] BPIR 458.
12 See Enterprise Act 2002 s. 258 which remodelled s. 289 of the Insolvency Act 1986.
13 *R v Mungroo* [1998] BPIR 784.
14 [2002] BPIR 1193.
15 [2002] EWCA Crim 748, [2002] BPIR 1213.
16 [2004] EWCA Crim 1025, [2004] BPIR 1073.
17 See Enterprise Act 2002 s. 263.
18 It is not an offence if the credit is to be supplied to a third party (such as a company) in which the bankrupt has an interest – see *R v Godwin* (1980) 11 Cr App Rep 97. Having said that the offence under section 360 is one of strict liability, see the Australian case of *R v Scott* [1998] BPIR 471.
19 [1964] AC 210 followed in *R v Miller* [1977] 3 All ER 986 (obtaining goods on hire purchase not seen as obtaining credit).

in 1985 by the enactment of what now appears as s. 360(2) in the 1986 consolidated legislation.

Disqualification (which may either be mandatory or subject to the exercise of bureaucratic discretion) is a significant impediment in theory for a bankrupt.[20] A perusal of Appendix A of the White Paper, "Insolvency: a Second Chance" will reveal that a bankrupt will lose the right to operate in many professions[21] and is disqualified from being an MP[22] or local government councillor.[23] The provisions here have been amended by the Enterprise Act 2002 as we shall see shortly. Police and prison officers lose their employment if they are declared bankrupt.[24] Holding office as a charity trustee is denied to an undischarged bankrupt.[25] Most serious of all, a bankrupt cannot become a company director without the leave of the court.[26] This prohibition, breach of which constitutes a crime of strict liability,[27] was introduced in 1929 as part of a general crackdown on company fraud rather than as a result of lateral thinking in bankruptcy law. The court does have discretion to lift this prohibition by granting leave, but it is clear from the comments made in *Re McQuillan*[28] that it is unlikely to do this. With short discharge periods now on offer this disability will lose much of its impact unless the individual director is made subject to a (BRO). Taken together, the aforementioned disqualifications may appear significant restrictions on opportunities, but for the average *consumer debtor* of humble background they are not real limitations upon career or lifestyle options. The position with regard to the disqualification of undischarged bankrupts was changed considerably by the Enterprise Act 2002. A number of specific disqualifications were lifted[29] and mechanisms introduced into the law to permit further changes.[30] More importantly, remaining forms of disqualification lost much of their impact because bankrupts could now be expected to be discharged after only a year.[31] Disqualifications would only continue to operate in circumstances where a bankruptcy restrictions order was imposed.[32]

The rules on BROs are detailed in the Enterprise Act 2002 and associated schedules.[33] Firstly, a few words on the procedure. The application for a BRO must be

---

[20]   The use of disqualification to underpin bankruptcy has an unfortunate aspect. Although in some cases the disqualification may be there to protect the public, in other instances one is left with the distinct impression that it is punitive and designed to reflect a judgment upon the moral character of the bankrupt. For discussion of comparable aspects of disqualification but in the context of disqualification following criminal conviction see A. Hirsch and M. Wasik [1997] CLJ 599.

[21]   Estate Agents Act 1979 s. 23. Bankruptcy will disqualify the debtor from judicial office and from sitting on tribunals – s. 146 Copyright, Designs and Patents Act 1988 (membership of Copyright Tribunal).

[22]   Insolvency Act 1986 s. 427. Note that a sitting MP can be made bankrupt – ibid s. 427(7).

[23]   Local Government Act 1972 s. 80.

[24]   This draconian penalty explains the great popularity of IVAs for such individuals.

[25]   Charities Act 1993 s. 72.

[26]   Company Directors Disqualification Act 1986 s. 11 as substituted by Enterprise Act 2002 s. 257(3) and Sched 21 para 5. See generally A. Griffiths and R. Parry [1999] Ins Law 199.

[27]   *R v Doring* [2002] EWCA Crim 1695, [2002] BPIR 1204, *R v Brockley*, [1994] BCC 131. On sentencing see *R v Theivendran* (1992) 13 Cr App Rep (S) 601.

[28]   (1989) 5 BCC 137.

[29]   Enterprise Act 2002 ss. 265–267.

[30]   Ibid s. 268.

[31]   Ibid s. 256.

[32]   Ibid s. 257 inserting s. 281A into the Insolvency Act 1986.

[33]   For BROs see now Sched 4A of the 1986 Act. See A.J. Walters [2005] 5 JCLS 65.

made either by the Secretary of State or by the Official Receiver. Private trustees cannot apply. In other words, a BRO falls squarely within the public law dimension of bankruptcy. Application must normally be made within one year of the commencement of the bankruptcy unless the court permits a later application or unless discharge is suspended. A BRO can only be made if appropriate. The precise grounds on which a BRO may be granted are itemised in para 2 of Schedule 4A. These include failure to keep/produce records, undertaking preferences or transactions at an undervalue, improper trading activities, failure to account for assets, failure to cooperate with trustee or Official Receiver, gambling, fraud, neglect of business affairs and making excessive pension contributions. Some of these concepts are new to bankruptcy law. It is interesting that two former bankruptcy offences (namely losses generated by gambling and failing to keep proper accounts) are included in this list.[34] Although "repeaters" (serial bankrupts) are not automatically bound to be subject to a BRO if the individual had been bankrupt within the previous six years, that fact is to be taken account of by the court as para 2(3) of Schedule 4A makes clear. In spite of this statutory guidance on criteria to be applied when considering a BRO most commentators expect a glut of litigation to add flesh to the bare bones of the legislation.[35] Where a BRO is granted the consequences are[36] as follows: further credit cannot be obtained and the ban on being a director is prolonged for the duration of the BRO as are other disqualifications generally removed from undischarged bankrupts by the Enterprise Act 2002. These consequences are imposed for a minimum of two years up to a maximum of 15 years. BROs are to be placed on a public register. Interim BROs are available pending full hearing if a prima facie case is made out. If the bankruptcy is annulled the BRO automatically falls away.

Drawing upon the model of director disqualifications the legislature has quite sensibly introduced an alternative to the BRO in the form of a legally binding undertaking which may be settled between the bankrupt and the Official Receiver (Sched 4A paras 7–9). Again we must wait to see if this proves to be an attractive option. The first BRU (for a six-year period) was arranged in November 2004 in respect of a female bankrupt with details posted on the Insolvency Service website via a press notice.[37]

Since the BRO procedure was introduced in April 2004 there have been few such orders granted with only one being referred to on the Insolvency Service press notice website (see 18 January 2005, where a three-year BRO was imposed). This compares with estimates at the time that ten per cent of bankrupts might become subject to this procedure. Clearly there is some mismatch in the figures here, but that may reflect initial teething difficulties. That said. attaining a ten per cent level of usage in an era of rising bankruptcy numbers seems unlikely.

Having noted the aforementioned adverse consequences associated with bankruptcy, matters are made worse from the bankrupt's viewpoint by virtue of the fact that his bankruptcy status is a matter for the public domain. Bankruptcy orders

---

[34] See paras 22j and 22a respectively.
[35] See A.J. Walters [2005] 5 JCLS 65.
[36] For the consequences of a BRO see Sched 21 of the Enterprise Act 2002.
[37] Press Notice dated 9 November 2004. For another BRU see Press Notice January 18 2005 (five-year undertaking).

have to be registered and can now be freely accessed.[38] However, the mere fact that such orders are in the public domain does not excuse a bankrupt from a positive obligation of disclosure in appropriate situations. Thus, in *Shephard v Wheeler*[39] Lawrence Collins QC (sitting as a Deputy Judge of the High Court) indicated that an undischarged bankrupt applying for the administration of the estate of a deceased person had to disclose that bankruptcy status and could not rely on the fact that the bankruptcy was a matter of public record. Adverse consequences flowing from bankruptcy may not always be the result of legislative provision. Many contracts or property dispositions contain provisions depriving the unfortunate bankrupt of the benefit of rights. Such provisions are valid in the eyes of English law (though they are frowned upon in some other jurisdictions). An example of this permissive approach is provided by the House of Lords ruling in *Cadogan Estates v McMahon*[40] where a provision in a lease entitling a landlord to re-enter in effect imposed an obligation on a tenant which carried over into a statutory tenancy and could deny a tenant of Rent Act protection in the event of bankruptcy occurring. This may be fair enough in the case of freely negotiated contracts but such provisions may have less to commend them in standard form contracts, (for example under pension schemes).[41] The fact that they have been allowed to stand, whereas in Contract Law generally provisions deemed penalties or amounting to exclusion clauses have been often assailed, might say something about traditional legal attitudes towards bankrupts.

The law does recognise that a bankrupt needs protection from being unfairly subjected to the bankruptcy procedure and from unjust treatment whilst undergoing bankruptcy. This protection is well established in bankruptcy law and can take many forms. We now must consider these protective mechanisms and ask whether these mechanisms are adequate. For many years the issue of whether bankrupts enjoyed rights over and above those identified at common law or under legislation was dormant. This fitted in perfectly with current contemporary attitudes towards bankrupts. However, with increased interest in the European Convention on Human Rights and the frenzy[42] surrounding the enactment of the Human Rights Act 1998 many difficult questions, which in the past have been sidelined, must now be addressed by UK bankruptcy law.

A Right to Access Bankruptcy ?

There is a real problem with the use of the bankruptcy institution. All commentators agree that there is a substantial cohort of debtors who do not take advantage of the

---

[38] Insolvency (Amendment) Rules 1999 (SI 1999/359) inserting rules 6.223A–6.223C into the Insolvency Rules 1986. For background see DTI Press Notice P/99/256. Australia has taken a step in the same direction with the creation of the National Personal Insolvency Index – see A. Keay (1997) 13 IL&P 149.
[39] The Times February 15 2000.
[40] [2000] 3 WLR 1555.
[41] For the new law on forfeiture of pension rights see Welfare Reform and Pensions Act 1999 s. 14 and the discussion above in Chapter 3.
[42] There are emerging signs that the courts are already concerned about the number of cases where human rights arguments are being raised on the flimsiest of grounds – *Daniels v Walker*, The Times May 17 2000.

opportunities that bankruptcy offers. Ignorance of the law may be one factor. Cost may be another. Is it in the public interest to maximise recourse to bankruptcy? There is no doubt that some debtors see bankruptcy as a safe harbour from pressing creditors and ultimately a route to a fresh start. Setting aside obvious abuses of the process,[43] can the law legitimately deny the debtor this opportunity to wipe the slate clean? This question was tested in the Court of Appeal in *R v Lord Chancellor ex parte Lightfoot*.[44] Here the Court of Appeal rejected an argument that the practice of requiring debtors to lodge a deposit (of £250) before petitioning for their own bankruptcy was unlawful. The Court of Appeal rejected the application for judicial review for a variety of reasons. Firstly, the deposit fee was not concerned with erecting a barrier to a citizen seeking to enforce a constitutional right of access to the courts;[45] rather it was to represent a contribution to cover in part the costs of the Official Receiver in administering the estate. In any case, it clearly had the imprimatur of Parliament. The deposit requirement did not interfere with the right of access to the courts as enshrined in Art 6 because that provision concerned access to justice in the event of a dispute as to rights. No such dispute existed here. Having rejected the application for judicial review Simon Brown LJ called for a reappraisal:

> ... it is not difficult to recognise the hardship and worry that many will suffer through their financial exclusion from the undoubted benefits of this rehabilitation scheme and, in the more compassionate times in which we now live, it may be hoped that the competing interests will be considered anew and perhaps a fresh balance struck.[46]

No such reappraisal took place and the deposit fee now stands at £310.[47] Another interesting slant on the same question is whether "creditors" denied the right to bankrupt a debtor are being denied their rights to protect property and possessions under Art 1 of the First Protocol ECHR. This scenario might arise if the debt is below £750, or if there is an administration order in place[48] or if the court uses its discretion to deny the bankruptcy remedy to a particular creditor, who may be acting through improper motive.[49] This issue remains to be tested in the courts.

Interference with Property

Article 1 of the First Protocol to the European Convention on Human Rights prohibits unjustified interference with the peaceable enjoyment of property rights except in

---

[43] For example self-induced bankruptcy designed to avoid affordable matrimonial provision – *F v F* [1994] 1 FLR 359.
[44] [2000] 2 WLR 318.
[45] The principle referred to was that laid down in *R v Lord Chancellor ex parte Witham* [1998] QB 575.
[46] [2000] 2 WLR 318 at 333.
[47] Insolvency Proceedings (Fees) Order 2004 (SI 2004/593).
[48] See County Courts Act 1984 ss. 112(4) and 114 which place restrictions on a creditor's right to petition if the debtor is covered by an administration order and the debt was less than £1500.
[49] The court is reluctant to bar a petition on these grounds – many peripheral motives may still be regarded as acceptable – *Leonard v LSC* [2002] EWCA Civ 744 [2002] BPIR 994.

the public interest and under the conditions prescribed by the law. A person who has been made bankrupt has his property seized and sold. Pre-bankruptcy transactions entered into by the debtor may be impugned. Are these forms of interference permitted in the context of fundamental rights? The issue of Art 1 was touched upon in the Court of Appeal in *Dennison* v *Krasner*[50] with regard to the deemed inclusion of pension benefits within the estate. Although this was not the major part of the case Chadwick LJ expressed the clear opinion that the appropriation of pension rights was carried out in accordance with the law and was therefore justifiable within the terms of the Convention.

> In my view it would be quite impossible to hold that Parliament did not take full account of what, in its view, the public interest required when, in 1986, it enacted s. 310 of the Insolvency Act 1986 in the form in which it did; or that, for Parliament to have failed to provide that the courts should have power to make income payments orders in respect of income derived from property which had vested in the trustee in bankruptcy would have been inconsistent with the United Kingdom's obligations under Article 1 of the First Protocol of the Convention.

The prospects therefore of the courts holding that a significant change in the law has been effected by virtue of the introduction of the ECHR into English law are slim. Most forms of interference with property rights are justifiable and proportionate.

Investigation of Bankrupts

The Cork Committee (para 238) was a strong advocate of having robust investigation procedures. Once again this may be linked to the idea of maintaining public confidence in the ability of the bankruptcy system to weed out abuse. The investigatory function rests primarily with the Official Receiver who used to be expected to investigate all bankrupts. That blanket and inflexible requirement was quite sensibly moderated by s. 258 of the Enterprise Act 2002 (which reconstituted s. 289 of the 1986 Act). Investigations are now only to be conducted if the Official Receiver deems it necessary. This judgment will rest upon bureaucratic guidelines as the legislation is silent on the matter. Canada moved in this direction a decade earlier.

A trustee in bankruptcy is an office holder and as such enjoys considerable powers of investigation. These powers of investigation are supported by the statutory obligation of a bankrupt to cooperate with the trustee and criminal sanctions are available to give this obligation added force. The court will support these investigation powers even in cases where the fact of bankruptcy is in dispute. Typically in *Official Receiver* v *Turner*[51] the court refused to exempt a bankrupt from scrutiny simply because the bankrupt was appealing the bankruptcy order; protecting the estate was the prime concern. A private investigation can be carried out under s. 366.[52] There are wide statutory powers available to both the trustee and the Official Receiver to support this process. In exercising discretion under s. 366 the court needs to balance the

---

[50]   [2000] BPIR 410 at 431–433.
[51]   [1998] BPIR 636.
[52]   See generally *Albert* v *Albert* [1996] BPIR 232.

interests of the trustee/estate against other competing interests (e.g. of the bankrupt).[53] The examination may extend not merely to the bankrupt but also to a spouse (or former spouse), to any person believed to have possession of property belonging to the bankrupt, or to be indebted to the bankrupt, or in a position to provide information about the bankrupt's affairs. This latter category clearly covers professional advisers and thus the vexed issue of professional privilege arises. In *Re Murjani*[54] Lightman J ruled that a solicitor can be compelled to disclose any information which the bankrupt himself could have been obliged on examination to reveal. Beyond that, professional legal privilege did apply. Moreover, the practice of seeking orders under s. 366 on an ex parte basis was criticised unless it was a case of genuine emergency. An unusual situation arose in *Re Ouvaroff*[55] where legally privileged documents had been handed over to the trustee by the solicitors of the plaintiff in error. The trustee had not induced this mistake nor had employed deception to obtain the documents. The court held that as they were now in the possession of the trustee they could be used to support the trustee's claim that the bankrupt had entered into a transaction at an undervalue; it was not unethical for the trustee to exploit this "windfall". Failure to attend (or a belief that an examinee may not attend) a s. 366 interview can lead to arrest. Those suspected of holding property belonging to the estate can be ordered to deliver it up and debtors can be ordered to pay the sums due to the trustee by virtue of summary powers in s. 367.

Public investigations of bankrupts, which were introduced in modern form[56] in 1869, used to be the norm They are now rare. The Insolvency Act 1976 represented a move away from their use in every case by permitting the court to waive the requirement to hold such an examination in appropriate cases. The Cork Committee felt that were still being used too extensively causing unnecessary humiliation for the bankrupt. The cost to the public exchequer may also have motivated a deregulatory desire. Section 290 permits the Official Receiver to call for a public examination of a bankrupt by applying to the court. Thus the burden is switched. Creditors holding more than half of the debt can compel the trustee to apply for a public examination. The procedure on a public examination (see IR 1986 rr. 6.172– 6. 177) is public and may involve questions being put to the bankrupt by various parties apart from the Official Receiver (including the trustee and creditors).[57] Failure to attend or to participate in a public examination may constitute contempt and could result in imprisonment.[58] An attempt to challenge these investigation procedures as such would probably fail because such procedures are necessary to underpin the effectiveness and integrity of the bankruptcy system.[59] A more complex issue to consider concerns

---

[53] For consideration of the relevant principles governing the exercise of judicial discretion under s. 366 see *Long v Farrer & Co* [2004] EWHC 1774 (Ch), [2004] BPIR 1218.

[54] [1996] 1 WLR 1498.

[55] [1997] BPIR 712.

[56] In fact they may be traced back to procedures introduced in 1604 when bankrupts had to appear before the commissioners to explain themselves.

[57] This reverses the more restrictive view taken in *Re Stern* [1982] 1 WLR 860.

[58] See *R v Scriven* [2004] EWCA Civ 683, [2004] BPIR 972. For general background see S. Baister [2000] Recov (Dec) 16.

[59] See *Re Leard* (1993) 23 CBR (3d) 233.

the use of the information gleaned from such investigations. In *Trustee of the Estate of Omar v Omar*[60] the court ruled that transcripts of a private examination could be passed on by the trustee to a third party who wished to bring proceedings for fraud against the bankrupt in respect of his conduct in the administration of an estate. Although this course of action was unusual, the strong indications of fraud permitted the court to authorise this.

Can the details provided by examination without the benefit of the right to silence be used to form the basis of a criminal prosecution? Section 433 of the Insolvency Act 1986 provides without qualification for the admissibility of any statement made during the course of insolvency proceedings. In *R v Kansal*[61] the Court of Appeal (Criminal Division) had no doubt on the basis of s. 433 that self-incriminating answers given by a bankrupt during the course of a public examination by the Official Receiver could be used to form the basis of a prosecution in respect of alleged offences under the Theft Act 1968 and the Insolvency Act 1986 (s. 354(2)) notwithstanding the fact that the bankrupt did not enjoy the right of silence during the course of that examination. The conviction of Kansal was referred back by the Criminal Cases Review Commission and this time the Court of Appeal concluded that developments in human rights law, particularly the enactment of the Human Rights Act 1998, meant that the conviction must be viewed as unsafe.[62] The Crown appealed that this attempt to give retrospective effect to the law would undermine the criminal justice system. On appeal to the House of Lords[63] their Lordships tended to agree with the Crown, though identifying the ratio is nigh impossible. More of this case later. In the intervening years this decision, and comparable authorities in Company Law, became the subject of uncertainty due to the ruling of the European Court of Human Rights in *Saunders v UK*[64] where it was held to be contrary to the right of fair trial (as enshrined in Article 6 of the Convention) for a prosecution to be based substantially upon compelled evidence extracted without the benefit of the right of silence. In the wake of this ruling the Attorney General issued new guidelines to prosecutors limiting recourse to confessions obtained under such circumstances.[65] An opportunity to reconsider the position in the specific insolvency context came in *R v Faryab*[66] where the issue was whether a confession given to an Official Receiver could be used to support a charge of theft. The Court of Appeal quashed the conviction. This change of attitude on the part of the English courts was fortunate because, when the *Kansal* case was taken to the European Court of Human Rights, the Court found in favour of Mr Kansal[67] on the basis that it was an infringement of rights for the prosecution to be so heavily based upon evidence gleaned without the privilege of a refusal of self-

---

[60] [2000] BCC 434
[61] [1993] QB 244.
[62] [2001] EWCA Crim 1260, [2001] 3 WLR 751.
[63] [2001] UKHL 62, [2002] BPIR 370.
[64] [1997] BCC 872. Followed in *IJL, GMR and AKP v UK* [2002] BCC 380. In *R v Ross* (1995) 31 CBR (3d) 273 the Canadian courts ruled that the use of evidence gleaned in bankruptcy investigations might contravene provisions in the Charter of Rights.
[65] Since then the *law* has been changed – Criminal Evidence and Young Persons Act 1999 s. 50.
[66] [1999] BPIR 569.
[67] [2004] BPIR 740.

incrimination. However one must be careful not to take matters too far. Fundamental rights legislation has not completely nullified investigatory powers. This is apparent from *Attorney General's Reference (No. 7 of 2000)*[68] where the Court of Appeal stressed that the use by the prosecution of information freely given but contained in documents whose delivery up to the Official Receiver had been compelled was not inappropriate.

Where a prosecution is launched against a bankrupt with respect to his conduct leading up to his bankruptcy the law is in effect retrospectively criminalising conduct that was not at the time it occurred illegal. The best example of this was provided by the offence of gambling.[69] How does this legal exercise square up with the expectations of human rights law? Doubts have been raised[70] as to whether this criminalisation was consistent with the guarantees contained in the Convention in Art 7. Nevertheless, in *R v Mithun Muhammad*[71] the English courts upheld this offence as being consistent with requirements of fundamental rights law. Ironically, the conduct in question was shortly thereafter decriminalised by the Enterprise Act 2002 though the conduct may be penalised through the imposition of a bankruptcy restrictions order.

Privacy Rights

The issue here concerns the right to private life as conferred by Art 8 of the Convention. A bankrupt must expect intrusions into his or her private affairs because the trustee has a duty to uncover assets and to enquire as to why debts were incurred which cannot now be met. One of the first consequences of bankruptcy is that the bankrupt becomes subject to the obligation in s. 288 to deliver a statement of affairs. This legal justification for interference with privacy was held in *Re Keene*[72] to be able to justify forcing an inventive bankrupt to disclose details of secret formulae which he had not previously been prepared to commit to writing.

One crude form of invasion of privacy concerns the statutory right of a trustee under s. 371 to have the bankrupt's mail redirected and opened. This facility (which can be traced back to 1869 and is found in other jurisdictions) looks suspect in the

---

[68]   [2001] EWCA Civ 888, [2001] BPIR 953. The case of *R v Brady* [2004] EWCA Crim 1763, [2004] BPIR 962 (which deals with corporate insolvency matters) is in a similar vein.

[69]   Matters become more curious when one is told that gambling debts are not legally enforceable and therefore cannot found the basis of a bankruptcy petition or be provable in a bankruptcy. On the other hand, J.S. Mill argued strongly in favour of the punishment of persons who could not meet their debts because of intemperance or extravagance – *On Liberty* (1859), Chapter IV "Of the Limits to the Authority of Society over the Individual". Similar objections may also be levelled at the criminalisation of a failure to maintain accounts (s. 361). This latter offence only applied to traders who might normally be expected to keep books of account – see *Re Mutton* (1887) 19 QBD 102.

[70]   See J. Wollaston (1987) 3 IL&P 42. Whatever the correct view on the legality of retrospective criminalisation it seems clear that the courts were keen to restrict the ambit of the gambling offence by introducing a double materiality element – see *R v P* [2000] BPIR 1308. Thus the gambling must have materially contributed both to the fact of the bankruptcy and to the extent of liabilities.

[71]   [2002] EWCA Crim 1856, [2003] BPIR 110.

[72]   [1922] 2 Ch 475.

light of Art 8 of the Convention. Section 371 has rarely come before the courts.[73] It was the subject of litigation in *Singh v Official Receiver*[74] and it is clear that Sir Richard Scott had considerable qualms about this procedure, particularly where it had been invoked on an ex parte basis. Jaconelli in reviewing this area of the law in 1994, expressed reservations as to whether it is compliant with the requirements of human rights law.[75] These reservations must now be assessed by the judgment handed down by the European Court of Human Rights in *Foxley v UK (Application No. 33274/96)*.[76] Here a corrupt civil servant had been bankrupted and subject to a receivership process designed to enforce a criminal compensation order. The trustee in bankruptcy had obtained a court order for the redirection of his mail. Under this order the bankrupt's mail was photocopied and then forwarded to him. This process of interception was applied to all of the correspondence of the bankrupt (including communications from legal advisers). It was also allowed to continue beyond the deadline specified by the court order. The European Court of Human Rights concluded that the interception of mail was justified by law because it had been carried out under the aegis of a court order. It was also a proportionate mechanism designed to support a legitimate socio-economic regime of bankruptcy.

> The Court observes that the trustee in bankruptcy sought and was granted the re-direction order to enable her to identify and secure the assets of the applicant, a bankrupt, with a view to their distribution to his creditors. Authorising the trustee in bankruptcy to have access to the applicant's correspondence during the period covered by the order can be considered to be in furtherance of the protection of the 'rights of others' within the meaning of Article 8(2) of the Convention.

However, once the deadline had expired the interception was no longer justified by law and did infringe the right of privacy. Moreover the interference with the correspondence from legal advisers could not be regarded as a proportionate response and must be viewed as infringing fundamental rights. The European Court of Human Rights revisited this territory in *Narinen v Finland*.[77] The approach taken in this case was much more sympathetic to the position of the bankrupt. The Court ruled that a practice in Finland of opening a bankrupt's correspondence did indeed infringe Art 8 for the reason that the relevant law was too general and gave no protection to the bankrupt and also because the legislative measure upon which the postal authorities were acting had in fact been repealed! Infuriatingly, *Foxley*[78] was not considered by the Court. As a result the state of jurisprudence here is in disarray with much depending upon the features of each national law.

The expectation of privacy which a private citizen enjoys extends to cover

---

[73]　A rare instance of the provision coming under judicial scrutiny is afforded by *Re Halberstamm, ex parte* Lister (1881) 17 Ch D 518 where the courts confirmed that it is not possible for an individual creditor to apply to the court to intercept a bankrupt's mail.

[74]　[1997] BPIR 530.

[75]　See the pieces by J. Jaconelli in [1994] Conv 370 and [1995] 8 Ins Intell 1.

[76]　[2000] BPIR 1009.

[77]　[2004] BPIR 914.

[78]　Supra.

information held by banks and lawyers. Thus, in *Barclays Bank v Eustice*[79] where prima facie evidence of an intention to defeat creditors for the purposes of s. 423 of the Insolvency Act 1986 was manifested the Court of Appeal held that it could order discovery of confidential communications between the debtor and his solicitors to clarify the matter. Again under English law a bankrupt is deprived of rights. In *Christofi v Barclays Bank*[80] a bank was held to be entitled to breach its implied duty of confidentiality to its client in order to respond to legitimate inquiries from the trustee in bankruptcy of that client's husband where the trustee was looking into property transactions between husband and wife. The implied duty of confidentiality was not absolute and the bank was entitled to respond to the lawful inquiries in the way that it had done. A similar invasion of privacy is anticipated by s. 369 which permits details of one's tax affairs to be disclosed for the purposes of an insolvency examination.

The issue of the protection of the right to privacy arose in dramatic form in the Jonathan Aitken case (*Haig v Aitken*).[81] Here, as we saw in Chapter 3, the question was whether the trustee in bankruptcy could sell private papers belonging to a bankrupt. These papers, which included correspondence with fellow politicians and foreign dignitaries, may well have had a commercial value. In his judgment Rattee J refused to allow the sale to proceed. Various reasons were suggested as to why such a sale would be "repugnant". Firstly, the judge reasoned although the documents in question were "property" within the meaning of s. 436 of the Insolvency Act 1986, Parliament must have intended that exceptions should exist; personal papers affecting one's status as a human being could not be regarded as part of the estate:

> In my judgment it is inconceivable that Parliament really envisaged by passing the Insolvency Act, that the effect of bankruptcy should be that a bankrupt's personal correspondence should be available for publication to the world at large by sale at the behest of the trustee in bankruptcy. In my opinion the concept of such a gross invasion of privacy is repugnant.[82]

Moreover, the papers in question did not relate to the "affairs" of the bankrupt within the meaning of s. 311 of the Insolvency Act 1986 because the word "affairs" must be construed as relating solely to the financial affairs of the bankrupt. In any case such a seizure of personal papers would infringe the bankrupt's right to a private life within the meaning of Art 8 of the Convention.

Freedom of Movement

The ancient writ of *ne exeat regno* has been available for centuries to prevent a debtor fleeing the jurisdiction. As noted in Chapter 1 there are some recorded instances of this writ being used successfully in recent memory. The Cork Committee would

---

[79]   [1995] 1 WLR 1238.
[80]   [1999] BPIR 855.
[81]   [2000] BPIR 462.
[82]   Ibid at 470.

generally be viewed as an enlightened body of experts on insolvency law and practice. However, in spite of these credentials, it did recommend (para 1852) that the freedom of movement of bankrupts, and in particular their right to travel abroad, be constrained. Thus, a person who has been made bankrupt may be subject to restrictions upon his or her right to travel abroad. This is clear from s. 358 of the Act. Passports may be seized.[83] This happened in *Re Greystoke (No. 2)*[84] where a bankrupt who had earlier failed to attend for private examination was refused permission to fly to the US to attend to urgent business matters. Although there was no likelihood of the bankrupt absconding there was a real concern that there might be interference with assets belonging to the estate and located in the US. It remains to be seen whether these restrictions are permitted under human rights law.

Access to the Courts

One of the most fundamental entitlements conferred by the European Convention on Human Rights is the right of access to the courts as created by Art 6. We have already seen that this right is often denied to bankrupts because the cause of action which they wish to pursue (or indeed any appeal right[85] or defence status[86]) becomes vested in the trustee.[87] Could it be argued that this legal metamorphosis constitutes a breach of Art 6? It should be remembered that if the trustee is not prepared to pursue the cause of action the bankrupt might be allowed to proceed by persuading the court to order the trustee to reassign the cause of action back to the bankrupt.[88] However, the court will not direct this outcome in many cases, preferring instead to back the stance of the trustee. Bankrupts may be barred from litigating on grounds of being a vexatious litigant.[89] This is a general feature of English law and is not limited to vexatious bankrupts; however, the exercise of this jurisdiction is ripe for challenge on the grounds that it contravenes fundamental rights. Having said that, where this matter has come

---

[83]   In Australia the bankrupt must hand over any passport to the trustee and travel abroad is therefore constrained – see Bankruptcy Act 1966 s. 77(a)(ii) and the account in J. Duns *Insolvency: Law and Policy* (2002). On the powers of the English courts generally in this area see *Re Caldwell* (B.D.) (unreported) noted by D. Archer in (1998) 142 Sol Jo 596 (an example of the court using its power under s. 39(1) of the Supreme Court Act 1981).

[84]   [1998] BPIR 77.

[85]   *Wordsworth v Dixon* [1997] BPIR 337, *Church of Scientology v Scott* [1997] BPIR 418, *Cummings and Fuller v Claremont Petroleum* [1998] BPIR 187.

[86]   *Seven Eight Six Properties Ltd v Ghafoor* [1997] BPIR 519.

[87]   *Stein v Blake* [1993] 1 WLR 1421. Strictly speaking an undischarged bankrupt loses only the right to pursue actions relating to the estate; personal actions (e.g. for defamation or a personal injury action) survive – see *Nelson v Nelson* [1997] 1 WLR 233 (right to instruct a solicitor in a personal claim preserved). Where a debtor enters an IVA his right to litigate is unaffected – *Envis v Thakkar* [1997] BPIR 189, *Frost v Unity Trust Bank* [1998] BPIR 469.

[88]   See above in Chapter 3 at p. 76.

[89]   See Supreme Court Act 1981 s. 42 and the inherent jurisdiction under the principle outlined in *Grepe v Loam* (1887) 37 Ch D 168 as exemplified by *Ebert v Venvil* [1999] 3 WLR 670. See also *Brown v Beat* [2002] BPIR 421. For guidance on the use of civil restraint orders see *Bhamjee v Forsdick (No. 2)* [2003] EWCA Civ 1113, [2003] BPIR 1252 and *Hurst v Bennett* [2004] EWCA Civ 230 [2004] BPIR 732. For comment see C. Gibson (2004) 25 Co Law 53.

before the courts. the judiciary have taken a robust view of the need to prevent legal proceedings being used as instruments of oppression. In *Re Thorogood (No. 1)*[90] Neuberger J explained the balancing exercise that had to be carried out; on the one hand an opportunity should be given to frustrated bankrupts to vent their grievances but at the same time the courts have to look after the interests of trustees and creditors, and indeed the wider community who make use of the courts. A less draconian restraint, as the Court of Appeal explained in *Hocking v Walker*,[91] is that security for costs would normally be required from a litigating bankrupt.

Discrimination Against Bankrupts

The law does nothing to remove the stigma from bankrupts.[92] Indeed, traditionally it has exacerbated matters by imposing formal disqualifications upon them and by demonising them through "whistleblowing" initiatives. This traditional approach (which admittedly is on the wane if the Enterprise Act 2002 is anything to go by) is in stark contrast to the position in the USA where s. 525 of the Bankruptcy Code contains various prohibitions on discrimination (e.g. in the sphere of employment). This provision (which was first introduced in 1978) puts into statutory language the sentiments expressed by the Supreme Court in *Perez v Campbell*[93] where an attempt by the state of Arizona to deny a driver's licence to an individual who had escaped liability for a civil claim by securing bankruptcy and discharge was ruled unconstitutional. This case dealt with discrimination by a public authority; the protection afforded to bankrupts was strengthened in 1984 when s. 525 was amended to prohibit discrimination by private parties. Although it is possible to offer some forms of protection to undischarged and former bankrupts, it is difficult to see English law interfering with the contractual right of counterparties to regulate their relationship with such debtors in such a way as to protect their own economic interests. Having said that, Michael Green, in his all-embracing report[94] on IVAs and personal insolvency, has suggested that private organisations should not be allowed to use public data on bankruptcies to impose a lengthier credit bar than that imposed by the State itself.

---

90 [2003] BPIR 1468.

91 [1997] BPIR 93. However, it seems that this is not an automatic conclusion – *Tormey v ESRI* [1986] IR 615 and *McCue v Scottish Daily Record and Sunday Mail Ltd (No. 2)* [1999] SC 322. The Canadian case of *Rahall v McLennan* [2000] BPIR 140 found that it was not a breach of the Canadian Charter of Rights to require a bankrupt appealing against a bankruptcy order to pay filing costs.

92 Certificates of misfortune, available under s. 26(4) of the Bankruptcy Act 1914 have not been retained in English law. Such certificates may have derived their inspiration from the ill-fated experiment with grading certificates of discharge which operated between 1849 and 1861. For judicial comment on certificates of misfortune see *Re A Debtor (No. 612 of 1960)* [1964] All ER 165. There is no equivalent of the Rehabilitation of Offenders Act 1974 to protect former bankrupts. Certificates of misfortune are retained in other jurisdictions – e.g. Canada (Bankruptcy and Insolvency Act s 175).

93 402 US 637 (1971).

94 Michael Green, "Individual Voluntary Arrangements: Over-indebtedness and the Insolvency Regime" (November 2002) (Short Report available on Insolvency Service website) Chapter VI at para 49.

Creditors Have Rights

The discussion up to now has proceeded on the assumption that the fundamental rights in question are those of the bankrupt. That is misleading in that it is clear that creditors may have the benefit of fundamental rights. It must always be remembered that the first successful challenge to a UK statute on the grounds of inconsistency with the Human Rights Act 1998 was mounted by a creditor, though that success turned out to be short-lived.[95] Apart from the examples noted above (at 33-34) where petitions may be curbed, there are a number of situations where potentially creditors may seek to challenge personal insolvency law reform.[96]

---

[95] *Wilson v First County Trust Ltd (No. 2)* [2001] EWCA Civ 633, [2002] QB 74 – declaration of incompatibility issued by Court of Appeal with regard to s. 127(3) of the Consumer Credit Act 1974. On appeal the House of Lords revoked that declaration – see [2003] UKHL 40, [2003] 3 WLR 568.

[96] See for example *Back v Finland* [2005] BPIR 1 (Finnish debt relief scheme found not to infringe fundamental rights of creditors). On the corporate insolvency front it has been suggested that the government backed away from abolishing administrative receivership as a remedial enforcement procedure for existing floating charges because of concerns that such a diminution of security rights might infringe Art 1 of the First Protocol ECHR.

Chapter 6

Balancing Non-Debtor Interests[1]

Wide Impact of Bankruptcy

When a debtor becomes bankrupt an extensive range of parties may be affected. Apart from the debtor and that debtor's creditors there may be family members involved. Married women have been subject to the bankruptcy regime since 1935, but the majority of cases show that in a family context it is the husband who is the bankrupt party.[2] The legal concept of family for these purposes has been extended by sched. 27 of the Civil Partnership Act 2004 with civil partners treated as equivalent to "spouses" for insolvency purposes. Business associates will undoubtedly be affected, particularly if there are cross guarantees used to support borrowing. The bankrupt may be in some other form of contractual relationship with a counterparty and the impact of bankruptcy upon that connection needs to be evaluated. The State, or some manifestation of the State, may be a creditor. The public also has a legitimate interest to see that the economic facility of credit, which its democratic representatives sanction, is not abused to the detriment of society. Last, but not least, professionals dealing with bankruptcy cases have a stake in the system. The function of the law must therefore be to arrive at an equitable *balance* between competing interests and legitimate expectations in situations of conflict on bankruptcy. This central mission of the law underpins much of bankruptcy litigation ranging from the initiation of the bankruptcy, through the activities of the trustee, to the mechanism of discharge and beyond. The problem of weighing competing interests on insolvency is not unique to

---

[1]   For an excellent review of the issues at stake see A. Keay (2001) 30 CLWR 206.

[2]   Prior to the enactment of the Law Reform (Married Women and Tortfeasors) Act 1935 s. 1(d) married women could not be made bankrupt. The 1935 Act was not retrospective and therefore did not apply to debts incurred before it came into force – *Re A Debtor* [1937] Ch 156, *Re A Debtor* [1938] Ch 694. The wife may often be dragged into dispute with the creditor because she has signed up to a mortgage of the family home as security for her husband's business debts or alternatively has personally acted as surety for her husband. This has been a fertile source of litigation – see *Barclays Bank v O'Brien* [1993] 3 WLR 786 and *Royal Bank of Scotland v Etridge (No. 2)* [2002] 2 AC 773. This litigation in turn has generated much academic discourse – see A. Arora [1994] JBL 242, A. Lawson [1995] 54 CLJ 280, S. Cooper [1995] JBL 384, M. Richardson (1996) 16 Leg Stud 368, M. Haley [1998] JBL 355 and S. Wong [2002] JBL 439. For an Australian (and significantly different) judicial perspective on this problem see the study by A. Finlay outlined in [1999] JBL 361. On the wider social issues arising here see B. Fehlberg *Sexually Transmitted Debt: The Surety Experience in English Law* (1997). This "STD" label has now entered the popular imagination and may even displace the more commonly understood meaning of the acronym – see for example *The Observer* (Cash Supplement), October 10 2004 at 2–3. But it would be a mistake to view female insolvency in purely "imposed" terms. The incidence of self-induced female personal insolvency is a growing and worrying phenomenon, reflected partly by the fact that the first two reported BRUs obtained under the Enterprise Act 2002 were against female bankrupts – see Chapter 7.

bankruptcy law; it is an ubiquitous legal conundrum. Comparable problems arise in corporate insolvency law, but there the disputes often feature the clash between secured/unsecured creditors and the demands of employees. Such contentious matters rarely come to prominence in bankruptcy law where there is not the same level of sophisticated lending and usually few employees are involved where a trader is adjudicated bankrupt.[3]

Creditor Interests

With the abolition of imprisonment for debt creditors' recovery rights have been focused upon the estate rather than the person of the bankrupt.[4] In more recent times the possibility of accessing future income has exercised the minds of creditors. Bankruptcy is seen as an important means of enforcing a legally enforceable[5] debt of at least £750.[6] This statutory right to enforce via bankruptcy proceedings is now conferred by ss. 264(1)(a) and 267 of the Insolvency Act 1986 (as amplified by s. 268). In determining whether a particular debt may be suitable to found a bankruptcy petition the court enjoys considerable powers of social engineering, because to treat a debt as a bankruptcy debt would be to significantly enhance prospects for recovery.

---

[3]   A rare example of a case featuring employee rights on an employer's personal insolvency is *Secretary of State for Trade and Industry v Henson* (EAT, unreported March 13 2000). Here it was held that for the purposes of the state guarantee system under the Employment Rights Act 1996 the insolvency of an employer is established by the employer being adjudicated bankrupt or entering into a formal arrangement with creditors but not if some private and informal arrangement is negotiated with a single creditor. An equally strict view was taken by the Employment Appeal Tribunal in *Secretary of State for Trade and Industry v Key* [2004] BPIR 214.

[4]   Certain special creditors may still pursue the person of the debtor, for example non-payment of rates (now council tax) may lead to committal. However, such ad personam remedies may be frustrated by the operation of s. 285 of the Insolvency Act 1986 if they are initiated too late in the day – see *Smith v Braintree DC* [1989] 3 WLR 1317 overruling *Re Edgcome* [1902] 2 KB 403 on this point.

[5]   Time-barred debts are not provable – *Re Benzon* [1914] 2 Ch 68, *Jelly v All Type Roofing Co* [1996] BPIR 565, *Re A Debtor (No. 647/SD/1999)*, The Times April 10 2000 (*Bruton v CIR* [2000] BPIR 946). Debts may be unenforceable for a variety of other reasons – *Maple Division v Wilson* [1999] BPIR 102 (breach of the Consumer Credit Act 1974). Only liquidated debts can form the basis of a petition – *Hope v Premierspace (Europe) Ltd* [1999] BPIR 695. Thus a statutory demand cannot be based upon a claim for an account – *Bennett v Filmer* [1998] BPIR 444. On the other hand the courts might be prepared to take notice of debts enforceable under Jewish law – *National Westminster Bank v Scher* [1998] BPIR 224.

[6]   The debt of £750 must still be outstanding when the petition is heard – *Re Patel* [1986] 1 WLR 221. When calculating the £750 you cannot add on the costs of the petition – *Lilley v American Express Europe Ltd* [2000] BPIR 70. For the procedural safeguards here see *Practice Note (Bankruptcy: Certificate of Debt)* [1987] 1 WLR 120. On the impact of an equitable set off see *TSB v Platts (No. 2)* [1998] BPIR 284. If the debtor is already subject to a county court administration order this figure is doubled to £1500 – see County Courts Act 1984 ss. 112(4) and 114. The thinking here is that if an administration order scheme is working it should not be frustrated by a single creditor unless the debt is particularly large. Creditors owed less than £750 have a problem; they can combine with other known creditors to present a joint petition. There is, however, no equivalent in bankruptcy law of winding up in the public interest (IA 1986 s. 124A) to deal with debtors who exploit the £750 minimum by incurring large debts in total due to many small creditors.

A good example of changing social priorities is reflected by *Re McGreavy*[7] where an unpaid rates demand was for the first time treated as a bankruptcy debt. Clearly other avenues exist to enforce rates arrears (now council tax) but to open up the option of bankruptcy was a boon to collecting authorities. A considerable percentage of bankruptcy cases are generated by the Inland Revenue pursuing taxpayers who are in default. Bankruptcy petitions can be based upon non-provable debts (e.g. family claims) but the courts will not accede to such a petition unless there are exceptional circumstances.[8] This may well be because the pursuit of bankruptcy in such cases could be viewed as a vindictive act unconnected with the recovery of debt.

The creditor facilitation view came to the fore in *Alliance and Leicester Building Society v Slayford*[9] where the court indicated that it was not an abuse of procedure for a secured creditor to exploit the bankruptcy mechanism in circumstances where this was a more advantageous strategy than the normal option of enforcing security. Peter Gibson LJ declared:

...there is no abuse of process in a mortgagee, who has been met with a successful *O'Brien*-type defence taken by the wife of the mortgagor, merely choosing to pursue his remedies against the mortgagor by suing on the personal covenant with a view as an unsecured creditor to bankrupting him, even though this may lead to an application by the trustee in bankruptcy for the sale of the property in which the wife has an equitable interest.

Equally it is not an abuse of procedure merely because the creditor may have mixed motives in pursuing bankruptcy[10] and simply because the debtor has no assets to realise is not an insuperable obstacle.[11] Access to the bankruptcy procedure is also not precluded by an arbitration clause in an underlying contract as this attempt to exclude the jurisdiction of the court and to take over a statutory right from a creditor would be deemed contrary to public policy.[12] A creditor who improperly seeks the bankruptcy of another may incur liability in tort but it has to be said that the court will be most reluctant to make a finding of malice against a creditor.[13] Notwithstanding this, a key point to grasp with regard to the bankruptcy process is that although it can be used to enforce debts owed to individuals it is nevertheless treated by the law as a

---

[7] [1950] Ch 269. Just to prove that the State might re-adjust social priorities to the disadvantage of a particular creditor, one could point to the removal of preferential status from rates arrears in 1985 and its own belated act of self-sacrifice in removing Crown preferential status via the Enterprise Act 2002.
[8] See *Russell v Russell* [1998] BPIR 259, *Wheatley v Wheatley* [1999] BPIR 431 and *Levy v Legal Services Commission* [2000] BPIR 1065 for discussion.
[9] [2001] BPIR 555. See also *Re Ng* [1997] BCC 507 for another illustration of a mortgagee exploiting advantages offered by bankruptcy which would not be available in traditional security enforcement procedures.
[10] *Hicks v Gulliver* [2002] BPIR 518. The fact that the debtor is in a predicament because of the alleged wrongful actions of another creditor is no bar to the petition succeeding – *Leicester v Plumtree Farms Ltd* [2003] EWHC 206 (Ch), [2004] BPIR 296.
[11] *Re Field* [1978] 1 Ch 371, *Shepherd v Legal Services Commission* [2003] BPIR 140. But compare *Amihyia v Official Receiver* [2004] EWHC 2617 (Ch) where the absence of assets, coupled with the lack of culpability of the bankrupt and the benefits in restoring him as a productive member of society, persuaded the court to grant an annulment.
[12] See *Shalson v DF Keane* [2003] BPIR 1045.
[13] See *Tibbs v Islington BC* [2002] EWCA Civ 1682, [2003] BPIR 743.

collective process not entirely within the exclusive control of a single creditor.[14] In modern parlance it represents a form of class action.

The court in many situations has to balance creditor expectations against those of the debtor. A prime example of this balance at work is to be found in the operation of the jurisdiction under s. 271(3) of the Insolvency Act 1986. This provides that the court shall not make a bankruptcy order if the debtor has made an offer to pay or secure the debts and this offer has been unreasonably rejected by the creditor. The review of the relevant case law (which was undertaken in Chapter 2) shows a marked reluctance on the part of the courts to go behind the decision of the creditor to reject such an offer. The decision on refusal is very much within the subjective prerogative of the creditor. In *John Lewis plc v Pearson Burton*[15] Pumfrey J held that it was not unreasonable for a petitioning creditor to refuse a proposal to complete repayment over the course of seven years. More importantly there was no requirement for the creditor to have exhausted all other potential remedies before resorting to bankruptcy.

Unsecured creditors have the right to take actions to enhance their position prior to bankruptcy but once bankruptcy intervenes they are to be treated *pari passu*. The principle of rateable distribution has a long ancestry in bankruptcy law and may be detected in the terms of s. 2 of the 1570 Act (13 Eliz I, c.7). Certainly it featured prominently in the reasoning in the 1584 *Case of the Bankrupts*[16] where an attempt to favour one creditor over the remainder was struck down by the courts. In more recent times in *Pritchard v Westminster Bank Ltd*,[17] a case dealing with the administration of the estate of a deceased insolvent, Lord Denning MR restated the principle thus:

> The general principle, when there is no insolvency, is that the person who gets in first gets the fruits of his diligence ... But it is different when the estate is insolvent...it is quite plain that, when an estate is insolvent, the bankruptcy rules apply ... and ... all debts proved are to be paid *pari passu*.

This is an equitable concept and admits of no discrimination between creditors linked to the date of their debt (unless it is time-barred) nor their financial circumstances. The *pari passu* rule has been the subject of much academic debate.[18] The consensus is that it may be said to be crude but just. Attempts have been made in recent times to support it by reference to the "creditors' bargain theory" of insolvency. Thus, academics such as Jackson would support a *pari passu* distributional tool because it appears to

---

[14]   See J. Finnis, *Natural Law and Natural Rights* (1980) at 189. See also Hart J in *Dickins v Inland Revenue* [2004] EWHC 852 (Ch).

[15]   [2004] BPIR 70.

[16]   (1584) 2 Co Rep 25a.

[17]   [1969] 1 All ER 999 at 1000–01. In Canada this rule is found expressed in s. 141 of the Bankruptcy and Insolvency Act. The Payne Committee in 1969 favoured the use of *pari passu* in dealing with priority disputes between creditors seeking to enforce judgments as an alternative to the grab for assets. In particular the idea of rateable distribution was to be managed by the Office for the Enforcement of Judgments – see Cm 3909 paras 40(h) and 323. Alas none of this came to fruition.

[18]   For discussion of the status of the *pari passu* rule compare V. Finch (1999) 62 MLR 633 and [2000] Ins Law 194 with R. Mokal [2001] CLJ 581. See also the article by Look Chan Ho in [2003] LMCLQ 95 and the paper by D. Milman, "Priority Rights on Corporate Insolvency" in A. Clarke (ed) *Current Issues in Insolvency Law* (1991) at 59.

reflect pre-bankruptcy expectations of unsecured creditors and is economically efficient.[19] Whatever the philosophical/economic justification, it has the great advantage of simplicity. To determine priority between unsecured creditors by reference to date of debt could involve time consuming (and expensive) investigations. Not surprisingly, the Cork Committee lent its support to this basic distributional tool (see paras 1220 and 1072). The *pari passu* rule does admit of exceptions; indeed some commentators would argue that these are so extensive as to place into question the existence of a general principle of rateable distribution. We will consider the position in relation to secured creditors shortly. However, there is an important distinction drawn between pre-bankruptcy creditors and those whose debts are incurred after the commencement of bankruptcy. The latter will normally rank as unsecured creditors governed by the *pari passu* rule. Nevertheless, they may bargain for special priority or may benefit from prioritisation under the expenses principle which permits certain post-bankruptcy creditors to rank their debts in priority to other claims. Jackson would justify this preference on the basis that the estate benefits from the supplies made by these creditors and indeed practical business politics requires such prioritisation.[20]

Secured creditors can exploit the bankruptcy procedure provided they are prepared to forego their rights to security. This is made clear by s. 269 of the Insolvency Act 1986 and this right of election to use what may appear to be an inferior procedure was upheld in *Zandfarid v BCCI*.[21] However, for the institution of bankruptcy to retain public respect it must not be seen as entirely in the service of the creditor lobby.[22] Thus, the courts have in some cases expressed concern that the trustee in bankruptcy may be seen to be acting too much under the influence of a particular creditor. In *Re Ng*[23] the so-called "hired gun" syndrome was much deplored. It must be remembered that trustees in bankruptcy are officers of the court and have a duty to act in the interests of all creditors and to behave honourably. Although they have the option of utilising bankruptcy, secured creditors will often prefer to rely upon their private rights and in particular to repossess and sell charged property. Bankruptcy leaves this right largely unmolested, except in so far as the realisation of the family home is concerned. The same is true of the IVA process which allows secured creditors to remain aloof from the haggling involved in agreeing the arrangement (see s. 258(4)).[24]

The relationship between unsecured and secured creditors, and indeed between secured creditors inter se, in bankruptcy law appears unsophisticated when compared to the position in corporate insolvency law. The reason for this is simple. The floating charge is not at present found in bankruptcy law. Sole traders and partners[25] might

---

[19] T. Jackson, *The Logic and Limits of Bankruptcy Law* (1986) Chapter 1.
[20] Ibid at 153.
[21] [1996] BPIR 501.
[22] Administrative receivership, unashamedly a collection device for secured creditors, underwent a cosmetic makeover in the Insolvency Act 1986 through the provision of a consultative creditors' committee but that did not save it from its prospective abolition under the terms of the Enterprise Act 2002.
[23] [1997] BCC 507.
[24] See also *Hylands v McLintock* [1999] NI 28.
[25] Floating charges are not likely to be introduced into partnership law in the immediate future – see Law Commission Report No. 283, *Partnership Law* (2003) (Cm 6015) para 13.30.

lament their inability to exploit this form of security to attract borrowing but its absence has rid bankruptcy law of much of the artificiality found in corporate insolvency law.

There is another group of unsecured creditors requiring special comment. These are involuntary creditors, such as the victims of torts committed by the bankrupt. If the bankrupt tortfeasor was insured, such victims could seek solace in their right to be subrogated against the insurer under the Third Parties (Rights Against Insurers) Act 1930 which was specifically introduced[26] to benefit such persons and to prevent the estate gaining a windfall in the event of the insurance company paying up on a policy held by a bankrupt tortfeasor.[27] This legislation has recently been held to apply to a wide range of circumstances.[28] Outside the insurance scenario the position of tort victims was less fortunate. The old rule prevented them from submitting claims in bankruptcy. As a result of the recommendations of the Cork Committee (para 1318) such claimants can prove provided the claim has become liquidated (i.e. by judgment) by the date of proof. This reflects the position now found in other jurisdictions.[29]

Creditors who do not enjoy the protection of security may nevertheless enjoy special rights either through legal privilege or through their economic muscle. The first category is represented by the preferential creditors. This preferential treatment goes back a long way. The courts were always careful not to extend the scope of the priority given by the legislation, a point exemplified by *Re Baker*[30] where the preference given in respect of local authority rates was held not to apply to water rates due to a water company. Until 15 September 2003 the main preferential creditor was the state in respect of certain so-called Crown debts. This preferential status was swept away by s. 251 of the Enterprise Act 2002 and the main remaining preferential creditors will be employees of the bankrupt owed specified debts up to a capped maximum.[31] Monopoly utility suppliers are not preferential creditors but if they are allowed to flex their economic muscles in an unregulated fashion they may defeat some of the social aims of the bankruptcy regime. Therefore, in recent times their powers to cut off essential supplies and services have been constrained. Under s. 372 of the Act the trustee in bankruptcy has a right to demand a continued supply of such utilities without first having to settle arrears run up by the bankrupt; these must be proved as bankruptcy debts.

Creditor interests are also reflected in the stewardship of the trustee. Witness the creditors' committee established under section 301 (supported by IR 1986 rr 6.150–

---

[26] The 1930 Act was specifically introduced to counteract two judicial decisions that had come to that conclusion – see *Re Harrington Motor Co Ltd* [1928] Ch 105 and *Hood's Trustees v Southern Union General Insurance Company of Australia Ltd* [1928] 1 Ch 793. Note also R. Bragg (1996) 17 Ins Law 2. In Ireland the same effect has been achieved by a different route in that if the insurance moneys are paid over to the bankrupt they do not form part of the estate but are held on trust for the victim – Civil Liability Act 1961 s. 61.

[27] See further *Re Bielecki* [1998] BPIR 655 at 670 where Richard McCombe QC suggested that the 1930 Act should apply to IVA cases. Note also *Jackson v Greenfield* [1998] BPIR 699.

[28] *First National Trinity Finance v OT Computers* [2004] EWCA Civ 653, [2004] 3 WLR 886, [2004] BPIR 932.

[29] In Ireland tort claimants can also prove – Bankruptcy Act 1988 s. 75. In Australia the position is different – see Bankruptcy Act 1966 s. 82(2).

[30] [1954] 2 All ER 790.

[31] For details see Insolvency Act 1986 sched 6 para 9 as supplemented by the Insolvency Proceedings (Monetary Limits) Order 1986 (SI 1986/96).

6.166). For example, the trustee is required by r. 6.152 to keep the committee informed about significant developments.

Family Rights

Family considerations can come to the fore in a number of bankruptcies and raise delicate legal issues.[32] These considerations are particularly sensitive where the bankrupt is deceased[33] and the family is left to face the consequences of unpaid debt. Clearly the fate of the family home is central, but that is not the only legal conundrum to be faced in this vexed area. The impact of the bankruptcy upon current and future income of the family must be considered, as must the interface between bankruptcy law and matrimonial law, particularly where the relevant principles are inconsistent and the courts are compelled to decide in favour of one or the other. The fact that the bankruptcy of one member of a family may produce difficulties for the rest of the family may attract sympathy from the courts but will not distract them from acting judicially, as Neuberger J stressed in *West Bromwich Building Society v Crammer*:[34]

> No one could be other than very sympathetic to his plight, and indeed that of his family. But it seems to me that sort of consideration cannot of itself justify the court setting aside a statutory demand, or refusing to make a bankruptcy order. No doubt most bankruptcies involve hardship to the bankrupt and their families. However, it is not as if bankruptcy leads to the debtor's incarceration as it might have done 150 years ago. That is not to underplay the unpleasantness, seriousness and stigma of bankruptcy.

The starting point here is to note that spouses are treated quite properly as separate persons for the purposes of bankruptcy law. English law has never subscribed to the principle of "kinship liability" which has been applied in some legal systems in the past.[35] The Cork Committee considered the idea of pooling their assets but decisively rejected the notion (para 1229). Notwithstanding this rejection, the Cork Report recognised (at para 1230) it would be foolish to treat spouses as totally independent in all respects. The "connected person/associate" idea was thus introduced by way of compromise. Its main impact is in the area of property transfers between spouses[36] where by invoking it time limits may be extended and burdens of proof reversed. When considering this issue we should note that under sched. 27 of the Civil Partnership Act 2004 civil partners are treated as equivalent to spouses and are regarded as "associates" of the bankrupt.

---

[32] For general practitioner reviews of this topic see W. Boyce, *Debt and Insolvency on Family Breakdown* (1994) and G. Schofield and J. Middleton, *Debt and Insolvency on Family Breakdown* (2nd ed, 2003). A more recent scholarly analysis of the issues at stake is G. Miller, *Family, Creditors and Insolvency* (OUP, 2004).

[33] For the regime governing deceased insolvents see Insolvency Act 1986 s. 421 and SI 1986/1999 (as amended). See also *Re Palmer* [1994] Ch 316 which is effectively reversed by Insolvency Act 1986 s. 421A.

[34] [2003] BPIR 783. See also *Re Citro* [1991] Ch 142 for comments in the Court of Appeal to similar effect.

[35] This concept appears to have been operated in early Irish law – see F Kelly, *A Guide to Early Irish Law* (1988) Chapter 6. It is also a feature of Jewish law.

[36] This term includes civil partners.

The family home has always been the focus of tension.[37] This is hardly surprising as it may represent the most significant asset owned (in whole or in part) by the bankrupt; there are no "homestead" exceptions operating in English law. Creditors clearly have a legitimate expectation that they can realise this asset to secure repayment of what is due to them. How is this expectation to be rated as against the social interest in protecting the stability of family life? Under the old law, as contained in s. 30 of the Law of Property Act 1925 if the property was jointly owned the trustee in bankruptcy could apply to the court for a sale order. Such an order would be granted as a matter of course unless there were wholly exceptional circumstances. Thus the interests of the chargee would normally prevail.[38] If the property was solely owned by the bankrupt the historic position was that the wife had no rights at all. This attracted adverse judicial comment[39] and her interest was first officially recognised by the Matrimonial Homes Act 1967.[40]

In reviewing this most difficult aspect of the law (at paras 1120–1131) the Cork Committee recommended that there should be a switch in the balance of power in favour of the family interest at the expense of creditor expectations. This was primarily to be achieved by allowing the sale of the family home to be postponed for an indefinite period. In considering whether this delay should be imposed the courts were to be directed to what were perceived to be relevant criteria. Generally, the banking community, which feared for the integrity of securities already taken, found the Cork proposals on the family home too much to stomach. By exerting their customary political influence they were able to persuade the government to water down the recommendations of the Cork Committee and in particular to ensure that any postponement in the sale would be only for a limited period.

The least controversial option in realising the family home is in fact not to realise it. A trustee enjoys the discretion to refrain from selling and instead to secure the creditors' position by having a charging order made against the property pursuant to s. 313 of the Act. This option will only be considered if the creditors are prepared to be patient. In practice it is not clear how frequently trustees make use of this facility. The Enterprise Act 2002 has made some changes here in order to further protect the interests of the bankrupt where a charging order is made by ensuring that the bankrupt gets the benefit of any uplift in property values.[41]

Returning to the scenario considered above what is the current position on competing rights to the family home on bankruptcy? Although there are some

---

[37] For analysis of the modern authorities see C. Hand [1983] 47 Conv 219, G. Miller (1999) 15 IL& P 176, M. Davey [2000] Ins Law 2.

[38] *Barclays Bank v Hendricks* [1996] BPIR 17.

[39] Lord Denning initiated the idea of a deserted wife's equity in *Bendall v McWhirter* [1952] 2 QB 466 but this was dismissed by the House of Lords in *National Provincial Bank v Ainsworth* [1965] AC 1175. Where the wife had acted as surety the courts also developed an equity of exoneration to protect the wife's interest in the family home – *Re Pittortou* [1985] 1 All ER 285.

[40] Matrimonial Homes Act 1967 later re-enacted as Matrimonial Homes Act 1983 s. 1 and then as s. 30 Family Law Act 1996. Initial recognition was tentative in terms of offering protection against the bankruptcy of a spouse. However, protection was available permitting the non-bankrupt spouse to make representations on an application for possession by a mortgagee under s. 36 of the Administration of Justice Act 1970 (see Chapter 1).

[41] See Enterprise Act 2002 s. 261(2).

differences in the law depending on whether the bankrupt is the sole owner of the property or merely a joint owner, in fact much depends on the exercise of judicial discretion. The basic rule governing realisation therefore is that once the initial 12 months period has expired then the interests of the creditors should prevail unless there are "exceptional circumstances". The use of such an imprecise test consequently vests considerable discretion in the judiciary.[42] Let us consider a few examples of how that discretion is exercised. In *Re Mott*[43] an elderly widow had lived in the family home for some 40 years and the bankruptcy involved her son (who had disappeared). As the main creditors were Crown departments with deep pockets, Hoffmann J had no hesitation in postponing sale indefinitely. Exceptional circumstances were found to be present in *Claughton v Charalambous*[44] where the wife of the bankrupt was disabled and an indefinite stay in the sale order imposed by Jonathan Parker J was deemed appropriate by the Court of Appeal which noted that in any case the creditors would not directly benefit because the proceeds of sale would be swallowed up by the bankruptcy expenses. In *Re Bremner*[45] the court imposed an indefinite stay on sale in order to allow the debtor to die peacefully in the family home. The evidence was that this event was likely to occur within the space of a few months.

In cases of joint ownership s. 335A of the Act states that after one year the interests of the creditors prevail unless there are exceptional circumstances present. In *Re Raval*,[46] a case dealing with s. 335A of the Insolvency Act 1986, Blackburne J, faced with the court having originally agreed to a six months breathing space to permit the bankrupt's family to relocate, then extended that to a full year. The relevant principles here were further reviewed by Lawrence Collins QC (sitting as a Deputy Judge of the High Court) in *Harrington v Bennett*.[47] "Exceptional circumstances" is a fluid concept that goes beyond the ordinary level of misery consequent upon bankruptcy. The learned judge was also at pains to point out that the existence of exceptional circumstances is no guarantee that the sale will be postponed. In *Re Bowe*[48] the facts were that a bankrupt held a joint beneficial interest in the matrimonial home which was subject to a charge. The trustee, having waited for one year to elapse after vesting, then sought a sale of that property but this was resisted by the bankrupt on the grounds that as the sale would only produce sufficient funds to repay the bankruptcy expenses no benefit would accrue to creditors and therefore this constituted exceptional circumstances within the meaning of s. 336(5) so as to justify the court refusing to order sale. Jonathan Parker J rejected this argument on the grounds that it was in the interests of creditors

---

[42]   A similar discretion is created by s. 61 of the Irish Bankruptcy Act 1988. See *Rubotham v Duddy* (Shanley J, unreported, May 1 1996) where a sale was delayed for some ten years in circumstances where both the wife and some of the children of the bankrupt were in poor health.

[43]   [1987] CLY 212. See also *Re Citro* [1991] Ch 142 where Hoffmann J imposed a five-year delay on the sale but this was then reduced to six months by the Court of Appeal (in a majority ruling) – for critique see J.C. Hall [1991] CLJ 45 and D. Brown (1992) 55 MLR 284.

[44]   [1998] BPIR 558.

[45]   [1999] BPIR 185.

[46]   [1998] BPIR 389.

[47]   [2000] BPIR 630.

[48]   [1997] BPIR 747.

that bankruptcy expenses be discharged in this way as that might leave residual (or after-acquired) assets available to provide a dividend for them. Where there are children in the home their interests need to be taken into account in any balancing exercise, as s. 337 makes clear.

There may be some need to reconsider the approach of the courts towards this question because it has been suggested that to adopt a conservative view of what constitutes exceptional circumstances might infringe rights of the bankrupt under Article 8 ECHR. Certainly, in *Barca v Mears*[49] Nicholas Strauss QC was of the opinion that this point was arguable and the earlier inconclusive Court of Appeal ruling in *Jackson v Bell*[50] points in the same direction. Having said that, the English courts have taken a sceptical view of similar arguments designed to water down legitimate enforcement rights of creditors.[51] Notwithstanding this reservation, it is clear that there has been a shift in the balance of power between secured creditors and family interests. That point was acknowledged by Neuberger J in *Mortgage Corporation v Shaire*,[52] where the point was made that the court enjoys much greater flexibility in deciding whether to order a sale.

Where one spouse has been allowed to remain in the family home (which has become vested in the estate) and continues to meet mortgage interest payments due credit should be given but equally it may be the case that such credit is neutralised by a notional occupation rent which the estate may levy. This balancing of accounts was the subject of judicial consideration in *Re Byford (dec'd)*.[53] Here Lawrence Collins J held that it was appropriate for a trustee to charge the spouse of a bankrupt who resided in the property until his death an occupation rent which coincidentally wiped out any benefit the wife would have gained by paying mortgage interest during this period.

The family home is not the only difficult "domestic" issue that bankruptcy law has to manage. The interface between bankruptcy law and matrimonial law has become one of the most vexed questions in recent years. Essentially the courts have had to grapple with the question of whether the bankruptcy regime should take priority over the law on family provision in circumstances where the governing legal principles come into conflict. One dispute has centred on the question of whether the power of the divorce courts to make property adjustment orders prevails over the estate protection rules in bankruptcy law. In *Re Flint*[54] the High Court ruled that s. 284 of the Insolvency Act 1986 could operate to nullify a matrimonial property transfer order made by the court under s. 24 of the Matrimonial Causes Act 1973 because a transfer of property pursuant to such an order was a disposition for the purposes of s. 284. Thus, insolvency law took priority over matrimonial law. This decision was criticised at the time it was handed down. It has been pointed out that an earlier

---

[49]   [2005] BPIR 15.
[50]   [2001] EWCA Civ 387, [2001] BPIR 612.
[51]   See the comments of Lord Scott in *Harrow LBC v Qazi* [2003] UKHL 43, [2003] 3 WLR 792 at para 135
[52]   [2000] BPIR 483 at 499.
[53]   [2003] EWHC 1267 (Ch), [2003] BPIR 1089.
[54]   [1993] Ch 319. See L. Doyle [1999] Ins Law 296.

authority of the Court of Appeal in *Burton v Burton*[55] had been ignored. These reservations appeared to have been confirmed by subsequent judicial pronouncements.[56] Questions were also being asked as to whether fundamental rights expectations were being complied with.[57] The interface was revisited in *Mountney v Treharne*[58] which is now the leading case on the subject. Here the husband had petitioned for his own bankruptcy after a wife had obtained a matrimonial property order in her favour. Although that order had not been executed by the date of the bankruptcy petition the Court of Appeal found that on the making of the order an immediate equitable interest had been created in favour of the wife and the trustee in bankruptcy took the estate subject to that interest. Jonathan Parker LJ was thus placed in the invidious position of having to declare that his earlier judgment in *Beer v Higham*[59] on this very same point had been decided in error because the binding authority of *Maclurcan v Maclurcan*[60] had been overlooked. Although he concurred Laws LJ clearly had some difficulty in squaring this old equity authority with the statutory rules governing property rights on bankruptcy:

> I do not think the result is satisfactory ... My difficulty is that I do not see how the evolution of equity can touch the operation of a statutory order as it may touch the operation of a common law rule.

Even though *Maclurcan*[61] had been followed in Australia, Laws LJ added:

> I have to say that I think it is a line of authority whose correctness is open to question as a matter of principle.

Re Flint[62] has suffered a bad press (one suspects because it is viewed as politically incorrect in certain quarters) but it has been given strong support by Lindsay J in *Treharne and Sand v Forrester*.[63] Here the court confirmed that a matrimonial property transfer executed by the court after the presentation of a bankruptcy petition could be viewed as a disposition within the meaning of s. 284 and was therefore void. An argument that such a transfer could not properly be viewed as a disposition by the person later adjudicated bankrupt was specifically rejected by the court. The only crumb of comfort for the disappointed ex-wife was that there might be a partial ratification of the transfer as there was evidence that she had expended considerable sums of money in unearthing her former husband's assets. This expenditure had benefited the estate and it was arguable that it should not receive a complete windfall without giving some credit to the wife.

55 [1986] 2 FLR 419.
56 See *Beer v Higham* [1997] BPIR 349 and *Harper v O'Reilly* [1997] BPIR 656.
57 See *Jackson v Bell* [2001] BPIR 612 for inconclusive comment.
58 [2002] EWCA Civ 1174, [2002] BPIR 1126.
59 Supra.
60 (1897) 77 LT 474.
61 Supra.
62 Supra.
63 [2003] EWHC 2784 (Ch), [2004] BPIR 338.

The position with regard to the family home has been further complicated with the coming into force of the Enterprise Act 2002. Under the newly inserted s. 283A of the 1986 Act a trustee in bankruptcy must take a decision on realisation within three years or else the home ceases to form part of the estate.[64] A principle of "use it or lose it" has thus been introduced to regulate the exercise of the trustee's powers. In the case of certain "low value homes" (where the equity owned by the bankrupt is worth less than £1K) even action taken within that three-year period is precluded.[65] Technical changes are also introduced to improve the rights of the bankrupt where the s. 313 charge procedure is used.[66]

Family members may be creditors. Spouses (and now civil partners) are regarded as deferred creditors as a result of s. 329 of the Insolvency Act 1986. In *Re Meade*[67] this disability was extended to cohabitees by means of extending common law principles rather than as a result of creative statutory interpretation. Difficulties arise with regard to debts arising purely through the relationship of marriage. It has been settled for many years that sums payable by a former spouse in respect of maintenance are not provable debts and therefore must continue to be paid notwithstanding bankruptcy.[68] The justification for this can only be the social prioritisation of such obligations above ordinary commercial commitments which are deemed capable of discharge. Lump sum payments are also not provables.[69] Indeed, the bankruptcy of a spouse does not preclude the court from making an order in matrimonial proceedings against the undischarged bankrupt spouse.[70] The downside of all of this is that matrimonial creditors may be placed at a real disadvantage in cases of bankruptcy and this has troubled the courts, as has been made clear on a number of occasions, most recently in the composite judgment of the Court of Appeal delivered in *Ram v Ram*.[71] Change here is likely in the near future. The bankruptcy procedure is nevertheless available to assist spouses (almost invariably wives) in recovering sums due under ancillary proceedings. Accordingly, it is clear that although matrimonial payments are not provable they can still be bankruptcy debts and found the basis of a petition.[72] Legal aid may also be available.[73] Alternatively, a wife may challenge the initiation of bankruptcy where it is clear that her spouse has used it as a stratagem to

---

[64] Enterprise Act 2002 s. 261 – see C. Hiley [2003] Recov (Summer) 18.
[65] Ibid.
[66] Ibid.
[67] [1951] Ch 774.
[68] *Re Linton* (1885) 15 QBD 239, *James v James* [1963] 2 All ER 465. The position may be different if payments have been agreed in the form of an annuity under a formal deed of separation – *Victor v Victor* [1912] 1 KB 247.
[69] Insolvency Rules 1986 r. 12.3. Note *Woodley v Woodley (No. 2)* [1994] 1 WLR 1167 where the Court of Appeal made the point that the 1986 reforms may have inadvertently changed the former position as reflected in *Curtis v Curtis* [1968] 2 QB 793. Compare *Re X* [1996] BPIR 494. However a spouse owed a lump sum may be bound by an IVA entered into by the debtor spouse – *JP v A Debtor* [1999] BPIR 206.
[70] *Hellyer v Hellyer* [1997] BPIR 85.
[71] [2004] EWCA Civ 1452.
[72] *Russell v Russell* [1998] BPIR 259, *Wheatley v Wheatley* [1999] BPIR 431. Having said that, the court will normally exercise its discretion and refuse to make a bankruptcy order on a petition by a spouse unless there exist exceptional circumstances.
[73] *Galloppa v Galloppa* [1999] BPIR 352.

avoid paying her what she is entitled to. Thus bankruptcies initiated by debtor petitions may be annulled in appropriate cases. For example, in *F v F*[74] the court annulled a bankruptcy initiated by her husband simply in order to defeat her claim for matrimonial provision. This stratagem employed by the husband was seen as an abuse of process. The fact that a spouse is a legitimate stakeholder in the bankruptcy of a spouse is also reflected by the fact that he or she enjoys locus standi to challenge the actions of the trustee in bankruptcy.[75]

Family considerations are also relevant when the court is contemplating making an income payments order. It has always been the case that the court would not hypothecate the income of a bankrupt to that bankrupt's creditors to such an extent that the bankrupt would not be able to live. In *Re Rayatt*[76] the issue arose as to whether private school fees for children could be taken into account. The court held that it was reasonable for the bankrupt to continue to make educational provision for children and any income payments order had to reflect that fact. This matter was revisited in *Scott v Davis*[77] with the court concluding that everything turns upon the precise facts of each case and therefore laying down hard and fast rules is not desirable.

Partners

Partnership (in the sense of the traditional legal concept, not the new style "civil partnership") is often characterised as a form of commercial marriage. It is not surprising that it has been necessary to develop special rules to handle bankruptcy within partnership. The starting point is that bankruptcy automatically dissolves a partnership. This rule, now found in s. 33(1) of the Partnership Act 1890, is inconvenient, particularly where the bankruptcy in question is attributable to the private affairs of the bankrupted partner.[78] A dissolution of a partnership is profoundly disruptive and may damage goodwill. Entry into an IVA by an individual partner does not necessarily have the same effect, unless the partnership agreement identifies such an occurrence as a ground for dissolution.

In practice where one partner is adjudged bankrupt this may have a domino effect and reduce all of the partners to that status.[79] One can therefore find concurrent insolvency regimes operating for both insolvent partners and insolvent partnerships. The Insolvency Act 1986 (s. 420) recognises the need for discrete provision to be made for insolvent partnerships and this special regime is developed through secondary legislation. The Insolvent Partnerships Order 1994 (SI 1994/2421),[80] which replaced

---

[74] [1994] 1 FLR 359. See also *Couvaras v Wolf* [2000] 2 FLR 107 and *Woodley v Woodley* (supra) at 1176 per Balcombe LJ.

[75] *Woodbridge v Smith* [2004] BPIR 247.

[76] [1998] BPIR 495. For a comparable Canadian authority see *Prochera v Prochera* (1969) 13 CBR (NS) 166 (sending a child to university not evidence of extravagance).

[77] [2003] BPIR 1009.

[78] See The Law Commission Report No. 283, *Partnership Law*, (Cm 6015, 2003) at para 8.101 for this problem and possible solutions.

[79] A debt owed jointly by partners can provide the basis of a bankruptcy petition against an individual partner – see *Schooler v Customs and Excise* [1995] 2 BCLC 610 and *Artman v Artman* [1996] BPIR 511.

[80] For comment see S. Frith and B. Jones (1995) 11 IL&P 14.

the badly drafted 1986 Order,[81] seeks to address the problems that can arise. Its basic approach is one of maximising flexibility, though at the price of making the law (much of which is beyond the scope of this book) hideously complicated. Where it is clear that all of the partners are individually bankrupt they can present a joint debtors' petition and the court may appoint a single trustee to realise their distinct estates.[82] A partnership voluntary arrangement (or PVA) is an innovation contained in the 1994 Order.[83] It is designed to promote rescue of distressed firms.

One problem that arises in the partnership context is that there may be two types of creditor claiming against a bankrupt partner. There may be creditors of the firm and creditors of the individual. Should the law discriminate between these two groupings? At common law the rule was that the two estates had to be strictly segregated with the creditors proving against each estate initially and participating only in the secondary estate once all of the creditors of that estate had been fully discharged.[84] This approach was adopted because it was felt that if a creditor had elected to prove against the joint estate it would be unfair to allow that creditor to prove in equal competition against the separate estate, the creditors of which enjoyed no such option. The Insolvent Partnerships Order 1994 changed that position by enabling unsatisfied joint creditors of the firm to have recourse to the separate estates and to rank *pari passu* with the separate estate creditors for those purposes.[85] This facility does not work in the opposite direction; a clear illustration of the law showing a preference for the rights of joint creditors. What is the justification for this discrimination? Presumably a desire to protect those who fund enterprise.

A related issue concerns the position of a partner who wishes to prove as a creditor against the estate of a partner (or the joint estate of the firm). The law here took a restrictive view. Such a proof would not be permitted until all of the joint creditors of the firm had been satisfied, if needs be against the separate estates of individual partners.[86] The thinking here is that it would be unjust for a partner, who might be jointly liable for partnership debts, to compete on equal terms with partnership creditors claiming against the estate of an individual partner (or joint estate of the firm).[87] These principles appear to have been largely unaffected by the Insolvent Partnerships Order 1994.

---

[81]   For criticism of the 1986 Order see *Re Marr* [1990] Ch 73 per Nicholls LJ.
[82]   Insolvent Partnerships Order 1994 Art 11.
[83]   For discussion of the PVA see A. Bacon (1994) 10 IL&P 166.
[84]   This rule is believed to date back to 1770. For the common law perspective see *Read v Bailey* (1877) 3 Ch App 94. The common law rule was embodied in section 33(6) of the Bankruptcy Act 1914. This common law solution did not apply if there was no joint estate to prove against (*Ex parte Elton* (1796) 3 Ves 238) nor if a joint creditor of the firm has petitioned successfully for the bankruptcy of an individual partner (*Ex parte Ackerman* (1808) 14 Ves 604).
[85]   Insolvent Partnerships Order 1994 Arts 8 and 10. For criticisms of the old law see Cork Committee (Cmnd 8558) para 1690.
[86]   *Ex parte Young* (1814) 2 Rose 40, *Ex parte Collinge* (1863) 4 De G & J 533.
[87]   This problem did not arise if the separate estate was clearly insufficient to fully satisfy the joint creditors because in such a case the joint creditors would have no claim on that fund – *Ex parte Topping* (1865) 4 De G J and Sm 551.

Contracting Counterparties

As a matter of common law the mere fact of bankruptcy does not terminate contracts.[88] A commercial contract will often contain a provision that the advent of bankruptcy will permit the other party to terminate the contract.[89] Such a provision is valid under English law.[90] Leases frequently contain such termination clauses,[91] though their impact may be denied by the debtor applying to court for relief against forfeiture under s. 146 of the Law of Property Act 1925. In cases where the contract makes no such provision recourse may be had to s. 345 of the Insolvency Act 1986 to terminate the contract. A comparable provision for contracts of apprenticeship is to be found in s. 348 of the 1986 Act.

Notwithstanding the general principle outlined above, the intervention of bankruptcy may be used to further the interests of the bankrupt's estate and ultimately creditors by permitting interference with existing continuing contracts. Thus extortionate credit bargains may be set aside pursuant to s. 343 of the Insolvency Act 1986. There is scant evidence of this provision being used in practice and this reflects the position generally on such contracts. The trustee in bankruptcy may disclaim an onerous continuing contract pursuant to s. 315 of the 1986 Act. One attraction in this strategy is that it may prevent obligations which might otherwise be regarded as expenses from being added to the list of priority claims on the estate. A landlord who suffers as a result of the lease being disclaimed can submit a claim in respect of his loss but this will often be much less than the amount he might have expected to receive had the tenancy continued. Can disclaimer be justified on legal principle? Critics of the mechanism argue that it discriminates unfairly against post-bankruptcy creditors and in favour of the estate. It interferes with pre-bankruptcy expectations and may undermine commercial confidence. To be set against this landlords should be aware of this possibility and should develop a risk management strategy – e.g. by demanding guarantees and sureties.

Sureties

A surety or guarantor who has committed itself to meet the financial obligation of a debtor in the event of default clearly has a legitimate interest in ensuring that its rights and obligations are properly addressed by bankruptcy law. These concerns have been with us since the earliest days of English law, and indeed they featured in the Magna Carta.[92] It is in the interests of the surety that bankruptcy operates effectively to enable maximum creditor recovery. On discharge of a bankrupt the creditor's rights

---

[88] *Brooke v Hewitt* (1796) 3 Ves Jun 253, *Re Stapleton* (1879) 10 Ch D 586.
[89] Even in the absence of such a clause the advent of bankruptcy may be seen either as a breach of contract or possibly a frustrating event depending upon the nature of the contract – see *Ex parte Chalmers* (1873) LR 8 Ch App 289.
[90] In Ireland forfeiture clauses in leases and hire purchase agreements are void – Bankruptcy Act 1988 s. 49. The same is true of Australia – Bankruptcy Act 1966 s. 301.
[91] See *Cadogan Estates Ltd v McMahon* [2001] BPIR 817.
[92] See Magna Carta 1215, article 9.

against any co-surety are unaffected, as s. 281(7) of the Insolvency Act 1986 makes clear.

One vexed area of the interface between bankruptcy law and the law of guarantees concerns disclaimer. If an insolvent party disclaims a liability, to what extent can the creditor have recourse to the surety. The original view, as expressed in *Stacey v Hill*[93] was that the guarantee fell with the disclaimer. That approach was rejected by the House of Lords in *Hindcastle v Attenborough*[94] with the result that the surety liabilities can now survive disclaimer. In so deciding their Lordships took the view that sureties are often demanded to deal with this very eventuality and it would be ludicrous for the court to frustrate what was the clear commercial purpose of the arrangement. Where a surety has been called upon by the creditor to honour the commitment in the guarantee then clearly the surety can lodge a proof against the estate of the bankrupt debtor.[95]

As might be expected, the surety issue has cropped up in several cases featuring IVAs. The basic question to be determined is whether an IVA featuring the realignment of the obligations of a co-obligor has a similar impact upon other parties obligated under the guarantee arrangement. The answer given by the courts has consistently been in the negative. Thus, in *Johnson v Davies*[96] the Court of Appeal indicated that as a general rule the entry into an IVA of a debtor does not release a surety or co-debtor, though it is possible with the assent of the creditor to produce such a result. However, the court was not minded to infer a term to that effect; express provision was required. Again in *Greene King plc v Stanley*[97] the Court of Appeal affirmed that as a general rule of law releasing a principal debtor through an IVA does not by implication release the surety; indeed on the facts of the present case the creditor had expressly reserved its rights as against the surety! The position here is therefore clear and release can only be arranged through negotiation and inclusion of a provision in the terms of the arrangement.

Public Interest[98]

This has been a vital component of bankruptcy regulation since the earliest days and continues to occupy a position of some prominence:

> Insolvency proceedings have never been treated in English law as an exclusively private matter between the debtor and his creditors; the community itself has always been recognised as having an important interest in them.

[93]   [1901] 1 KB 660.
[94]   [1997] AC 70.
[95]   Timing is critical here and the surety must wait until the creditor has had recourse under the guarantee – *Re Glen Express Ltd* [2000] BPIR 456 (rule against double proof must not be infringed).
[96]   [1999] 1 Ch 117. For comment see R. Munro (1998) 14 IL&P 230.
[97]   [2001] EWCA Civ 1966, [2002] BPIR 491. See also *Lombard Nat West Factors v Koutrouzas* [2002] EWHC 1084 (QB), [2003] BPIR 444.
[98]   On the public interest generally in insolvency law see A. Keay (2000) 51 NILQ 509.

So concluded the Cork Committee in 1982 (para 1734). The public interest surfaces in bankruptcy law for a variety of reasons. The institution of credit is deemed vital for the health of the economy and therefore the law should be adequate to ensure its effective operation by providing a default mechanism. Equally it may be argued that there is a public interest in encouraging the rehabilitation of debtors to enable them to make a productive contribution to society in the future (thereby removing them from the list of welfare claimants and enabling them to pay taxes). If we remain focused on this more selfish viewpoint the State may be a creditor and may be looking to recover its dues from the estate. In this context it is important to note s. 434 of the Insolvency Act 1986 which makes it clear that the general provisions governing creditor rights apply to the Crown. However, the Crown has in the past benefited from the award of preferential status. There is a legislative self-serving tradition here going back to 1849 and a common law predisposition of much greater antiquity. The Enterprise Act 2002, with its abolition of preferential status for Crown debts, breaks that tradition; not before time many would say. The State also has a legitimate interest in insolvency in that bad debts attract tax relief; facilitating repayment schemes that do not involve a crude fire sale of assets may thus produce fiscal maximisation.[99] The clearest manifestation of the public interest is through the role accorded to the Official Receiver as reflected by the provisions in ss. 399–401 of the Insolvency Act 1986 (as supported by Part 10 of the Insolvency Rules 1986). Apart from being a member of the bureaucracy an Official Receiver is also afforded the status of an officer of the court (s. 400(2)). One curious omission in the law lies in the fact that the State as such has no power to petition the court to bankrupt an individual except in its capacity as a private creditor. There is no facility comparable to petitions to wind up companies in the public interest pursuant to s. 124A of the Insolvency Act 1986. It is unclear whether this is a serious lacuna or a mere legislative quirk of no practical significance. The public interest is relevant in the corporate context because of the potential harm that limited liability can wreak. That is not to say, however, that there is a lack of public interest in all cases where the question of whether an individual should be bankrupted arises.

The role of the State in administering the system has been controversial for the last 150 years. Creditors complain about the cost of operating a bankruptcy regime. Private practitioners saw an opportunity to move into an area of activity. In a Consultative Document in 1980 the newly elected Conservative government saw an opportunity to roll back the boundaries of the State by withdrawing the Official Receiver from the bankruptcy arena. This proposal met with outrage and was then decisively rejected by the Cork Committee (see paras 714 and 717) which viewed the institution as vital to maintaining public confidence in the bankruptcy system. The committee was "diametrically opposed" to what the government was suggesting and was convinced that to go down the path that the government intended would lead to the sort of public scandal that was common before the Official Receiver was introduced in 1883. In its opinion the public interest was a key constituency in bankruptcy law and that

[99] In recent years the State has been keen to extend bad debt relief to rehabilitation schemes such as the IVA. Apart from the social desirability of promoting rescue the State undoubtedly has an eye on future tax revenues to be gleaned from keeping a debtor afloat.

had to be paid for. The current system of funding it via interest earned on what is now the Insolvency Services Account was viewed with some scepticism. A preference was expressed for funding through general taxation (para 857):

> The administration of insolvency is a vital public service, an essential part of the maintenance of law and order. In our view, it is no more appropriate for it to be provided at the expense of creditors than for police pay to be provided at the expense of the victims of crime.

The Insolvency Act 2000 (s. 13) represents a considerable change in policy by the government by permitting insolvency practitioners acting as trustees in bankruptcy to maximise realisation investments outside the confines of the Insolvency Services Account. Changes in the Enterprise Act 2002 (ss. 270–272) will improve both the position of the ISA vis-à-vis the Consolidated Fund and will allow insolvent estates to benefit from increased rates of interest on balances held in the ISA. The Enterprise Act 2002 makes further changes in this area. The 2002 legislation changes the role of the Official Receiver in a number of ways. Firstly, the oversight role is reduced in more mundane bankruptcy cases because the statutory duty to investigate is reduced to a mere discretion.[100] However, the Official Receiver is expected to have a key input into the operation of the bankruptcy restrictions order regime which has been introduced as a mechanism to deal with abusive bankrupts.[101] The 2002 Act also reflects a new approach in that the management of the post-bankruptcy IVA is to be vested exclusively in the hands of the Official Receiver.[102] The thinking here is that with the economies of scale this solution will be cost effective. The problem with this strategy is that the market for such a service may well be limited, particularly as bankruptcy will become a much gentler regime, thereby removing the need for alternatives.

Professional Interests

It must always be borne in mind that many professionals make their living out of bankruptcy. We are not merely talking about insolvency practitioners holding appointments – many lawyers, information specialists and other professional advisers depend upon bankruptcy to maintain their own way of life. Such "parasitic" constituencies have a legitimate stake in the operation of the bankruptcy system. In particular, they are entitled to expect that their fees and expenses incurred whilst administering the estate are recoverable. The acceptance of this expectation is reflected in many cases. The court has repeatedly said that in deciding whether to grant permission for the realisation of an asset, it will not refuse permission simply because

---

[100] Enterprise Act 2002 s. 258 replacing IA 1986 s. 289.
[101] Ibid s. 257 – inserting s. 281A and Sched 4A into IA 1986.
[102] Ibid s. 264 – inserting IA 1986 ss. 263A–G.

the main beneficiary will be the insolvency practitioner who is applying to the court.[103]

This right of reward cannot be an absolute expectation. Scrutiny of claims for fees and expenses is generally accepted within the professions. Thus, there are official scales for fees[104] and in theory there exists the opportunity to challenge the level of fees claimed. This right of challenge is now to be found in Insolvency Rule 6. 142 which allows a creditor with the support of the holders of 25% of the debt to challenge fees which are alleged to be excessive. The inherent jurisdiction of the court can also be used as a mechanism to control fees.[105] In *Engel v Peri*[106] the court was asked to consider whether its review jurisdiction in s. 303 could be used to review fees. It answered this question in the negative, though it did point out that the general review power conferred by s. 363 could be so invoked. This matter was revisited by Registrar Baister in *Woodbridge v Smith*.[107] Here the wife of a bankrupt, who was seeking to have the bankruptcy annulled, had managed to settle all of the bankruptcy debts apart from the professional fees charged by the trustee. On a request for a breakdown of the fees the trustee simply provided the final figure without a detailed itemisation. That figure was then approved by a creditors' meeting which had been called with inadequate notice. Registrar Baister held that the wife had locus standi to use s. 303 because she clearly had a legitimate interest in the matter. Moreover, this case could be distinguished from *Engel v Peri*[108] because the wife was not seeking to use s. 303 to challenge the final figure, but rather to ascertain how that total had been arrived at. In any case the court enjoyed jurisdiction both under s. 363 and by virtue of its inherent jurisdiction to control its officers to review the issues in question. The issue of professional fees in insolvency cases came to the fore in *Maxwell*.[109] This case arose out of the mysterious death of Robert Maxwell and the financial chaos left in its wake. A receiver was appointed to realise the personal estate of the deceased. The proceeds of realisation were swamped by the costs of the receiver (remuneration and disbursements).[110] When the matter came before Ferris J he was most critical of the state of affairs. Shortly afterwards a joint working party headed by Mr Justice Ferris

---

[103] See *Trustee of Estate of Bowe v Bowe* [1997] BPIR 747. In *Harrington v Bennett* [2000] BPIR 630 where the sale of property jointly owned by a bankrupt and her spouse was allowed to proceed notwithstanding that the proceeds were likely to be swallowed up in meeting the trustee's costs of realising the estate. Compare *Claughton v Charalambous* [1998] BPIR 558 and *Vadher v Weisgard* [1998] BPIR 295 where the court agreed to terminate an IVA on the petition of the supervisor because the income produced by the debtor was being swallowed up by administration costs with the creditors getting minimal benefit.

[104] The Official Receiver's scale is not appropriate for private practitioners – *Upton v Taylor* [1999] BPIR 168. Note generally IR 1986 rr. 6.138–6.142.

[105] See *Upton v Taylor* (supra) where the rule in *Ex parte James* (1874) LR 9 Ch App 609 (duty of court officers to act honourably) was cited as authorising such intervention.

[106] [2002] EWHC 799 (Ch), [2002] BPIR 961.

[107] [2004] BPIR 247.

[108] Supra.

[109] *Mirror Group Newspapers v Maxwell* [1998] BCC 324.

[110] When the case came before Chief Taxing Master Hurst the professional fees and disbursements were largely upheld – see [1999] BCC 684 for an unprecedented report of such a ruling. There is limited guidance on what is an acceptable disbursement. Solicitors' fees have to be taxed and we do know that a suggested fee claim by a litigant in person of £1000 per hour (!!) did not impress the court in *Customs and Excise v Chitolie* [2000] BPIR 275.

was set up to review remuneration practices. This body reported in July 1998.[111] As a result of this process a new Statement of Insolvency Practice 9 was introduced in December 2002.[112] A further regulatory measure appeared in the summer of 2004 with the publication of an important Practice Direction[113] offering guidance to practitioners where applications are made to the court. Independently of this guidance the courts are becoming more censorious of claims for remuneration and expenses.[114]

The professional interest does not merely extend to matters of fee income. Standard rules governing professional privilege may come into conflict with bankruptcy procedures. In *Barclays Bank v Eustice*[115] the court was considering whether a property transfer infringed s. 423 of the 1986 Act. The Court of Appeal held that where a prima facie breach of s. 423 was established it was appropriate to lift professional privilege to investigate the true motives of the debtor. There should also be in place adequate procedures to allow trustees to resign office should they consider such a step appropriate. Although a trusteeship in bankruptcy carries with it many obligations, there is no requirement to remain in office until the commission is completed. The personal circumstances of the trustee may dictate the need for a change – e.g. ill health or a career move. It is vital in this situation that transparent but cost-effective procedures exist for a substitution. This need is further magnified when one considers that an insolvency practitioner may hold many such appointments concurrently.[116] English law[117] still retains the quaint notion that offices are held by individuals rather than the firms for which they practice. This may reinforce notions of professional integrity but it does produce real practical difficulties in an era where "star" practitioners move between firms with the same regularity as Premier League footballers! The fact that it is also out of touch with reality is apparent when one considers that much of the day-to-day management of the estate is conducted at a lower level within the firm through the agency of managers rather than by the partner named as office holder.[118] The possibility of block transfer orders has attracted guidance from the courts both in individual instances[119] and through general guidelines.[120]

Insolvency practitioners are not the only professional group who make their living out of the financial difficulties of others. Money advisers, companies offering to roll

---

[111] On the Ferris Report see Sir F. Ferris [1999] Ins Law 48 and K. Theobald (1998) 14 IL&P 300.

[112] Noted in [2003] 15 Ins Intell 8.

[113] [2004] BPIR 953 (Registrar Baister).

[114] Witness the scathing comments of the district judge in *Boyden v Watson* [2004] BPIR 1131.

[115] [1995] 1 WLR 1238.

[116] See *Re A & C Supplies Ltd* [1998] 1 BCLC 603 where a partner held no less than 165 appointments!

[117] Not so in Canada where the appointment is vested in the firm.

[118] This fact of life is apparent from a perusal of the facts in *Re Alt Landscapes Ltd* [1999] BPIR 459 and from *Boyden v Watson* [2004] BPIR 1131 at [3].

[119] See for example *Re Equity Nominees Ltd* [1999] 2 BCLC 19, *Cork v Rolph*, The Times December 21 2000 and *Saville v Gerrard and Pick* [2004] EWHC 1363 (Ch), [2004] BPIR 1332 where Lewison J adopted the most cost-effective manner of carrying out the block transfer but made it clear as the transfer had been necessitated by reorganisation within the firm that the cost should not be borne by the insolvent estates. The court, however, cannot backdate a block transfer order – *Darrell v Miller* [2003] EWHC 2811 (Ch) [2004] BPIR 470. For general discussion of block transfer orders see *HM Customs and Excise v Allen* [2003] BPIR 830.

[120] See *Practice Direction: Insolvency Proceedings* [2000] BCC 92 para 1. 6.

up personal debts into a single repayment scheme and credit reference agencies all have a stake in the system. The needs of the latter came to the fore in *Re Austintel Ltd.*[121] Here a company specialising in collecting data on bankrupts sought permission under rule 7.28 of the Insolvency Rules 1986 to make a mass search of bankruptcy records for photocopying purposes. Permission was initially refused by Jonathan Parker J. On appeal the Court of Appeal came to the same conclusion though mainly because it decided that it lacked jurisdiction to hear an appeal on such an exercise of discretion. Nevertheless the lords justice who were on the bench recognised that there was a need for this area of law to be reviewed by the Insolvency Rules Committee and Ward LJ gave a strong hint that the position should be changed The case has lost much of its significance with the introduction of a national record of bankrupts in 1999 (now detailed in Part 6A of the Insolvency Rules 1986) but it does offer revealing insights into the mindset of the judiciary.

Getting the Balance Right

This is always a difficult task in any area of regulation. The relative position of competing interest groups will ebb and flow with the passage of time and changing social attitudes. One reform will often cancel out another. For instance, the possibility of improved financial returns for unsecured creditors ushered in by the financial and institutional changes in the Enterprise Act 2002 (such as the surrender of preferential status by the Crown and the changes made to the Insolvency Services Account) may be diminished by affording greater rights to bankrupts and their families over estate assets. There is no doubt, however, that the interests of the bankrupt have been advanced considerably by the legislature in the 30 years since 1976. It may be that we are due for a reversal of that trend in the years to come. Such a flow reversal may be triggered by an adverse public response to any perceived abuses thrown up by the Enterprise Act 2002 reforms.

---

[121] [1997] BCC 362 [2000] BPIR 223.

Chapter 7

Rehabilitation

The Rehabilitation Strategy

It has been the case for many years that official social/economic policy favours the rehabilitation of debtors through bankruptcy as a legitimate goal of personal insolvency law.[1] Thus, it is well settled that it is not contrary to public policy to permit a person in debt to exploit the bankruptcy procedure to clear outstanding debts.[2] In *Re Stern* Lawton LJ explained the rationale thus:

> The modern law of bankruptcy has its origins in a number of Victorian statutes which were intended to relieve those in financial difficulties from the burden of debt and the possibilities of loss of liberty in a debtors' prison and to enable them to make a fresh start free from debt. The price they had to pay for these benefits was the surrender to their creditors of all their property...[3]

Debtors thus have the statutory right conferred by s. 272 of the Insolvency Act 1986 to petition for their bankruptcy provided they are insolvent. Looking at the issue of rehabilitation from a different angle, the "tools of the trade" exemption from the catchment of the estate (discussed above in Chapter 3) clearly reflects this policy, as does the availability of income payment orders (and now income payment agreements) as an alternative to repaying debts from forced capital realisations.

---

[1] For the origins of the "fresh start" idea in the USA see *Local Loan v Hunt* 292 US 234 (1934) at 244. It is not however an aim that prevails over all other considerations – *Re Eileen Davies* [1997] BPIR 619.
[2] See *Re Dunn* [1949] 1 Ch 640 at 647 per Lord Evershed MR and *Collins v Official Receiver* [1996] BPIR 552. Indeed in *Boyden v Watson* [2004] BPIR 1131 at [18] District Judge Jones (perhaps tongue in cheek) even recommended this as a possible strategy to a bankrupt who might have to meet a large costs bill once his first bankruptcy was discharged! Having said that, the courts may be more hostile to the use of the bankruptcy mechanism to avoid judgment debts – see *Kozack v Ritter* (1974) 36 DLR (3d) 612. The opportunitistic use of bankruptcy has exercised the minds of recruitment officers in law firms when faced with questions from prospective trainees saddled with substantial education debts as to the attitude of employers to such a strategy. This idea of wiping the slate clean only applies to certain civil liabilities and does not extend to obligations under the criminal law – *Guppy v Redbridge Magistrates* [1997] BPIR 441.
[3] [1982] 1 WLR 860 at 866. That said, it is recognised that discharge can cause injustice, particularly to those creditors who cannot afford to write off the loss – see J. Finnis, *Natural Law and Natural Rights* (1980) at 191.

Bankruptcy Not a Terminal Process

Bankruptcy differs fundamentally from the liquidation of a company in that it does not anticipate the demise of the debtor. Bankruptcy thus is essentially a transient state of affairs that holds out the promise to the debtor of redemption through discharge. The realisation that bankruptcy is not a terminal condition is reflected in the fact that it is possible for an individual to undergo successive bankruptcies.[4] Statistics on UK serial bankrupts are hard to come by, but anecdotal evidence[5] suggests that they are comparatively rare birds at present but with relaxed discharge periods being introduced that position may change. In the USA it has been estimated that they represent less than three per cent of all recorded bankrupts.

We are told by s. 278 that bankruptcy commences on the making of the order and concludes when discharge occurs. That simplistic chronology however does not tell the full story; bankruptcy law can certainly have an impact on events occurring after the date when the successful petition was presented, and indeed before that date. Where s. 423 is invoked a detailed examination of events occurring years before the commencement of the bankruptcy may be required. Conversely, it is clear from s. 281 that the trustee's powers of realisation with regard to the estate survive discharge, as do income payments orders if the order indicates this or if the conditions of discharge so specify (s. 310(6)). Such eventualities have up to now however been apparently rare, though with the new one-year automatic discharge period introduced by the Enterprise Act 2002 one would expect the residual income payments order scenario to become the norm. As always, there is a lack of hard data on how long trustees on average continue to exercise their powers after discharge. The existence within the Insolvency Service of a Protracted Realisations Unit (which apparently has several thousand cases on its files) might be a useful pointer, though with the new rules on the prompt sale of the family home coming into effect on 1 April 2004 the days of this Unit seem numbered.

Discharge

The concept of discharge from debt is a feature of a number of legal systems.[6] Occasionally a discharge or debt amnesty has been introduced for political reasons to maintain social order or by way of recognition that some debts will never be repaid.[7] It has been said that it reflects the virtue of forgiveness and may even be justified by

---

[4]   This is implicit in s. 279 of the Insolvency Act 1986. Indeed it seems possible to have concurrent bankruptcies – ibid ss. 334, 335 – though the author is not aware of many instances of this happening. For a rare illustration of concurrent bankruptcies see *Hardy v Buchler* [1997] BPIR 643.

[5]   Serial bankrupts rarely feature in the law reports of bankruptcy cases.

[6]   Debt relief for poor countries is a high profile aspect of this tradition.

[7]   For historic examples see M. Radin (1940) 89 Pen L Rev 1 at 6. In modern times the campaign to write off Third World debt might be noted.

reference to The Bible[8] and other religious texts.[9] There are utilitarian aspects to it in that even taking into account the suffering of creditors a greater number of persons (in the form of the bankrupt's family and society at large) may benefit from a debtor being released from debts which he cannot possibly pay. Thomas Jackson offers an interesting insight into an economic rationale for discharge.[10] In a modern enlightened state where there is a decent social welfare net debtors may have limited incentive to control personal debt. By allowing debtors to escape debt through discharge society puts the burden of policing debt on the credit industry because they are the main losers from a liberal discharge regime. To quote in full:

> If there were no right of discharge, an individual who lost his assets to creditors might rely instead on social welfare programs. The existence of these programs might induce him to underestimate the true costs of his decisions to borrow. In contrast, discharge imposes much of the risk of ill-advised credit decisions not on social insurance programs but on creditors. The availability of a limited, non-waivable right of discharge in bankruptcy therefore encourages creditors to police extensions of credit and thus minimizes the moral hazard created by safety-net programs. Because creditors can monitor debtors and are free to grant or withhold credit, the discharge system contains a built-in checking mechanism.[11]

Another telling point made by Jackson is that as a society we in effect allow companies to escape debt by liquidation and dissolution, therefore it would appear harsh to deny individuals a comparable facility.[12]

One intriguing question that has not been tested is whether the system of discharging debts via a bankruptcy process infringes the property rights of a creditor protected by Art 1 of the First Protocol ECHR. It would be a surprise if such a conclusion were arrived at but it is a matter that should be considered by those pushing for more and more relaxed bankruptcy regimes. In *Back v Finland*[13] a debt extinguishment system was challenged but the European Court of Human Rights ruled that in the circumstances it represented a proportionate tool to achieve the social goal of rehabilitating debtors.

The discharge mechanism was first introduced into English law in the 1705 Act (4 and 5 Anne, C.17) specifically to benefit traders. Daniel Defoe, himself a failed trader, had been a key protagonist behind its enactment.[14] Non-traders (who could

---

[8] See the *New Testament* book of *St Matthew* chapter 6 verse 12 (forgive us our debts, as we forgive our debtors"). In the *Old Testament* book of *Deuteronomy* chapter 15 verses 1–11 we are offered an exhortation in favour of cancelling debts every seven years. See generally J. Kilpi, *The Ethics of Bankruptcy* (1998). J. R Sutherland provides a good account of the so-called Jubilee discharge tradition in (1988) 7 Jo of Bus Eth 917 at 923.

[9] *The Koran* (Al Baqarah) – "If your debtor be in straits, grant him a delay until he can discharge his debt; but if you waive the sum as alms it will be better for you, if you but knew it". For attitudes in Jewish Law where a distinction may be maintained between the right of a creditor to insist on payment and the obligation of society to promote rehabilitation, see M. Tamari (1999) 9 Jo of Bus Eth 785.

[10] See T.H. Jackson (1985) 98 Harv L Rev 1393 at 1402.

[11] Jackson at 231.

[12] Ibid at 229–230.

[13] [2005] BPIR 1.

[14] For background see M. Quilter (2004) 25 Jo of L Hist 53. It appears that the 1705 Act was merely intended as a short-term measure designed to help out traders hit by wartime disruption – see *ex parte Burton* (1744) 1 Atk 255 per Lord Hardwicke.

not utilise the relative leniency of the bankruptcy regime) were denied the opportunity of discharge unless all debts were paid. To the disappointment of Defoe there was an adverse reaction to this radical legislation and under the 1706 Act (5 Anne, c. 22) it was necessary for traders to obtain the support of some 80% of creditors before discharge could be given but this figure was reduced to 60% in 1809. In the years until 1842 the grant of discharge was still essentially in the hands of creditors and there were a number of recorded instances of it being refused for vindictive reasons. The procedure for discharge involved first obtaining the requisite support from creditors, then the approval of the bankruptcy commissioners and finally the agreement of the Lord Chancellor. The prerogative writ of *mandamus* could not be employed to compel the commissioners to agree to a discharge.[15] Special rules applied to the discharge of Crown debts: the consent of the Treasury had to be obtained in such cases. The 1849 Act (12 and 13 Vict, c. 106) introduced an element of moral judgment into the process by grading certificates as either first, second or third class depending upon the moral responsibility of the bankrupt for his reduced circumstances. This experiment proved controversial and was discontinued in 1861.[16] Under the watershed 1883 Act the position was arrived at in s. 28 where discharge could be obtained through application to the court with the court being required to refuse discharge where misconduct was shown to have taken place. Under this same provision of the 1883 Act creditors were allowed to make representations to the court. Generally, the latter half of the 19th century witnessed a number of restrictions being imposed incrementally (in 1861, 1869 and 1890) upon the grant of discharge; these legislative preconditions are best viewed as checks and balances introduced to protect creditors who had been deprived of their right of veto in 1842. One difficulty with the discharge mechanism (which required individual review of each case) was that it was not suited to large numbers of bankrupts flooding the court with requests that their bankruptcy be terminated. The statistics show a considerable increase in the numbers being declared bankrupt through the course of the 20th century. An even bigger problem was that many bankrupts could not be bothered to seek a discharge and this apathy was deemed socially undesirable. In 1976 a significant change of policy was introduced with the advent of *automatic* review of potential discharge cases after five years.[17] In future it would not be required for the undischarged bankrupt to go to court[18] to secure a discharge but the system would trigger the review. This sounded nice in theory but created an administrative nightmare and much wasted court time. The 1986 Act simplified matters by introducing an *automatic* discharge mechanism that did not require the imprimatur of the court. Thus, under s. 279 discharge would inevitably follow on after a specified period (three years) unless there were circumstances present deemed sufficient to displace this presumption. Under s. 279(3) non-cooperation with the trustee or Official Receiver

---

[15] *Ex parte King* (1805) 11 Ves Jun 417, (1806) 13 Ves Jun 181, (1808) 15 Ves Jun 127. For an account of the trials and tribulations of Mr King see M.S. Servian (1987) 3 IL&P 7.

[16] For an excellent account of this grading system see B. Weiss, *The Hell of The English* (op cit) at 44–45.

[17] For a good example of the transitional difficulties caused by this reform see the episode discussed by D. Morgan in (1980) 43 MLR 221. Australia provided the model for five-year automatic discharge through the operation of s. 149 of the Bankruptcy Act 1966.

[18] Statistics indicated that under the old system the vast majority of bankrupts did not bother to seek a discharge – see I. Fletcher (1977) 40 MLR 192 at 194.

constitutes grounds for refusing an automatic discharge, a point made with some force in *Hardy v Focus Insurance Co Ltd*.[19] An application under s. 279(3) can only be made by the Official Receiver (and not by individual creditors) but a creditor can make use of the complaints mechanism under s. 303 to induce a trustee to use his influence with the Official Receiver to intervene to block automatic discharge.[20] The fact of an earlier bankruptcy within the previous 15 years would also deny the automatic discharge. Where the bankrupt is undergoing the experience for the second time in 15 years, he or she is required to wait five years before applying to the court for a discharge.[21] It is also the case that the court retains a residual discretion to delay discharge if there are compelling reasons for taking this course of action.[22] To some extent the change in the law favouring automatic discharge was meant to represent a relaxation in the treatment of bankrupts. Undoubtedly, however, it was intended to reduce the number of legal proceedings.

The position on discharge has been changed by the Enterprise Act 2002. Discharge will now occur (even for repeat bankrupts) after a maximum of one year.[23] If the Official Receiver gives the green light it may occur before those 12 months have expired. Although this timescale is attenuated, it is worth remembering that the initial government proposals suggested (with a lack of realism) a six-month automatic discharge period! Many commentators think that the period enshrined in the 2002 legislation is too short, though we shall have to wait for a period of settling in before we can conclude definitely on this reform. Early indications from the Insolvency Service are positive. By way of comparison Australia, having adopted a short discharge period in 1996, then reverted to a more substantial duration in 2002.[24] Discharge periods on the continent of Europe are usually of considerable duration (in jurisdictions where they exist at all).[25] There has been a traditional antipathy towards notions of discharge, but in recent years several European jurisdictions have introduced the alternative of debt adjustment schemes under which repayments can be rescheduled and, in some cases, written off altogether.[26]

---

[19] [1997] BPIR 77. See also *Singh v Official Receiver* [1997] BPIR 530.
[20] *Hardy v Focus Insurance Co Ltd* (supra).
[21] Insolvency Act 1986 s. 280. In the US a debtor who has completed the Chapter 7 process has to wait six years before entering another bankruptcy.
[22] See *Holmes v Official Receiver* [1996] BCC 246 and *Jacobs v Official Receiver* [1998] BPIR 711.
[23] Enterprise Act 2002 s. 256.
[24] Bankruptcy Amendment Act 2002 – Australia reverts to a three-year minimum discharge period. A six-month early discharge optional facility was used in Australia in 1991–2002 but the onus was on the bankrupt to apply for discharge – Bankruptcy Act 1966 s. 149S. If such an application was not made the standard period for automatic discharge in Australia was three years. This early discharge facility was dropped in 2002. See J. Ziegel, *Comparative Consumer Insolvency Regimes: A Canadian Perspective* (2003) at 102–3.
[25] Discharge periods in Germany are fixed at six years. There is a three-year period in The Netherlands and 12 years in Ireland. There are no fixed periods specified in France and Italy where discharge is extremely difficult to obtain. In Canada automatic discharge is available after nine months – Bankruptcy and Insolvency Act s. 168. See "A Fresh Start" at para 4.2 et seq.
[26] See Chapter 2 in J. Niemi-Kiesilainen, I. Ramsay and W. Whitford (eds), *Consumer Bankruptcy in Global Perspective* (2003).

The effect of discharge is explained by s. 281. In short it releases the bankrupt from obligations in respect of provable debts;[27] the bankruptcy process therefore involves a trade-off, with original creditor rights being substituted for distribution rights in bankruptcy against the estate.[28] The law defines provable debts widely in order to permit the slate to be wiped clean[29] but certain debts (which are not provable on bankruptcy) persist. Fines[30] and liabilities in respect of family maintenance orders or lump sums are the clearest illustrations of this genre. The former exception can be justified by reference to the paramount importance of maintaining respect for criminal sanctions. The second exception (which is found in most developed countries) has an unashamed social rationale[31] though it may also reflect the indeterminate nature of the potential liability.[32] Fraud claims survive discharge,[33] though in English law the concept of fraud has been narrowly construed by the courts to prevent the survival of too many residual claims. In *Mander v Evans*[34] Ferris J indicated that any liability in respect of what might be termed constructive fraud was discharged on bankruptcy:

> I find it readily comprehensible that the legislature should consider that a bankrupt who has obtained his discharge should not be relieved of liability for his actual fraud committed before his bankruptcy. I find it much less comprehensible that he should remain liable for constructive fraud, which covers a wide range of conduct regarded by equity as unconscionable but not necessarily involving actual dishonesty.

The fraud exception has engendered debate in the US with some major credit suppliers arguing that it could be used to preserve debts owed by bankrupt credit card users when those debts were incurred at a time when repayment was unlikely. It will be interesting to see if this line of argument is invoked in the UK. Hypothetical liabilities are also not wiped away by discharge if in fact they crystallise at some later date.[35]

---

[27] It is for this reason that an IVA cannot be entered into by a discharged bankrupt for the simple reason that at this stage the debtor is no longer regarded as a debtor – *Re Ravichandran* [2004] BPIR 814.

[28] For a lucid explanation of this process, which demands an inclusive interpretation of what is a provable debt see *Re Hide* (1871) 7 Ch App 28 at 31 per James LJ.

[29] See *Sheffield and Regional Properties Ltd v Wright and Gilbert* (September 17 2003, unreported but noted in (2003) 19 IL&P 224 (contingent liability to specific performance discharged by bankruptcy). For discussion of the position on housing debts see J. Kruse (1996) 12 IL&P 193.

[30] See Insolvency Act 1986 s. 281(4) (fines non dischargeable) and Insolvency Rule 1986 r. 12.3(2)(a), which in effect reverses the position at common law as reflected by *Re Pascoe (No. 2)* [1944] Ch 310, a reform urged by the Cork Committee (Cmnd 8558, para 1330). Criminal compensation orders are viewed in like fashion and are non-provable – *R v Barnet JJ ex parte Phillippou* [1997] BPIR 134. Confiscation order liabilities are treated in similar fashion – IR 1986 r. 6.223. On the other hand, tax penalties are provable – *Re Hurren* [1983] 1 WLR 183, *Count Artsrunik v Waller* [2005] BPIR 82 – as are penalties imposed by professional associations which may be characterised as contractual debts (*Marcus v Institute of Chartered Accountants* [2004] EWHC 3010 (Ch)).

[31] Such items are provable debts in Australia – Bankruptcy Act 1966 s. 82.

[32] *James v James* [1963] 2 All ER 465.

[33] See the discussion in *Masters v Leaver* [2000] BPIR 284. There have been suggestions in the US that credit card companies have been testing this exception to deal with irresponsible credit card users who then declare themselves bankrupt. We must see if a comparable trend develops in the UK.

[34] [2001] BPIR 902. See also *Woodland-Ferrari v UCL Group Retirement Benefits Scheme* [2002] BPIR 1270.

[35] *Glenister v Rowe* [1999] BPIR 674 (risk of an adverse costs order). Compare *Re A Debtor (No 46 of 1998)*, The Times July 20 1998.

The list of liabilities that survive discharge has been extended in the wake of the Higher Education Act 2004. This legislation deals with the vexed position on student loans. Under 1990 legislation the assumption was that liability in respect of student loans survived discharge.[36] In the discussion over the implications of the early discharge provisions in the Enterprise Act 2002 the Insolvency Service indicated that student loans might indeed be wiped out on bankruptcy,[37] hence the need for clarifying provisions under the terms of the 2004 Act which preserve liability for student loans.[38] In the meantime it has been suggested[39] that some 899 students exploited this loophole in 2003.

The significance of the social policy favouring a fresh start is reflected in the decision in *Anglo Manx Group Ltd v Aitken.*[40] Here it was held that limitation periods do not cease to run during the period of bankruptcy. Thus the court held that it was not possible for a prospective claimant, realising that the putative defendant is about to enter bankruptcy, to delay issuing proceedings until after the bankruptcy has been discharged because by that stage there was a fair chance that the limitation period will have expired. Whether that reasoning holds good in a climate where discharge will be available after a maximum of one year remains to be seen.

Moreover discharge does not necessarily terminate the powers of the trustee vis a vis the estate.[41] On discharge the estate that automatically vested in the trustee does not then revest in the erstwhile bankrupt. Moreover, in *Oakes v Simms*[42] the Court of Appeal held that a trustee could conduct a private examination pursuant to s. 366 of the Insolvency Act 1986 with regard to a discharged bankrupt. Discharge, therefore, is not a panacea from the viewpoint of the bankrupt. What it does do, however, is to remove the burden of the stigma of being an undischarged bankrupt from the shoulders of the debtor and thereby relieves him or her of the attendant disqualifications and disabilities. With the reduction of disabilities imposed on undischarged bankrupts effected by the Enterprise Act 2002 ironically discharge will lose some of its relative benefits. Indeed, discharge will not prevent a prospective employer or supplier of goods and services from requiring confirmation of one's previous credit history. Michael Green, in his report on IVAs and insolvency regimes, has suggested statutory limitations on the storage and use of bad credit history.

---

[36] Education (Student Loans) Act 1990 sched 2 para 5(2) – see now Higher Education Act 2004 s. 42.
[37] See the note in [2003] 16 Ins Intell 24.
[38] Higher Education Act 2004 s. 42 and reg 5 of the Education (Student Support) (No. 2) Regulations 2002 (Amendment) (No. 3) Regulations 2004 (SI 2004/2041). In Australia such loans are also non-dischargeable on bankruptcy – see Higher Education Funding Act 1988 (Cth) s. 106YA and the discussion in J. Duns, *Insolvency: Law and Policy* (2002) at 412. Social policy and the need to protect the public exchequer has also induced the Canadians to provide that discharge will not be allowed to operate to relieve the bankrupt of the duty to repay student loans – the loan is not discharged until ten years have elapsed. The US has adopted a similar approach with s. 525(a)(8) of the Bankruptcy Code making educational loans non dischargeable on bankruptcy. For a critique of the US position see R.F. Salvin (1996) 71 Tul L Rev 139.
[39] See The Guardian, 14 February 2004.
[40] [2002] BPIR 215 – for comment see A. McGee [2002] Ins Law 133.
[41] *Re A Debtor (No. 6 of 1934)* [1941] 3 All ER 289.
[42] [1997] BPIR 499.

When considering whether to grant discharge the courts enjoy considerable flexibility. They can make it conditional, suspend it, or do both.[43] Thus, in *Jacobs v Official Receiver*[44] the anticipated discharge was delayed to enable further investigations to be undertaken into the conduct of the bankrupt and particularly as to the possibility of undisclosed income. In such circumstances an interim order to suspend discharge pending further inquiries was deemed appropriate. The options of the court were reviewed in *Bagnall v Official Receiver*[45] where an ex parte interim order to suspend discharge for a short period was upheld. Evans-Lombe J held that there was power to make such an order under the terms of IR 1986 r.7.4 and that the exercise of such power did not infringe Art 6 ECHR. On appeal the Court of Appeal[46] confirmed the order, though it did indicate some concern that late applications to suspend discharge need careful consideration

One criticism of current discharge arrangements is that they do little to offer constructive guidance on future debt management to the bankrupt who is being discharged. This is hardly surprising as successive governments have failed to act on the issue of debt counselling.[47] In 1992 Canada introduced a controversial procedure in which discharge is made conditional upon mandatory counselling.[48] This requirement has to be seen against the context of automatic discharge after a mere nine months. Clearly such a process may be regarded as demeaning but it would be interesting to be able to assess its impact.[49] Certainly the present government is receptive to discussion that there may be some merit in this mechanism. In its Consultative Document, "Bankruptcy: A Fresh Start", the possibility of employing these in English law was floated.[50] However, the idea was not pursued in the subsequent White Paper, "Insolvency: A Second Chance" (Cm 5234 para 1.5) with the result that it did not feature in the Enterprise Act 2002.

Repayment of Debts via Income not Estate

Bankruptcy involves the realisation of "hard" assets for the benefit of creditors. Many debtors, however, possess other intangible and future assets, such as human capital and the ability to continue to earn, which might offer alternative recovery prospects for creditors. Increasingly legal systems have identified this as a possible way of repaying creditors without destroying all hopes of salvation for individual debtors. This strategy also complemented the well-recognised desire of many debtors

---

[43] *Re Miller* [1966] 1 All ER 516.
[44] [1999] 1 WLR 619 – following the Scottish case of *Re Whittaker* [1993] SCLC 718.
[45] [2003] EWHC 1398, [2003] BPIR 1080.
[46] [2003] EWCA Civ 1925, [2004] 1 WLR 2832.
[47] In 1969 the Payne Committee (Cm 3909 paras 1209 et seq) recommended that the state extend the remit of social services to cover debt counselling – this proposal was never implemented.
[48] Bankruptcy and Insolvency Act s. 157 as explained by a Directive from the Office of Supervision (December 21 1994). See J. Ziegel, *Comparative Consumer Insolvency Regimes – A Canadian Perspective* (2003) at 50–51.
[49] Indications from Canada suggest that bankrupts perceive the counselling sessions as quite useful – see Ch 10 in J. Ziegel, *New Developments in International Commercial and Consumer Law* (1998).
[50] "Fresh Start" at paras 7.19–7.21.

to pay off all of their debts in the fullness of time.[51] In *Ex parte Vine, in re Wilson*,[52] James LJ, after indicating that on bankruptcy the estate as a general rule vested in the trustee, went on to declare:

> But an exception was absolutely necessary in order that the bankrupt might not be an outlaw, a mere slave to his trustee; he could not be prevented from earning his own living.

This sentiment that the law should look to the long term was manifested by the advent of the income payments order procedure.[53] In fact such a procedure existed under s. 51 of the 1914 Act but was rarely used.[54] One reason for this was that the law took a very narrow view of what was "income" for these purposes; prospective earnings of a professional person were not included.[55] Under s. 310 of the Insolvency Act 1986 the court may grant an income payments order on the application of the trustee, but only to the extent of reserving for the bankrupt sufficient income to meet the reasonable domestic needs of the bankrupt and his or her family.[56] This provision is amplified by Insolvency Rules 6.189–6.193. Income received from a pension is taken into account for the purposes of this assessment. An income payments order may take the form of requiring direct payments from the bankrupt or an attachment of payments to the bankrupt. Any existing attachment of earnings order may be varied by the court. In order for such an order to be made it is a prerequisite that there is available "income". What is income for these purposes is not always easy to determine. Certainly a lump sum may be so regarded if it can be treated as an income surge.[57] What is clear is that sums of money in the possession of a bankrupt as a result of a student loan are not available to fund an income payments order.[58]

In considering whether to grant an income payments order the court will not reduce a bankrupt to a state of affairs that is incompatible with modern notions as to what is an acceptable minimum standard of living. This concept is one that must be sufficiently

---

[51] This human characteristic was noted by Lord Mansfield in *Trueman v Fenton* (1777) 2 Cowp 444. The imperative desire of the character Mr Tulliver, who had been forced into insolvency through ill-judged litigation, to pay his debts to the last penny was central to the plot of *The Mill on the Floss* (1860) by G. Eliot (see Books Third, Fourth and Fifth). This is described by Eliot as an old fashioned approach in the prevailing notions of commerce but today it is a characteristic exhibited by a number of bankrupts. Sir Walter Scott wielded his pen to great effect as part of his resolve to repay his business debts. The same trait was manifested by Mark Twain in the US when a company he had invested in failed – Twain undertook a five-year world tour (1895–1900) to generate sufficient funds to repay the company's creditors in full.

[52] (1878) 8 Ch D 364 at 366.

[53] On the income payments regime see G. Miller (2002) 18 IL&P 43. Outside bankruptcy the attachment of earnings procedure (discussed in Chapter 1) fulfils a similar role.

[54] The former procedure in s. 51 of the Bankruptcy Act 1914 was rarely used – see Cork Committee (Cmnd 8558 para 1159).

[55] *Ex parte Benwell* (1884) 14 QBD 301 (a case dealing with s.60 of the 1869 Act). The ratio decidendi was based upon the fact that such professional earnings were fluctuating in nature and therefore not sufficiently stable to provide the basis for such an order. See also *Re Graydon* [1896] 1 QB 417.

[56] For the Canadian equivalent see Bankruptcy and Insolvency Act s. 68.

[57] *Kilvert v Flackett* [1998] BPIR 721 – this case typifies a purposive construction of the legislation.

[58] Higher Education Act 2004 s. 42 and Education (Student Support)(No. 2) Regulations 2002 (Amendment) (No.3) Regulations 2004 (SI 2004/2041) reg 5 – this reverts to the position under the Education (Student Loans) Act 1990 sched 2 para 5(1).

flexible to move with contemporary notions. In *Re Rayatt*[59] the issue was whether a bankrupt should be left with sufficient funds to pay for his children's private school fees arose. The High Court held that such expenditure might in certain cases fall within the reasonable domestic needs of the family, a concept that was not to be interpreted simply as basic needs. Michael Hart QC (sitting as a Deputy Judge) made the point that the law allows the bankrupt to make provision for reasonable domestic needs and providing for the private education of one's children might be seen as reasonable in a wide range of circumstances. Bankrupts must not be deprived of the right of choice and education choice was specifically protected by Art 8 of the European Convention on Human Rights. The court could weigh up the balance of hardship; here the creditors would gain minimally if the IPO was upheld but the child would suffer. In this particular case the children were already attending an independent school and the income payments order that disregarded their position had to be set aside. This matter was revisited in *Scott v Davis*[60] where it was emphasised that each case would turn on the question of what was reasonable in the circumstances. The bankrupt with mortgage obligations was the focus of attention in *Malcolm v Official Receiver*.[61] Here the court took a much less sympathetic approach. The bankrupt (a single person) was directed to find new accommodation if he could not afford to maintain his high mortgage costs together with the amounts that were properly payable under an income payments order. In *Albert v Albert*[62] the critical question of the interface between a bankrupt's obligations to a spouse and his creditors once again surfaced. In particular the issue at stake was whether the trustee in bankruptcy could be joined as a party to ancillary divorce proceedings in which the wife of the bankrupt was seeking a periodical payment. The Court of Appeal held that it was not appropriate to join the trustee as he was not at this stage seeking an income payments order. Millett LJ took great pains to explain the respective roles of the Family Division and the Insolvency Court in such cases. The Family Division could proceed to make an order for periodical payments but the amounts payable might subsequently be reduced if an income payments order was then granted in favour of the trustee. Rather than being joined as a party to the matrimonial proceedings the trustee should use his powers under s. 366 of the Insolvency Act 1986 to gather information necessary to protect the interests of the estate. An extraordinary application for an income payments order was rejected by District Judge Jones in *Boyden v Watson*.[63] Here the figures clearly showed that even if the most nominal amount were ordered to be paid, that would then put the bankrupt in a position of being unable to pay. The district judge clearly felt that the purpose of the application was to put the trustee in funds to cover his claim for remuneration and expenses. The application was dismissed with costs being awarded to the bankrupt.

If an income payments order has been granted it can be varied. However, such a variation should only be made if there has been a material change in circumstances.[64]

---

[59]   [1998] BPIR 495. For similar sentiments see *Prochera v Prochera* (1969) 13 CBR (NS) 166.
[60]   [2003] BPIR 1009.
[61]   [1999] BPIR 97.
[62]   [1996] BPIR 232.
[63]   [2004] BPIR 1131.
[64]   *Jones v Patel and Brent LBC* [1999] BPIR 509.

In view of the short-term nature of most income payments orders at present this facility is rarely resorted to. Again, statistical evidence in the public domain is sadly lacking.

The income payments order regime has not been a great success as was observed in "Bankruptcy: A Fresh Start". There appear to be two problems. Firstly, the courts seem reluctant to extend such an order beyond the three-year period for automatic discharge. The reasons for this reticence are not clear, but this is a pity as the legislation clearly anticipates such an extended period (see s. 310(6)). Secondly, the usage of such orders is limited by virtue of the fact that many bankrupts have poor income prospects. A debtor with good income prospects these days is much more likely to avoid bankruptcy by exploiting a voluntary arrangement. As a result of these factors it was estimated by the Insolvency Service ("Fresh Start" at para 7.7). that income payments orders are used in only ten per cent of cases and in that cohort many orders simply fail to deliver the promised returns for the estate. The income payments regime was modified in a number of respects by the Enterprise Act 2002. Firstly, technical weaknesses in the current regime were addressed. Thus the position with regard to income payments after discharge required clarification with shorter discharge periods being in vogue. Procedures for variation of IPOs were modified. More significantly, an alternative of an income payments *agreement,* which could be put in place without the need for a court order,[65] was introduced. This scheme, detailed in the newly inserted s. 310A, operates as follows. The bankrupt makes a written agreement with the trustee or Official Receiver under which either the bankrupt makes specified payments or such payments are made by a third party. The general rules relevant to an IPO then apply. Early indications are that this innovation has proved a great success and that since its introduction the vast majority of income payments arrangements are via this method. Indeed in the first three months since the April 2004 reforms were introduced, some 3300 income payment arrangements were made (mainly via undertakings) which represents more than the entire figure for 2003. At present we are looking at about 700 per month, which represents significant usage. The acid test, however, will be whether the promised income does indeed flow to the estate.

In order further to promote the rehabilitation strategy in 2000 the Insolvency Service produced a novel concept of "a post-bankruptcy IVA". This idea, which was influenced by models operating in North America, was given a formal basis by the Enterprise Act 2002. This mechanism (which is described below at 136) is designed to allow more bankrupts to use ongoing income to settle old debts. The scheme will be administered by Official Receivers so with the economies of scale the management costs should be modest. Corners are cut with the procedures associated with setting up a standard IVA model to further reduce costs. Anything that enables a bankrupt to make a fresh start whilst maximising returns to creditors must be applauded, but one wonders whether the introduction of yet another regime might not create confusion in the minds of advisers. Evaluating options can have hidden costs. Would it have not been simpler to fine tune the income payments order regime and (if that is a problem) make it more cost effective?

---

[65]   In Australia the trustee can gain access to a bankrupt's income via an administrative procedure that has its own in-built review mechanisms – Bankruptcy Act 1966 ss 139J–139ZI.

Arranging to Forestall Bankruptcy: the Genesis of the IVA

Once the idea had taken root that bankruptcy was legitimately concerned with rehabilitating the bankrupt it did not require a great leap of imagination to conceive that in some cases debt repayment procedures and debtor salvation might be facilitated outside bankruptcy. One reason why alternatives to bankruptcy have developed is that they may offer better returns to creditors. Equally there may be much to commend non-bankruptcy arrangements to debtors. This possibility has been noted since the early part of the 19th century. The 1825 Act (6 Geo IV, c. 16) introduced the notion of binding statutory compositions by which the holders of 90% of the debt could force their fellow creditors to accept a composition with the debtor. This figure was reduced to 60% by the 1849 Act. Registration of private arrangements and compositions became mandatory in 1861. Deeds of arrangement were introduced in 1914. None of these schemes were motivated by a desire to rehabilitate, but rather in response to the failings of the bankruptcy model as a debt recovery tool. By the latter half of the 20th century the deeds of arrangement model was obsolete. There were procedures under section 16 of the Bankruptcy Act 1914 providing for compositions and schemes of arrangement but these could only be activated once bankruptcy had commenced and by this stage this option was often too late. When the Cork Committee reviewed Insolvency Law it recommended significant changes in this sphere by further promoting the social goal of rehabilitation.[66] Strangely its recommendation that deeds of arrangement be scrapped (para 366) was never implemented, though the last recorded deed of arrangement entered into in English law was in 1998. The ensuing legislation accepted the basic arguments of the Cork Committee but tinkered with the precise model suggested.

The individual voluntary arrangement procedure as laid out in Part VIII of the Insolvency Act 1986, Part 5 of the Insolvency Rules 1986[67] and Statement of Insolvency Practice 3 has in terms of absolute usage appeared to have been an unqualified success.[68] In recent years on average a quarter of all personal insolvencies go through this route. In 1999 there were 21,611 recorded bankruptcies and 7,195 IVAs entered into. The figures for 2003–04 show that, of a total of 36,328 personal insolvencies, some 8,307 featured IVAs. Looking behind these headline figures there are worrying indications that many IVAs fail and others represent an inefficient recovery tool. The relative attractiveness of IVAs as compared to the newly deregulated bankruptcy model is also giving cause for concern. These issues will be discussed later.

The IVA Initiation Procedure

---

[66] Another indication of the tide in favour of arrangements rather than bankruptcy is to be found in s. 273 of the Insolvency Act 1986 which provides that where a debtor petitions for bankruptcy and the case is regarded as a small bankruptcy, an insolvency practitioner should be appointed to investigate the possibility of an IVA. As the community of debtors (and their professional advisers) becomes more alert to the IVA option this mechanism is likely to be rendered of marginal utility.

[67] Note also *Practice Direction* [1992] 1 WLR 120.

[68] The statistics for the year 1999 record 7,195 IVAs, which represents an increase of 46% over the previous year. For comment on the IVA regime in general see F. Oditah [1994] LMCLQ 210, K. Pond (1988) 4 IL&P 66, (1988) 4 IL&P 104, [1995] JBL 118, (1998) 14 IL&P 324, (2002) 18 IL & P 9, N. Doherty and K. Pond (1994) 10 IL&P169, and P. Walton [1997–98] 3 RALQ 277. The leading practitioner text on the subject is by S. Lawson, *Individual Voluntary Arrangements* (3rd ed, 1999).

Setting on one side the theoretical possibility of the court initiating the procedure,[69] the IVA procedure involves a debtor presenting his predicament to an insolvency practitioner (the nominee).[70] If the nominee believes that an IVA might offer a viable solution[71] he will assist the debtor to prepare a proposal to be put to creditors. While this is happening the debtor applies to the court for an interim order under s. 253. Section 252(2) informs us that such an order protects the debtor's assets for 14 days (unless extended) from most forms of hostile action.[72] Indeed it should be noted that the moratorium is operational by virtue of s. 254 on the making of the application for an interim order. The courts have been supportive of the moratorium associated with the interim order as the ruling of the Court of Appeal *Clarke v Coutts & Co*[73] suggests. As a result of changes introduced in the Insolvency Act 2000 (s. 3 and Sched 3) it is no longer obligatory for a debtor wishing to take advantage of the IVA facility to seek an interim order. In some cases, for example where all of the creditors are prepared to support the proposal, seeking an interim order may be an unnecessary and expensive step. The finalised proposal is then put to creditors and if it secures the required majority of three fourths in value of creditors' debt[74] the nominee (now described as the supervisor) is charged with carrying it out. Once the proposal is approved s. 260 provides that all creditors who had notice of the meeting and who were entitled to vote are bound by the scheme;[75] the moratorium is thus continued through the mechanics of a statutory contract. If the proposal becomes unviable or the debtor fails to live up to promises,[76] s. 276 requires that the supervisor should petition for bankruptcy.

---

[69] The court can do this under 273 of the Insolvency Act 1986 on receipt of a debtor's petition in a small bankruptcy case by inviting an insolvency practitioner to look into the possibility of an IVA. The insolvency practitioner will then report under s. 274 on viability and whether the debtor wishes to use the IVA scheme. There are no statistics on how often this option is used but one suspects that it is rare.

[70] An IVA can also be entered into by a trustee on behalf of an undischarged bankrupt – such an eventuality is very rare but things may change with the new rules on fast track IVAs introduced via the Enterprise Act 2002 (see below). To prevent abuse by repeat players in the IVA game an interim order is not to be granted if an earlier application had been made within the previous 12 months – s. 255(1)(c).

[71] *Cooper v Fearnley* [1997] BPIR 20, *Hook v Jewson Ltd* [1997] BCC 752 and *Knowles v Coutts & Co* [1998] BPIR 96. See now Insolvency Act 1986 s. 256(1)(a) inserted by Insolvency Act 2000.

[72] Protection is not total. For example, society may prioritise other social goals in preference to debtor rehabilitation – *Re M* [1991] TLR 192 (need to combat drug trafficking), *R v Barnet JJ ex parte Phillippou* [1997] BPIR 134 (enforcing quasi fines). At common law landlords retained the power to forfeit leases – *Re A Debtor (Nos 13A and 14A of 1994)* [1995] 1 WLR 1127 but their power to levy distress for unpaid rent has been blocked by the Insolvency Act 2000 (s.3, Sched 3, para 2). That legislation also took away the right to forfeit and re-enter.

[73] [2002] EWCA Civ 943, [2002] BPIR 916 (charging order absolute set aside).

[74] Insolvency Rules 1986 r. 5.23. Creditors with debts which are not provable on bankruptcy can participate – *Re A Debtor (488 IO of 1996)* [1999] 2 BCLC 571.

[75] In practice matters may be more complex with certain creditors being bound by the scheme with respect to some of their debts but outside the scheme for other debts – *Re Hoare* [1997] BPIR 683. The position with regard to sureties of the creditor is also difficult and depends very much upon the documentation in each individual case – see *Johnson v Davies* [1999] Ch 117.

[76] On the problem of debtor non-cooperation see D. Evans and K. Pond (1995) 11 IL & P 95.

The attraction of this scheme for the debtor is that the stigma of bankruptcy (and attendant disqualifications) is avoided. Creditors gain financially because the dividend payable to them will invariably be greater than the recovery they might have expected on bankruptcy. This economic alchemy is achieved because the costs of a supervisor will be much lower than the administration costs on bankruptcy. The creditors can also benefit from funds lodged in a bank by the supervisor; there is no requirement to lodge funds in the Insolvency Services Account. Having said that, it should be noted that this comparative advantage over bankruptcy has disappeared in the wake of reforms embodied in the Insolvency Act 2000. Other relative attractions have also been diluted in the wake of the Enterprise Act 2002. The law recognises the relative attraction of an IVA to a debtor, as opposed to bankruptcy and has put in place criminal sanctions to discourage debtors from including false or misleading particulars in their proposals in order to win the support of their creditors.[77]

The Role of the Courts

The courts have played a key role in promoting the successful operation of the IVA procedure.[78] They are involved at the initiation stage because without the protective effect of an interim order the scheme may never get off the ground.[79] Having said that, they prefer to leave questions as to the viability of the proposed arrangement to the nominee[80] and creditors to evaluate. Thus, they will not intervene simply because the creditors appear to gain little from what is proposed.[81] On the other hand, the court will not rubber stamp proposals that are manifestly hopeless cases[82] nor ratify proposals that have not been approved by the debtor.[83] Nor indeed will they allow the IVA scheme to be used to provide a binding framework for proposals which can neither be characterised as compositions nor schemes of arrangement.[84] If a proposal does not fall under either of these headings it cannot be subsequently brought under the IVA aegis by late modification.[85] In exceptional cases the courts have been prepared to intervene if they have doubts about the proposed level of remuneration for the nominee/supervisor.[86] The courts have attempted to protect the perceived integrity of

---

[77] Insolvency Act 2000 s. 3, sched 3, para 12 inserting a new s. 262A into the 1986 Act.
[78] There are many examples of decisions that may be regarded as supportive – *Doorbar v Alltime Securities* [1996] 1 WLR 456 being an early illustration of the genre. See generally D. Milman, "The Challenge of Modern Bankruptcy Policy: The Judicial Response", Chapter 13 in S. Worthington (ed) *Commercial Law and Commercial Practice* (2003).
[79] Having said that there are instances of voluntary arrangements being operated without the protective effect of an interim order. This manifestation has now received official recognition with the passage of the Insolvency Act 2000.
[80] By imposing an obligation on the nominee to be satisfied as to viability – see *Cooper v Fearnley* [1997] BPIR 20, *Hook v Jewson Ltd* [1997] BPIR 100, *Shah v Cooper* [2003] BPIR 1018.
[81] *Knowles v Coutts & Co* [1998] BPIR 96.
[82] See *Re A Debtor (No. 101 of 1999)(No. 2)* [2001] BPIR 996 and *Davidson v Stanley* [2004] EWHC 2595 (Ch).
[83] *Reid v Hamblin* [2001] BPIR 929, *Re Plummer* [2004] BPIR 767.
[84] *IRC v Bland and Sargent* [2003] BPIR 1247.
[85] *IRC v Bland and Sargent* (supra).
[86] *Re Julie O'Sullivan* [2001] BPIR 534 – see M Strong [2002] Recov (June) 16.

the voluntary arrangement concept by adding a duty of continuing disclosure which acts upon the debtor up to the time when his proposal is voted upon.[87]

The judiciary also act as referees if disputes arise as to procedure or as to fairness. Thus under s. 262 they can hear petitions by creditors complaining of "material irregularity" or "unfair prejudice". The Court of Appeal stressed in *Doorbar v Alltime Securities (No 2)*[88] that it will only accept the former complaint if the irregularity is such as to be likely to have affected the outcome of the meeting. A refusal to admit a vote[89] or the inclusion of erroneous particulars[90] in the debtor's proposal are almost certainly good grounds for alleging material irregularity. Equally unfair prejudice will only prove fatal if the complainant can show that its interests as a creditor (and not in some other capacity) have been unfairly affected.[91]

As with any new statutory procedure lacunae were bound to be uncovered. The courts have been quite adept in plugging these. Thus the practical difficulties faced by chairs of creditors' meetings in dealing with disputed and unascertained debts have been eased by the application of a fair degree of judicial commonsense.[92] Subsequently the Insolvency Rules were amended to help out with residual difficulties.[93] The profession both individually and collectively have displayed ingenuity in getting the IVA to work. R3 deserves particular praise for creating model IVA terms[94] in 2002 (revised in November 2004) in an effort to drive down IVA costs, though some practitioners have been loathe to ditch their own tried and trusted models with the result that many IVAs are not cost effective. Its booklet ("Is an IVA Right for Me?") (revised April 2004) has also proved helpful.

However the creativity of the courts has its limitations. They have refused to vary the terms of arrangements in cases where the creditors have not agreed to such a modification.[95] This cautionary approach has a beneficial effect in that it will surely encourage IVA drafters to include express variation clauses in proposals, though the courts have indicated that these are not without dangers.[96] Having said that, if every participating creditor favours a modification the court will not stand in its way, a point made clear by the Court of Appeal in *Raja v Rubin*.[97] Peter Gibson LJ explained:

---

[87] *Cadbury Schweppes v Somji* [2001] 1 WLR 615 – see N. Griffiths (2001) 17 IL & P 104. See also *Fender v IRC* [2003] BPIR 1304 and *Stanley v Phillips* [2003] EWHC 720 (Ch), [2004] BPIR 632.
[88] [1995] BCC 1149.
[89] *Emery v UCB Corporate Services Ltd* [1999] BPIR 480 – this may also be viewed as unfairly prejudicial.
[90] *IRC v Duce* [1999] BPIR 189.
[91] See *Re Cancol* [1996] BPIR 252. For a successful use of an unfair prejudice challenge see *Re A Debtor (No. 101 of 1999)* [2000] BPIR 998.
[92] *Re Cranley Mansions* [1994] BCC 576, *Doorbar v Alltime Securities* [1996] 1 WLR 456.
[93] See now Insolvency Rules 1986 Part 5 which were remodelled by SI 2002/2712 and then further changed in the wake of the Enterprise Act 2002.
[94] For this initiative see P. Hughes-Holland [2002] Recov (June) 32, C. Boardman (2003) 19 IL&P 75 and the editorial note in [2002] 15 Ins Intell 40.
[95] See *Re Alpa Lighting Ltd* [1997] BPIR 341. Compare *Horrocks v Broome* [1999] BPIR 66 (variation power included in IVA). Conversely the courts will not uphold an IVA where it is clear that the debtor has not agreed to modifications – *Reid v Hamblin* [2001] BPIR 929, *Re Plummer* [2004] BPIR 767.
[96] See *Horrocks v Broome* (supra) at 71 where Hart J adopted a flexible interpretation of a variation clause but also warned of their potential dangers if drafted too widely.
[97] [1999] 3 WLR 606.

Here, in my judgment, the position is no different from that which obtains under the general law where there is a multilateral contract. It is always open to some of the parties to agree a variation of their rights as between themselves if they can do so without affecting the rights of the other parties.

The courts have declined to validate IVAs which have been embarked upon without the precondition of an interim order.[98] Equally, they have not been prepared to resurrect arrangements which according to their stated terms have expired by effluxion of time.[99] In essence the courts have conceptualised an IVA as being in essence a contract. Having so approached the issue many questions can be determined by reference to standard questions of contractual interpretation. For example, has a participating secured creditor waived a right of recourse to his security?[100] Alternatively the question of the identification of assets comprised in the arrangement can be determined by this simple methodology[101] as can a determination of the obligations of the debtor.[102]

One of the most intractable difficulties facing the courts has involved the legal implications of an IVA failing[103] and being followed by a bankruptcy. Equally complex issues arise where the IVA continues to run but creditors outside the arrangement successfully petition for bankruptcy. The position here has required clarification from the Court of Appeal.[104] Peter Gibson LJ, seeking to enhance the policy of the legislature set down *five* principles equally applicable to all types of voluntary arrangement:

(i)   The setting aside of assets by a debtor under the terms of a voluntary arrangement for the benefit of IVA creditors in effect creates a trust.
(ii)   The effect of bankruptcy of the debtor on that trust depends upon the terms of the voluntary arrangement.
(iii) The terms of the voluntary arrangement therefore determine consequences.
(iv)   If the terms of the arrangement are silent the default rule is that the trust survives bankruptcy.
(v)   Participating IVA creditors can prove in the bankruptcy for any balance owed to them not recouped from the trust fund.[105]

---

[98] *Fletcher v Vooght* [2000] BPIR 435.
[99] *Strongmaster Ltd v Kaye* [2002] EWHC 444 (Ch), [2002] BPIR 1259.
[100] Compare *Khan v Permayer* [2001] BPIR 95 (security waived through IVA participation) and *Whitehead v Household Mortgage Corp* [2002] EWCA Civ 1657, [2003] BPIR 1482 (no waiver through secured creditor participating).
[101] *Welburn v Dibb Lupton Broomhead* [2002] EWCA Civ 1601, [2003] BPIR 768.
[102] *Stanley v Phillips* [2004] BPIR 632.
[103] It should be stressed that in determining whether an IVA is failing the court is not concerned with questions of culpability – *Re Keenan* [1998] BPIR 205. Equally the fact that defaults on the part of the debtor have been rectified by the time the supervisor's petition for bankruptcy is heard is no guarantee that bankruptcy will be avoided – *Carter-Knight v Peat* [2000] BPIR 968.
[104] *Re Gallagher NT & Sons Ltd* [2002] 1 WLR 2380. This case dealt with CVAs but the court stressed on several occasions that the principles applied equally to IVAs. This judgment of the Court of Appeal did much to resolve the inconsistencies of earlier case law – see *Davis v Martin-Sklan* [1995] BCC 1122, *Re Essengin Hussein* [1996] BPIR 160, *Kings v Cleghorn* [1998] BPIR 463, *Re McKeen* [1995] BCC 412, *Re Bradley-Hole* [1995] 1 WLR 1097.
[105] [2002] 1 WLR 2380 at 2396, [2002] BPIR 565 at 581.

These rules clearly favour IVA participating creditors at the expense of post-IVA creditors. That is a clear policy decision designed to encourage creditors to sign up to IVAs.

What the law does not tell us are the financial characteristics of a successful IVA. Pond has conducted valuable empirical research[106] in this respect and his findings suggest that if there is a strong asset base to the arrangement the prospects of success are greatly enhanced. In 2001 the Insolvency Service presented some data[107] to suggest that the average duration of an IVA was four years, with some 38% of IVAs lasting for five or more years. A more recent study carried out by Michael Green provides a goldmine of data and much food for thought.[108] Green concludes on the basis of his study of many IVAs entered into and concluded in recent years that the regime has lost its way. It has become over-legalistic, is inefficient and fails to deliver promised returns to all stakeholders. Its failure rate in terms of successfully completed IVAs is very high. It is also an institution that has been resorted to overwhelmingly by consumer credit debtors rather than by struggling traders. Having accepted all that, it still needs to be recognised that the returns are vastly improved on what a creditor might expect from a bankruptcy. Green makes many suggestions for reform. These include: reducing required levels of creditor support from 75% to 50%; compelling creditors to participate in IVAs instead of pursuing bankruptcy; nationally fixed pricing for IVAs; granting VAT concessions; more scientific procedures for licensing IPs and firms involved in IVA work. In spite of these perceived areas of action Green believes that the IVA has the potential to be the primary legal institution for dealing with personal insolvency and should therefore relegate bankruptcy to a secondary role. Bankruptcy should only be used to deal with those debtors who have the ability to repay debts but who refuse to participate in constructive solutions.

The original IVA model provided in 1985–86 has been upgraded as a result of the Insolvency Act 2000. The moratorium has been strengthened to encompass landlords' distress rights thereby overturning a number of decisions[109] of the courts. More significantly, the interim order has been decoupled from the arrangement by allowing IVAs to proceed without the need for a prior interim order. This should reduce costs and be particularly useful in cases where there are no hostile creditors likely to launch a smash and grab operation. These improvements from the viewpoint of debtors and practitioners must, however, be set against a more precise duty on the part of practitioners when reporting to the court under s. 256 on the viability of the proposal and a need to undertake more extensive investigations into possible debtor misconduct. There has been a feeling in some quarters that the IVA procedure has been exploited by some debtors looking for an easy ride; these changes should at least compel them to rethink their strategy. The 2000 Act modifications also introduce a number of technical solutions to the problem of unidentified creditors.

---

[106] See [1995] JBL 118 where Pond outlines the findings of a valuable empirical study.
[107] See D. Flynn [2001] Recov (July) 18.
[108] Michael Green, "Individual Voluntary Arrangements: Over-indebtedness and the Insolvency Regime" (November 2002) (short form report available on Insolvency Service website).
[109] *McMullen & Sons v Cerrone* [1994] BCC 25.

A New IVA Alternative

The Enterprise Act 2002 (s. 264 and Sched. 22) further modified the general IVA regime. Significantly, it introduced the variant of the post-bankruptcy "fast-track" IVA which was to be made available to *undischarged bankrupts*. The key provisions are located in ss. 263A–G of the Insolvency Act 1986 and permit the Official Receiver (and no other person) to promote this scheme. The Official Receiver will only assume this role if an IVA promises a better return for creditors than available on bankruptcy. It is not suitable for complicated cases. Basically we are looking at cheap and cheerful proposals that are offered to creditors on a "take it or leave it" basis; modifications are not permitted. If the creditors approve the proposal (and no formal meeting is required for these purposes) the Official Receiver will procure the annulment of the bankruptcy and the assets (unless included in the IVA) are returned to the bankrupt. This new type of IVA became available after 1 April 2004. Since that date the evidence suggests that it has not been taken advantage of widely. This is hardly surprising in that discharge is available after a maximum of one year. The only attraction would be freeing up the bankrupt from the attention of the trustee though the price to be paid involves being tied down to the terms of an IVA. The game might not be worth the candle.

The Future of the IVA

On one level (i.e. compared to bankruptcy numbers) the IVA has proved a statistical success. As a recovery tool it is infinitely more effective than bankruptcy, though there is still considerable scope to enhance its efficiency. When set against the number of debt management agreements being entered into the IVA has underperformed – this may be because it is less well publicised than debt management schemes as highlighted dozens of times a day via television adverts.[110] Even accepting this point there are always going to be real problems in providing legally backed effective "solutions" for relatively small scale consumer debtors.[111] We have seen that the report by Michael Green[112] contains many suggestions but his broad thrust is that the IVA should be seen as the primary model for dealing with personal insolvency and that bankruptcy should be reserved for serious cases where the conduct of the debtor requires investigation. This conclusion harks back to the impressions that influenced the Cork Committee. To effect such a switch in model usage would require major legislative engineering. The Enterprise Act 2002 has frustrated such a policy goal by

---

[110] See M. Allen [2004] Recov (Spring) 20.
[111] This problem has been encountered in other jurisdictions. For example, in 1996 Australia, recognising that its model of voluntary arrangements (Part X Bankruptcy Act 1966) was not working in a cost-effective manner in the consumer debt area, introduced a new instrument (debt agreements under Part IX) – for accounts of this reform see A. Keay (1997) 13 IL&P 149 and [1997] 20 Ins Law 10. An up-to-date summary of the rules governing Part IX debt agreements is also found in J. Duns, *Insolvency: Law and Policy* (2002) at 439–444.
[112] "Individual Voluntary Arrangements: Over-indebtedness and the Insolvency Regime" (November 2002) (short form report available on Insolvency Service website).

making bankruptcy (with all its weaknesses as a recovery device) more attractive to debtors than the IVA appears to be. The future of the IVA is therefore uncertain. Some commentators think that it has no future with the advent of "bankruptcy-lite". Others are more circumspect and insist that it has a continuing role to play.[113] Both creditors and debtors will have to think carefully about their positions. Debtors might decide that the short-term misery of bankruptcy is preferable to the drawn out commitments involved in an IVA. Creditors may have to be prepared to take a lesser dividend than they would want on an IVA proposal or else the debtor could opt for a complete discharge via bankruptcy.

---

[113] See P. Boyden [2004] Recov (Spring) 16.

Chapter 8

Final Reflections: The Challenge of Personal Insolvency Law

Does Bankruptcy Work?

If we can return to the question posed at the beginning of this survey we must now pass judgement on bankruptcy law. We noted in the introduction to this study that if popularity is a measure of success then bankruptcy would be regarded as in rude health. The problem with this criterion is, of course, that bankruptcy in itself is an admission of failure. By definition on bankruptcy there has been an inability by the debtor to meet obligations and a failure by the creditor to arrange appropriate repayment. The legal and financial system should also acknowledge some responsibility for this state of affairs. Looking at bankruptcy from a different angle it may also be said to have succeeded because it has instilled sufficient confidence in lenders to enable them to increase substantially the amount of consumer credit in circulation.[1]

Trying to judge bankruptcy on statistical criteria encounters a major difficulty in that the data is deficient.[2] Things have improved in recent years and are certainly much better than 1991 when the Deputy Inspector General of the Insolvency Service had to admit to the existence of a "black hole".[3] However, there are still many critical gaps in our knowledge, a situation which JUSTICE has deplored.[4] One interesting statistic that the Deputy Inspector General highlighted as critical was the number of second bankruptcies. If evidence could be adduced that this figure was rising a reasonable person might conclude that the strategy of going easy on debtors and offering rehabilitation might have to reconsidered. Some ten years on this key statistic remains unknown.[5] What statistical information do we have on returns to creditors?

---

[1]   J.K. Galbraith, *The Affluent Society* (1984, 4th ed) draws together the link between debts and the rise of consumerism/the production economy in chapter 13.

[2]   There have always been difficulties with bankruptcy statistics going back to the very early days – see S. Marriner (1980) 33 Econ Hist Rev 351. This lack of hard data is a problem in other jurisdictions – see T. Sullivan, E. Warren and J. Westbrook, *As We Forgive Our Debtors* (1989) at 4, though this particular book and its successor *The Fragile Middle Class: Americans in Debt* (2000) do much to remedy this defect in analysing the US system.

[3]   See D. Flynn, in Chapter 7 of H. Rajak (ed) *Insolvency Law: Theory and Practice* (1993) at 111.

[4]   "An Agenda for Reform" (1994). See S. Rajani (1995) 11 IL&P 24.

[5]   We are also in the dark as to the number of serial IVA debtors. As far as the US is concerned Sullivan, Warren and Westbrook estimate the number of "repeaters" to be as low as three per cent (op cit at 196–197).

A useful source of information here is provided by the Annual Surveys carried out by the Association of Business Recovery Professionals (or R3 for short), the organisation formerly known as the Society of Practitioners of Insolvency. The evidence then is that ordinary creditors do not get much out of bankruptcy whereas much better returns are on offer if an IVA can be worked out. Figures from the Insolvency Service referred to by Michael Green in his study produce the amazing conclusion that there is no distribution to creditors in some 80% of bankruptcies; the realisations are simply swallowed up in professional fees and overheads. A major reason for this in the past was the relatively high administration costs of bankruptcy and the fact that interest on sums collected by the trustee for the benefit of creditors was diverted to the public exchequer. The State also benefited from the unjustifiable preferential claims regime. The changes introduced by the Insolvency Act 2000 and the Enterprise Act 2002 should improve the prospects for ordinary unsecured creditors, though it will take some time for this improvement to be reflected in any data. Quite frankly any improvement will hardly make a radical difference.

When considering creditors it is important to distinguish between one-off players and repeat creditors (i.e. professional lenders). The former may be shocked by the low returns on offer. The latter may be more philosophical and indeed calculate that it is more cost effective to accept these low dividends than to impose high monitoring costs at the point of the credit decision.[6] A question for policymakers is whether lenders should be allowed the freedom to make such a choice.

From the perspective of justice a number of features of the present law must be criticised. Of course, our notion of justice must now encompass the fundamental rights criteria in the European Convention on Human Rights and now in the Human Rights Act 1998. Having said that, fundamental principles of bankruptcy law have stood up well to challenges under this new legislation. That said, it is clear that the law has softened its approach towards debtors in the last 150 years. Imprisonment for debt is now rare, a good thing because this would not be permitted by the European Convention (Art 1, Fourth Protocol). This liberalisation in English law is further evidenced by its approach to discharge, rehabilitation, exempt assets, and its willingness to permit a delay in the sale of the family home to allow for an adjustment to the changed financial circumstances. The Enterprise Act 2002 continues the trend in favour of introducing measures that improve the lot of debtors. Nevertheless the English law system of bankruptcy could still be characterised as "pro creditor".[7] We have a long way to go before Professor Wood would rank English bankruptcy law alongside the heavily pro debtor French model or the more middle of the road US model.[8]

As an economic institution bankruptcy is controversial. Of particular difficulty is the relatively high administration cost. All one can say here is that it is spread between the creditor body at large. There is some public subsidy. The funding of the system through interest earned on the Insolvency Services Account operated to the interests

---

[6] See Sullivan, Warren and Westbrook (op cit at 323).

[7] English law is not isolated in this bias in favour of creditors – Ireland and Australia may be cited as jurisdictions adopting a pro creditor stance.

[8] P. Wood, *Maps of World Financial Law* (3rd ed, 1997) Map 5. See also Philip Wood's piece in [1995] 4 IIR 94 and 109.

of the State for many years. The financial arithmetic has changed in recent years but that seems largely to be due to the costs of funding the director disqualification regime. Steps are in hand to control that latter head of expenditure. More significantly the Insolvency Act 2000 and the Enterprise Act 2002 represent a move away from the strategy of using profits on the Insolvency Services Account to fund the bankruptcy system.

Turning to the potential consumers of the product we see that small debtors are still not adequately catered for. There is in effect an underclass of the poorest debtors who are left to the mercies of more draconian methods of debt enforcement, procedures which do not offer the possibility of discharge for unremitted debt.[9] This has been a long standing problem that caused much angst in the days of imprisonment for debt and was most recently commented upon by JUSTICE in its 1994 report entitled "An Agenda for Reform".[10] The long awaited introduction of the revamped county court administration order procedure is the main hope here. This has been discussed in the July 2004 Consultative Document from the Department of Constitutional Affairs which dealt with the subject of overindebtedness.[11]

One criterion for judging the effectiveness of an institution is its adaptability. It is apparent from the ongoing study that bankruptcy law has proved itself to be a flexible institution over the ages. It has reinvented itself to cater for changing socio-economic conditions. Both Parliament and the courts have been receptive to changed circumstances. A perfect example of this is provided by the demise of the reputed ownership doctrine in the light of the development of hire purchase and consumer credit. Can we be equally confident that bankruptcy will meet the challenges of the future? To answer that question we need first to identify what those challenges might be.

Personal Insolvency in a Shrinking World

The fact that individuals may incur debts and own assets in a number of jurisdictions is not a new phenomenon. However, we are already beginning to encounter the impact of "globalisation" upon bankruptcy law on an increasingly regular basis. There have always been cases where a bankrupt has assets located in a number of jurisdictions but with the growth of second homes abroad and the widespread marketing of timeshare interests this is an increasingly encountered issue. In cases of cross-border bankruptcy several legal questions must be addressed. Firstly is it appropriate that a particular debtor be bankrupted under English law? The position here was for many years governed exclusively by s. 265 of the Insolvency Act 1986. Jurisdiction under s. 265 is conferred if the bankrupt was domiciled here, or was resident or had carried on business. Generally speaking the policy of the English courts has been to adopt a liberal view of carrying on business. For example, it is well settled that a business is

---

9   See J. Ford and M. Wilson, Chapter 6 in H Rajak (ed) *Insolvency Law: Theory and Practice* (1993).
10   Op cit at para 4.26.
11   *A Choice of Paths: Better Options to Manage Over-indebtedness and Multiple Debt* (CP 23/04), Dept of Constitutional Affairs (2004).

being carried on up to the time when obligations are settled.[12] However, in *Re Brauch*[13] the Court of Appeal indicated that a director of a company cannot be said to be carrying on business in the jurisdiction merely by acting in his capacity as a director. This is consistent with the notion of separate corporate personality. The position is different if the individual is in the business of managing or promoting a series of companies as part of an independent business activity, as was the case in *Re Brauch*.[14] In *Re Thulin*[15] the High Court permitted a debtor to be made bankrupt in England notwithstanding the fact that bankruptcy proceedings were already in motion in Sweden. Thus, foreign citizens (unless they enjoy diplomatic immunity) can be bankrupted under English law. Even though the terms of s. 265 are not met, the bankruptcy jurisdiction of English law may be invoked on a successful application by a foreign court under s. 426 of the Insolvency Act 1986.[16] This judicial comity provision is more usually encountered in the context of corporate insolvency but it is not so restricted. Indeed it must be pointed out that this provision originated out of s.122 of the Bankruptcy Act 1914, which in turn can trace its antecedents back as far as 1849.

Bankruptcy proceedings may be based upon a foreign debt provided the jurisdictional test is satisfied. Indeed, an English creditor can serve a statutory demand upon a foreign debtor without first requiring the leave of the court.[17] Moreover it was made clear by Morritt J in *Re A Debtor (No. 51/SD of 1991)*[18] that a statutory demand can be based upon a debt specified in a foreign currency. Foreign creditors[19] thus do have a right of proof but if they wish to exercise that right it might be necessary for them to hand over any recoveries from the bankrupt gained in a foreign jurisdiction or at least wait until domestic creditors have received an equivalent dividend before being allowed to participate in a distribution.[20] Cross-border issues arose in *Masters*

---

[12]   *Theophile v Solicitor General* [1950] AC 186 and *Re Bird* [1962] 1 WLR 686. Compare *Wilkinson v IRC* [1998] BPIR 418. See also *North v Skipton Building Society* Lewison J, June 13 2002, unreported, but noted in (2002) 18 IL & P 135 where issues of domicile of choice and place of business were considered and the bankruptcy was annulled for lack of jurisdiction on the part of the English courts.

[13]   [1978] Ch 316.

[14]   Supra.

[15]   [1995] 1 WLR 165, distinguishing *Robinson's case* (1883) 22 ChD 816.

[16]   A similar provision is to be found in Irish law in the form of section 142 of the Bankruptcy Act 1988. In jurisdictions with a federal structure it is necessary to make the bankruptcy courts of component states assist each other – for example see the provision in section 188 of the Canadian Bankruptcy and Insolvency Act.

[17]   See *Practice Note (Bankruptcy: Service Abroad)* [1988] 1 WLR 461.

[18]   [1992] 1 WLR 1294.

[19]   The exception to this rule concerns foreign states' claims in respect of tax debts – *Government of India v Taylor* [1955] AC 491. This exclusionary approach was confirmed in *QRS Aps v Frandsen* [1999] 1 WLR 2169. This prohibition sits very uneasily alongside protestations in favour of comity but it is an approach favoured in Ireland – *Buchanan v McVey* [1954] IR 89 and *Re Gibbons* [1960] Ir Jur 60. For discussion see J. G Miller [1991] JBL 144, K. Dawson [2000] Ins Law 81 and [2001] 4 RALQ 345, P. Fidler [2000] Ins Law 219 and P. St J. Smart (2000) 116 LQR 360. In insolvencies governed by the EC Insolvency Proceedings Regulation (1346/2000) it seems likely that this particular rule will not operate (see Art 39 of the Regulation) but it will still apply where there are no EC Regulation issues at stake.

[20]   This is the so-called hotchpot rule – see *Banco de Portugal v Waddell* (1880) 5 App Cas 161.

v Leaver[21] where the Court of Appeal was asked to consider the impact of discharge upon a foreign debt.

To what extent do the powers of the trustee to claim assets apply to foreign property? The short answer, as reflected by the comments of the court in *Pollard v Ashurst*,[22] is that a trustee is under an obligation to recover such assets but practicalities may preclude this. Proceedings may have to be launched in a foreign court to establish title and this may not be cost effective. Avoidance provisions may have extraterritorial effect[23] but again the cooperation of the foreign jurisdiction is required. There are signs that the English courts are seeking to improve procedures for the realisation of foreign assets. For example, in *Pollard v Ashurst*[24] a trustee of an English bankrupt who was the joint owner of property in Portugal secured an order from the English courts for vacant possession and sale of that property. This case may not be as dramatic as it appears at first sight because the other joint owner appears to have been within the jurisdiction of the English courts and the order seems to have been intended to operate in personam against her.

A problematical authority is *Re Tucker*,[25] a case decided under the now superseded s. 25 of the Bankruptcy Act 1914. Here it was held by the Court of Appeal that it was not possible for a trustee in bankruptcy to seek the public examination of an individual who was now resident abroad. Section 25 was not designed to have an extraterritorial effect and moreover it was not possible to compel an individual resident abroad to submit to the jurisdiction of the English courts. This decision has been heavily criticised and certainly it sits uneasily alongside later authorities in the corporate insolvency field.[26] It is therefore doubtful if it would be applied in the context of the current provision found in s. 290 of the 1986 Act.

Cross-border litigation is fraught with difficulty. The Brussels Convention does not extend to bankruptcy litigation. However, the courts in Europe, mindful of the need for some order in this field, have interpreted this limitation narrowly. A good example of this approach is provided by *Re Hayward*[27] where Rattee J ruled that the insolvency exclusion was limited to litigation which could only arise on liquidation or bankruptcy. The mere accident of bankruptcy could not take the case out of the Brussels Convention and thus the action to recover the Spanish villa property had to be brought in Spain because that is what the Convention indicated.

How will the position on cross-border bankruptcy be affected by the European Insolvency Proceedings Regulation?[28] This Regulation came into force on 31 May 2002 and applies to all insolvency proceedings opened in any Member State (with the exception of Denmark). The Regulation does not seek to harmonise substantive

---

[21] [2000] BPIR 284.
[22] [2001] BPIR 131. See also *Singh v Official Receiver* [1997] BPIR 530.
[23] See *Jyske Bank (Gibraltar) v Spjeldnaes (No. 2)* [1999] BPIR 525.
[24] [2001] BPIR 131.
[25] [1990] 1 All ER 603.
[26] See *Re Seagull Manufacturing Co Ltd* [1993] Ch 345.
[27] [1997] Ch 45, [1996] 3 WLR 674. See also *Pollard v Ashurst* [2001] BPIR 131.
[28] The Insolvency Proceedings Regulation (EC No. 1346/2000) was made on 29 May 2000. A vast literature on the subject has sprung up in the intervening period – see G. Moss, I. Fletcher and S. Isaacs *The EC Regulation on Insolvency Proceedings* (2002), H. Rajak [2000] CFILR 180, K. Dawson [2001] 4 RALQ 345, P. Omar [2000] Ins Law 211 and [2002] Ins Law 122, K. Gaines [2001] Ins Law 201.

bankruptcy law but rather to provide a set of working rules to deal with thorny disputes over jurisdiction and to establish cooperative mechanisms in cross-border and multi-jurisdictional insolvencies. The English courts will have jurisdiction to open bankruptcy proceedings against an individual who has his centre of main interests (COMI) in the jurisdiction. Whether the COMI is located in the jurisdiction will depend upon the facts with regard to each debtor. Unlike in the case of companies there are no legislative presumptions at work to determine COMI. If the COMI is not within the jurisdiction nor within an EU Member State jurisdiction will continue to be based upon Insolvency Act 1986 s. 265.[29] Many cases on determining COMI have come before the courts of Europe; most involve companies. One interesting English authority on COMI in the personal insolvency context is *Shierson v Vlieland-Boddy*.[30] Here the point was stressed by Mann J that in determining the jurisdiction of the English courts to open proceedings, the COMI must be within the jurisdiction at the date of the bankruptcy order; the fact that the bankrupt may have had a COMI here when the debts were incurred or even when the petition was presented is not determinative of the matter. Having said that, Mann J stressed that the courts should be alert to abusive changes of COMI designed to frustrate bankruptcy jurisdiction. One positive feature of the Regulation is that it allows for a more sensible solution to the problem of jurisdictional conflicts by permitting a secondary bankruptcy to be initiated first. The concept of determining primacy by virtue of the court first seized test has not been adopted. In reality the Regulation will merely firm up a move towards cooperation in insolvency matters that has been visible in judicial pronouncements across Europe for the last few years.

The advent of the Regulation will help but its utility will be limited by inherent territorial constraints. A broader international concordat will be required. The UNCITRAL Model Law[31] represents a step in the right direction and the introduction of an adoption facility by s. 14 of the Insolvency Act 2000 means that this will soon become a feature of English law (probably in late 2005). Having said that, the fundamental problem still remains – there is no harmonisation of substantive principles on the horizon and unlikely to be so for many years to come. Why has substantive harmonisation proved to be so difficult to achieve? The real difficulty is the fact that there are intractable differences on fundamental substantive rules and these differences themselves are founded upon cultural diversity. For example, there are sharp differences between English law and other jurisdictions on the acceptability of set off, the operation of preference rules and more importantly on basic objectives of bankruptcy law. The balance between creditor interests and debtor protection lies at the heart of the fissure. As we have seen in the common law world the UK is noted for its emphasis on creditor protection. This emphasis has influenced other jurisdictions,

---

[29]   See *Geveran Trading v Skjevesland* [2002] EWHC 2898 (Ch), [2003] BPIR 924 confirming [2003] BPIR 73. Where the Regulation applies its primacy is confirmed by s. 265(3) of the Insolvency Act 1986.
[30]   [2004] EWHC 2752 (Ch).
[31]   The text of this Model Law is available on the UNCITRAL website at *www.uncitral.org*. For discussion see M. Steiner [1997] Insolv Pract (Dec) 18, M Prior (1998) 14 IL & P 215 and P. Omar [2002] Ins Law 228. There is also a useful discussion to be found in P. Omar, *European Insolvency Law* (2004) at 42–43.

notably Australia. On the other hand, the US is more inclined towards debtor rehabilitation and, not surprisingly, the Canadians have followed suit.

In spite of these real difficulties with substantive harmonisation there are signs that the matter is beginning to be taken seriously at a European level. The coming into effect of the EC Insolvency Proceedings Regulation will inevitably serve to generate the interest of harmonisers in this field. In September 2003 a report of a group of experts was published by the Enterprise Directorate of the European Commission.[32] This report, entitled "Best Project on Restructuring, Bankruptcy and a Fresh Start", seeks to encourage entrepreneurial conduct by *inter alia* relaxing the rules on bankruptcy discharge and by reducing the stigma associated with bankruptcy. The report surveys the position in a number of EU national legal systems and it is quickly apparent that English law is well ahead of the game here compared to its EU partners. There is no sign of firm proposals for an EU measure in this area but that is surely only a matter of time.

New Technology

The increased usage of new communications technology poses a test for many established principles of law. Although there is no specific reference to bankruptcy in the Electronic Communications Act 2000 that legislation is likely to have an effect in a variety of ways. In particular the Insolvency Service is considering a scheme that will allow debtors to file their petitions on line in order to reduce costs. We already have in place an experimental internet scheme for the enforcement of uncontested debts in the county court. We experienced this factor of technological stress in *Re Austintel Ltd*.[33] Here the Court of Appeal had to grapple with the practice of searching insolvency records for commercial purposes by a credit reference firm. Under the Insolvency Rules 1986 there existed a procedure that allowed insolvency records kept by the courts to be searched with the leave of the courts. However, in this case it was held that this procedure was predicated on the traditional system of personal searches in ledgers and was not appropriate to modern systems of computerised records. Leave was therefore refused to permit mass searches and photocopying by a commercial searcher. The court did however express its concern that the law was antiquated and invited the Insolvency Rules Committee to investigate the position. Whether that investigation was carried out is unknown but shortly afterwards the Insolvency Rules were amended[34] to set up a public register of bankruptcy records.

In bankruptcy the impact of new technology is likely to be encountered in the procedural sphere. It seems clear that statutory demands in bankruptcy can be served

---

[32]   This report may be accessed at the following Commission website *http://europa.eu.int/comm/enterprise/ entrepreneurship/support_m.*
[33]   [1997] 1 WLR 616. Note especially the comments of Morritt and Potter LJJ at the conclusion of their respective judgments.
[34]   SI 1999/ 359. Generally much more information about insolvencies is freely available on the internet.

by fax.[35] The acceptance of this principle is apparent from case law and the Civil Procedure Rules 1998.[36] Creditors can also exercise proxy votes by using fax.[37] The acceptance of such communications by electronic means seems an inevitability. It does not require great intuition to guess at other ways in which the practice of bankruptcy might be affected. The conduct of business and the creation of debt across borders will become more commonplace throwing up an increasing number of jurisdictional problems. We are not far from virtual meetings of creditors. Interrogation of bankrupts can be carried out via video conferencing. Indeed in many cases at present the vital information gathering process is conducted through the completion of questionnaires. The operations of insolvency practitioners will be varied with the advent of new technology. We have already seen this in a very minor way with the introduction of a facility under which payments into the Insolvency Services Account can be made electronically.[38] Finally awareness of bankruptcy law will be promoted by the march of technology. Bankruptcy cases appear on the internet virtually immediately through the system of neutral citation.[39] The Insolvency Service and other public bodies have extended the range of information on offer. The Insolvency Service website which can be accessed at *http:/www.insolvency.gov.uk*, is a mine of useful information. The days when bankruptcy was the preserve of a niche group of professionals have long gone.

New Social Priorities

The political consensus for much of the past 50 years has been to support the institution of credit. What would happen to bankruptcy law if that consensus broke down? The growth of personal debt, particularly amongst young people, is alarming. It is estimated that there are nearly 60 million credit cards in issue. For a society that is becoming increasingly paternalistic in its approach to activities that may be viewed as self-harming a strange blind spot arises when it comes to the availability of credit in inappropriate cases. Late in the day the dangers posed are becoming apparent. Well-recorded suicides of individuals whose debts have run out of control have influenced the debate and there have been calls to limit credit card availability by means of a central register. If politicians decided to restrict credit, one tool they might adopt would be to return to a more draconian system of bankruptcy. What might this involve? Limitations upon discharge rights would figure high on this putative agenda. The use of counselling, as operated in parts of the US and Canada, is another possibility.[40]

---

[35]   An indication of the growing acceptance of fax is to be found in the procedures under which a qualifying floating charge holder can appoint an administrator under Schedule B1 of the Insolvency Act 1986 by filing notice with the court through a dedicated fax number.

[36]   SI 1998/3132, L. 17.

[37]   *IRC v Conbeer* [1996] BPIR 398 (an IVA case).

[38]   Insolvency (Amendment) Regulations 2000 (SI 2000/485).

[39]   For neutral citation see *Practice Direction (Judgments: Neutral Citation)* [2002] 1 WLR 346.

[40]   In Canada a trustee is under a statutory obligation to counsel the bankrupt and may also choose to offer guidance to his family – see Bankruptcy and Insolvency Act s. 157 and the Directive from the Office of the Supervisor of Bankruptcy (21 December 1994).

Other strategies would be to curb irresponsible lending and to educate the young on how to manage credit. The UK government has embraced both policies in recent years. As far as controlling the offering of inappropriate credit significant reforms are in the pipeline. A new Consumer Credit Bill has been included in the Queen's Speech for November 2004.[41] This will change the test used to challenge inappropriate lending practices from extortionate[42] to unfair. The reforms likely to be enacted have been hailed as the most radical changes since the Consumer Credit Act 1974. The Michael Green report suggests further radical controls upon lenders including the removal of a right to enforce debt recovery in some cases and the imposition of a duty of care upon lenders.[43]

On the educational front progress has been made. In 2000 a pilot study involving the teaching of financial awareness in secondary schools was launched with the support of the Financial Services Authority.[44] Research findings[45] based upon this pilot project have recommended that the initiative should be extended generally. However, the issues of constraints upon finance within the education system (and the problem of an overloaded curriculum) loom large.

Dealing with Debt: A Comparative Overview

This book has been written on the assumption that bankruptcy is the most widely accepted procedure for dealing with debt. That assumption is hard to test but some consideration of other legal systems might help. Comparative research has in the past impacted upon our bankruptcy laws. The inspiration of the Scottish model lead to the introduction of the deregulated creditor control regime in the years between 1861 and 1883. That legal transplant did not work. The current government is clearly influenced by US philosophy when considering the options for bankruptcy reform. However, all comparative research should bear a health warning. One mechanism might operate perfectly well in one jurisdiction but fail abysmally in another due to differences in background "cultural" factors. Having issued that *caveat* one should not be deterred from examining one's own procedures in a comparative light.

Under Greek law serfdom for debtors was abolished in the 6th century BC as it was believed to threaten the stability of society. This change of approach was attributable to the work of that great jurist Solon.[46] However this relaxation of the law only applied

---

[41]   On this see Bill 16, introduced into House of Commons on 16 December 2004 and available on DTI website (*www.dti.gov.uk*).
[42]   This test used in s. 138 of the Consumer Credit Act 1974 (and s. 343 of the Insolvency Act 1986) is very difficult to satisfy – for a rare case where this provision was considered see *London North Securities v Meadows* (unreported, October 28 2004, county court ruling by Judge Howarth).
[43]   See Michael Green below at 155.
[44]   This initiative was launched in the wake of a study by the Centre for Research in Social Policy at Loughborough University on the low levels of financial awareness in poorer families – see FSA Press Notices PN/038/2000 and PN/039/2000. For the later development of FSA schools initiative see for example FSA Press Notice PN/113/2000 (5 September 2000) and FSA Press Notice PN/ 007/2002.
[45]   Brunel University (January 2004). This report indicates that some 300 schools had been teaching personal finance issues as part of this new initiative.
[46]   Solon, Athenian statesman 638–559 BC.

to the sanctions operating with respect to private debt. A public debtor who owed money to a State institution was subjected to a wide range of disabilities[47] and these sanctions could be transferred to his successors until the debt was repaid. Here we see early evidence of the State's preference as a creditor, a feature of the law that has persisted up to modern times. On the other hand, Roman law originally adopted a draconian approach towards debtors. Under Table III of the notorious Twelve Tables judgment, debtors ran the risk of arrest, slavery and death.[48] Later Roman law as developed through the formulary system presided over by the praetor developed a relatively sophisticated system of bankruptcy through the concepts of enforced seizure/ sale of assets (*bonorum venditio*) with the additional sanction of *infamia* (legal stigma) for debtors whose estate proved insufficient to settle the debt. Then came a notion of a voluntary surrender of assets by a debtor (*cessio bonorum*) which avoided the risk of imprisonment with the added attraction that legal stigma would not ensue. However, this latter concept was only available for debtors who could satisfy the praetor that the bankruptcy was due to misfortune.[49] A model similar to *cessio bonorum* was used in Scotland up to the beginning of the 20th century. This model was transported into civil law jurisdictions generally. One feature of civil law that is important is the Paulian action[50] which enables transactions to be unravelled. This mechanism is still found in many jurisdictions, including Quebec. Roman law has never had much of an impact on English law in the area of bankruptcy; a typical position in English commercial law.[51] Civil law concepts have influenced jurisdictions all over the world. Apart from the effects of imperialism some countries have voluntarily adopted Continental models. A good example of this happening is Japan whose 1922 Bankruptcy Law owes much to the French and German influences.[52]

The pervasive influence of English law transported through the effects of Empire has left many jurisdictions using a bankruptcy system based upon English law, though countries such as Australia, Canada, Ireland and New Zealand have all since moved on, introducing personal insolvency regimes that reflect appropriately on social conditions prevailing in those countries.

Bankruptcy is a major social phenomenon in the US with more than one million "consumers" experiencing it every year.[53] Indeed bankruptcy features in the US

---

[47] For a detailed analysis of the harsh treatment meted out to public debtors (e.g. seizure of assets, public humiliation, etc) see A.R.W. Harrison *The Law of Athens (Procedure)* (1971) at 172–5.

[48] Thirty days grace from the date of the judgment was given. The debtor could then be imprisoned for 60 days and if the debt was not settled the creditor could either kill the debtor or sell him into slavery. If there were several creditors at this final stage each creditor had a right to a portion of the body. One can see that this may have provided the inspiration for William Shakespeare's *The Merchant of Venice* (1596). This draconian aspect of the Twelve Tables was modified in BC 326 by the lex Poetelia which provided for continued imprisonment with enforced labour after the 60 days period of grace had expired.

[49] For a lucid account see A Borkowski (1994) *Textbook on Roman Law* pp 70 et seq.

[50] See Cork Report (Cmnd 8558) para 1200.

[51] Judges who have tried to introduce civil law ideas derived from Roman law have often encountered criticism from colleagues and judicial successors – Lord Mansfield became typical.

[52] See S. Baister (1992) 7 IL&P 181.

[53] The figure for 1999 was 1,442,549, which represented a decrease of 8.5% on the previous year – see American Bankruptcy Institute web page *www.abiworld.org*. This figure comprises Chapters 7 (individual and business debt repayment), 11 (business reorganisations), 12 (farm schemes) and 13 (income schemes). The crucial constituencies of Chapters 7, 11 and 13 produce an aggregate of personal filings of 1,281,581.

Constitution as a matter which the Congress may legislate for by uniform laws (Article I, Section 8). As with early English bankruptcy statutes, the motivation for this high profile treatment seems to have been the need to combat financial fraud – in this case by "state hopping".[54] Certainly, US bankruptcy law has, since 1898, been largely the province of the federal legislature and federal courts enjoy exclusive bankruptcy jurisdiction.[55] However, individual States continue to enjoy some independence of choice particularly with regard to the question of which assets are exempt from the estate.[56] A key point to note about US bankruptcy law is that there is much less State control than is found in English law; there is no equivalent of the Official Receiver. Instead the governing philosophy favours direct negotiation between debtor and creditors (or, more likely, between lawyers who play a central role in US bankruptcy operations). The underlying antipathy of US citizens to State intervention has also played its part in shaping the bankruptcy system.[57] The lack of a universal welfare state means that bankruptcy fulfils a safety net role (by preventing debtors being ruined) in the US in a way that is not encountered in Western Europe. Major changes in US bankruptcy law were introduced in 1978 after much deliberation[58] and several pieces of amending legislation have been enacted since that date.[59]

An individual debtor in the US has the choice of Chapter 7 of the Bankruptcy Code, which provides for a liquidation of assets to be used to repay debts. No recourse is

---

These figures need to be viewed in the context of a total US population of over 268 million. For discussion of the US bankruptcy phenomenon see D. Skeel *Debt's Dominion: A History of Bankruptcy Law in America* (2001), T. Sullivan, E. Warren and J.Westbrook *The Fragile Middle Class: Americans in Debt* (2000) and J. Ziegel in Chapter 3 of *Comparative Consumer Insolvency Regimes* (2003). An excellent analysis is also to be found in W.D. Warren and D. J. Bussel, *Bankruptcy* (6th ed, 2002).

[54] See the explanation offered by Madison in the celebrated *The Federalist Papers* (1788) (paper 42) – "The power of establishing uniform laws of bankruptcy is so intimately connected with the regulation of commerce, and will prevent so many frauds where the parties or their property may lie or be removed into different States, that the expediency of it seems not likely to be drawn into question".

[55] There were various short-lived federal statutes in the early 19th century but it was only at the end of that century that the need for permanent legislation to combat the problems of debt was appreciated. For the early history of US bankruptcy law see M. J. Horwitz *The Transformation of American Law (1870– 1960)* (1992) at 150–151. The fact that federal regulation dominates is an indication of the perceived importance of bankruptcy regulation – a similar priority is accorded in Canada and Australia where federal regimes provide the dominant regulation.

[56] A debtor must choose between the list of exemptions provided by federal law or the list available under State law. There must be no cherrypicking. Some 40 US States require debtors resident on their territory to adopt the local State list of exemptions. The issue of exemptions has been one of the most vexed questions in US bankruptcy law, provoking not merely disputes between consumer and creditor lobbies but also raising constitutional questions about federal power in the States – see *Hanover National Bank v Moyses* 186 US 181 (1902).

[57] Alexis de Tocqueville, *(Democracy in America* (1848)) writing in the mid 19th century, attributes the lack of legislation to combat fraudulent bankrupts to the fact that most Americans preferred to take their chance at being bilked rather than to take the risk of being subjected to an oppressive bankruptcy regime (see Volume I, Part II, Chapter 5, "American Democracy's Power of Self-Control".

[58] The subject was reviewed by the Brookings Commission which reported in 1973. Much debate ensued in Congress as to the way forward and in particular the best way of dealing with the rising tide of consumer bankruptcies.

[59] For example in 1984 the law was changed to frustrate automatic access to Chapter 7. For analysis of the modern law see D. Boshkoff (1987) 3 IL&P 178.

had to ongoing income. A debtor who files under Chapter 7 gets an automatic stay against hostile actions and is entitled to a discharge once the estate is realised and final dividend paid. Discharge may be delayed on cause shown. The process of liquidation and repayment is managed by a trustee. This procedure can also be used by a creditor seeking to recover a debt, though the statistics here show very little use by creditors. In the case of an involuntary Chapter 7 case there must be a least three creditors with debts totalling $5000. As far as consumer debtors are concerned creditors often recover very little in the way of dividend as once the exempt assets are removed from the pot there is little to distribute. The alternative US procedure, which is found in Chapter 13 (introduced in 1938 by the Chandler Act in the wake of the Great Depression), allows for the debtor to operate a regulated payment scheme under which creditors are to be repaid out of future earnings according to a plan which would normally run for three years. This option can only be used if the dividend received by creditors is at least as much as they would receive from an immediate liquidation. It is not available to debtors whose debts (both unsecured and secured) exceed specified limits (currently $290,525 and $871,550 respectively). Chapter 13 can only be used by debtors; creditors cannot impose it on a debtor. A trustee is responsible for implementing the plan and the court is involved in approving it. Although the assets of the debtor have to form part of the plan, they are not realised and revest in him. Again there is an automatic stay but discharge will be delayed until the plan has run its course. A Chapter 13 discharge is generally more favourable in its terms than the comparable Chapter 7 facility, particularly in the event of a later bankruptcy. The sad fact is that many Chapter 13 repayment plans fail to deliver with perhaps as many as two thirds of the plans agreed falling into this category. It should be noted that procedures exist to convert a Chapter 7 liquidation of a bankrupt's assets to a Chapter 13 repayment plan (and vice versa) if circumstances dictate.

Much debate has ensued in the USA as to the relative merits of these options. In particular questions have been raised as to what motivates debtors in making their choice of Chapter. Economists such as Meckling[60] have argued that the law should be modelled in such a way as to facilitate rational decision making and their arguments have attracted legislative backing. Other academics[61] dispute the view that decision on Chapter is simply a matter of rational economic choice. Other factors may come into play, such as the prejudices of professional advisers, cultural influences affecting particular debtors and attitudes of local courts to the alternative bankruptcy models. As in the UK there is a lack of hard data to prove or disprove any particular thesis. Generally the bankruptcy regimes so described are more pro debtor than their UK equivalents. This is reflected in the range of exempt assets, the relative ease of securing discharge and in the fundamental constitution protections on offer to prevent

---

[60]   (1977) 41 Law and Cont Prob 13.

[61]   T.A. Sullivan, E. Warren and J. Westbrook (1988) 13 Law and Soc Inq 661. Legal writers such as Schuchmann and Countryman were sceptical about the economic analysis model as an exclusive tool for determining debtor choice. Economists continue to make stimulating contributions to bankruptcy discourse – witness the paper by B. Adler, B. Polak and A. Schwartz in (2000) 29 Jo of Leg Stud 585 calling for debtors to be able to make prior contractual arrangements with lenders about eventual choice of bankruptcy Chapter in the event of borrowing default. This paper also laments the "over-legalisation" of the US bankruptcy regime, suggesting that the vested interest of lawyers serves as a constraint on reform.

discrimination against bankrupts. Where they have other options creditors prefer not to make use of bankruptcy to recover debts. The reason for this particular bias is the dominance of the risk/enterprise culture in the USA and also possibly the fact that many of the early Americans were transported debtors. Recent statistics suggest that the ratio of usage of Chapter 7 as compared to Chapter 13 is 70/30, a profile that indicates the relative attractions of Chapter 7 for consumer debtors with few assets to lose.

For many years in the 1960s, 1970s and 1980s discourse favoured liberalised bankruptcy law in the interests of debtors, but there is evidence that the worm has turned. The future of US bankruptcy law has been the subject of public debate over the past three years. The finance industry, alarmed at the increase in bankruptcies (there were 1.4 million filings in 1999), has sponsored legislation which seeks to swing the balance back in favour of creditors. Thus in 1984 the terms of Chapter 7 were modified to prevent its abusive usage by debtors who could properly participate in a Chapter 13 repayment plan. This has provoked much soul searching[62] and criticisms of credit practices.

Socialist countries (such as those in Eastern Europe) are having to reintroduce systems of bankruptcy as they move further in the direction of a market economy. The position with regard to bankruptcy under Islamic law is fundamentally different. Usury, of course, decriminalised in English law in the mid 19th century, continues to be proscribed by the Sharia.

What do we learn from this brief excursion into comparative bankruptcy law? Firstly all legal systems have to deal with the social problem of insolvency. Secondly, although there are common strands these owe much to shared legal/political/cultural experiences in those societies rather than reflecting a consensus on optimum bankruptcy models. Where there are real differences in any of these areas bankruptcy models diverge. Bankruptcy is therefore a parochial form of legal regulation much more so than other areas of commercial law.[63] An understanding of this fact of life explains why harmonisation of substantive bankruptcy law has been hard to achieve.

New Directions for Bankruptcy Law

The debate has started as to the appropriate model of bankruptcy to adopt for the new century. One possibility would be to return to the two-dimensional approach that was abandoned some 150 years ago. It would be possible to conceive of a system of bankruptcy law that dealt with entrepreneurial traders differently from basic consumer debtors. This distinction is already found in consumer credit law and there is no reason why it should not be carried over into bankruptcy regulation. At the heart of the debate about consumer bankruptcies is the question of responsibility. The period since the mid 1970s has seen a great increase in the regulatory burden imposed upon

---

[62]   See *The Washington Post*, 18 February 2000 ("Bad Ideas on Bankruptcy") and compare *The Wall Street Journal*, 11 February 2000 ("Bankruptcy Reform is a Moral Issue").
[63]   See T. Sullivan, E.Warren and J. Westbrook, *As We Forgive Our Debtors* (1989) at 341.

prospective lenders.[64] However, there is a general perception that the credit industry is still not sufficiently discriminating when offering credit opportunities. Human nature is such that the headline opportunity to take credit often leads to the regulatory small print being disregarded by the prospective borrower. A much stronger culture of caution must be developed, but this can only be achieved if there is adequate data on consumer bankrupts. Defenders of the present system would argue that the credit industry is capable of protecting itself through market forces and there is no need for further regulation.

The Payne Committee (Cmnd 3909) looked at this issue in 1969 and considered whether reckless lenders be reduced to the status of deferred creditors. Such a move would be controversial and probably unworkable. The Committee (at para 853) rejected such a general discipline to control lenders. With the massive growth of consumer credit debt in the past thirty years the idea of imposed subordination may merit revisiting. The issue of responsibility must also be addressed by individuals or by policymakers on their behalf. Should we as a society continue to allow thousands of our fellow citizens to over-extend themselves? Should the law place more general restrictions on the availability of credit than are presently operated? The Payne Committee (at paras 55 and 848) toyed with this idea in 1969 but baulked at decisive general action instead favouring the idea that the courts may have a role to play in placing disabilities on irresponsible borrowers in individual cases. Again, the unpalatable idea of imposed paternalistic austerity might need reconsideration in changed socio-economic conditions.

Is there a role to be played here by education? This question must be answered in the affirmative. I have always found it strange that our system of education fails to provide adequate information on the basic legal/financial system which will govern the lives of children when they become adults. This lacuna is made much more serious by the amount of enticing advertising thrust in the face of young people who are encouraged to borrow without a proper explanation of the consequences if they fail to meet their obligations. This deficiency in our system of education is now officially recognised and, as we mentioned above, the Financial Services Authority has launched an initiative to promote financial awareness and the National Curriculum introduced an optional financial awareness component from September 2000.[65]

Immediate Reform

In spite of the degree of reform of bankruptcy law introduced in the past 20 years further change is likely. The report by Michael Green,[66] although ostensibly concerned with IVAs, has much to say about the bankruptcy system as a whole. The stark fact is that it has an appalling record as a recovery tool and makes no contribution whatsoever

---

[64]   The regime instituted by the Consumer Credit Act 1974 produced in the wake of the report of the Crowther Committee (1971) (Cm 4596) exemplifies this trend. The European Union has added to the layers of regulation here.

[65]   For details see footnote 44 above.

[66]   Michael Green, "Individual Voluntary Arrangements: Over-indebtedness and the Insolvency Regime" (2002) (short form report available on Insolvency Service website).

to the social goal of rehabilitating debtors. In those circumstances Green argues[67] that bankruptcy should be relegated to a secondary regime in the topography of personal insolvency law, with the IVA (subject to suitable reforms) being regarded as the primary gateway. In the summer of 2004 the Department of Constitutional Affairs produced a major consultation document dealing with possible strategies to tackle the problem of over-indebtedness. This document, entitled "A Choice of Paths: Better Options to Manage Over-Indebtedness and Multiple Debt",[68] identifies a number of weaknesses in the current law and raises the possibility of significant reform. The methodology underpinning this document is interesting. In paragraph 22 of this report debtors are divided into *three* groups:

(i)   **Those who can't pay**. These would include low income debtors. The main suggested solution here would be the introduction of a debt relief scheme managed by the Insolvency Service described as NINA (No income, no assets). A maximum debt limit of perhaps £15,000 would be prescribed here and discharge from all liability would occur 12 months after the order was made. As there are no realisation costs and no need for investigation, administration costs should be minimal.

(ii) **Those who could pay**. These include debtors with the ability to pay but who are experiencing short-term cash flow difficulties. Amongst the strategies favoured here would be a court order imposing a moratorium against debt enforcement by unsecured creditors. Such an order would be denominated an Enforcement Restrictions Order (or ERO for short). This would offer protection for a period of between 6–12 months but would not preclude action by secured creditors. The order would only be granted by the court to protect individuals experiencing genuine and unforeseen difficulties. Ongoing payments to creditors during the moratorium period would also be part of the package. Individuals falling into the "could pay" category might also be suitable material for long-term debt management plans operating outside the court.

(iii) **Those who won't pay**. This category includes debtors who play the system but also those who dispute the existence of the debt. Little is said about this group and the assumption must be that bankruptcy may be the only option available.

One consequence of these proposals being implemented is that administration orders may become redundant and suitable for abolition. These proposals are interesting and do reflect what is happening on the ground in other countries, particularly with regard to debt relief schemes. Certainly, the move towards customised regimes for small/consumer debtors is marked.[69]

---

[67]   Ibid at Chapter VI para 3.
[68]   (CP 23/04) (July 2004) (available on *www.dca.gov.uk*).
[69]   Australia introduced a new debt agreement procedure in 1996 under its Bankruptcy Legislation Amendment Act 1996 as part of an effort to deal with small scale debtors – see A. Keay [1998] 11 Ins Intell 57.

A Personal Agenda for Reform

Having reviewed the issues in a critical manner it is time to put my cards on the table. These are the areas where personal insolvency law could be usefully reformed. In making these suggestions we acknowledge the debt owed to the 2001 INSOL International Report on Consumer Debt.[70]

(i) **Development of cost-effective alternatives to bankruptcy.** Statistics show that bankruptcy provides a poor return to creditors and therefore its rationale needs to be rethought. The development of the "No income, no assets" (or NINA) model (currently being studied by the Insolvency Service) is to be welcomed provided there are suitable safeguards set in place to deal with opportunistic conduct by debtors. It is interesting that a similar scheme for small debtors (NAP or "No Assets Procedure") is being included in proposals for the reform of New Zealand insolvency law.[71]

(ii) **Improving IVA procedures by cutting back on excessive formality and developing customised models for modest amounts of indebtedness.** Both private and public sector stakeholders are actively investigating this matter at present.

(iii) **Simplification of the law.** This is never an easy task but some progress could be made by abolishing deeds of arrangement, striking out criminal bankruptcy provisions from the Act (and Rules) and (in the event of poor take-up) accepting that post-bankruptcy IVAs will need to be revisited in the light of increasingly deregulated bankruptcy law and the possible introduction of NINA.

(iv) **Return to a longer basic discharge period for cases deemed appropriate for bankruptcy.**[72] A minimum period of two years should be the norm and that should be coupled with a system of counselling (proof of constructive participation in which might justify earlier discharge). The need for an effective system of independent debt counselling was reflected in Recommendation 7 of the INSOL Report. An absolute minimum of debts should survive discharge (see Recommendation 5) and therefore the issue of the non-dischargeability of student loans should be revisited. Many graduates proceed to professional lives and informal constraints operated at that career level may have a greater impact in deterring bankruptcy abuse.

(v) **Promotion of awareness of risks of credit in the wider community.** This objective, which relates back to the notion that prevention is better than cure, is manifested in Recommendation 8 of the INSOL Report referred to above. The current initiatives

---

[70] "Consumer Debt Report: Report of Findings and Recommendations" (2001).
[71] Full details of the New Zealand proposed reforms can be found on their Ministry of Economic Development website. A reform Bill will be introduced into the NZ Parliament in 2005. This Bill will completely revise the Insolvency Act 1967 and will involve the adoption of the UNCITRAL Model Law.

here in the schools need enhancement, though the problem of curriculum squeeze should not be underestimated. It is pleasing to see that the Insolvency Service is beginning to play a role here.

(vi) **Limiting availability of credit**. We should seriously consider limiting advertisement of credit services in the same way that curbs are placed on the sale of alcohol and tobacco. The idea of making lenders more responsible for imprudent lending[73] needs to be urgently re-examined. For example, there may be justification in reducing commercial lenders to the status of deferred creditors unless they could prove that they took reasonable steps in lending to this particular debtor. Another possibility, floated by Michael Green in his report,[74] would be to impose a duty of care on lenders, though the mechanics of this (and in particular the calculation of loss flowing from any breach of duty) would be difficult to envisage. At the very least, lenders should improve monitoring programmes (see Recommendation 9 of the INSOL Report). The extension by s. 98 of the Courts Act 2003 of the data kept on the Register of County Court Judgments (to be rebranded as the Register of Judgments and Orders) so as to include High Court judgments and fines will help in extending the pool of information in the public domain with regard to individuals with poor credit records and should encourage more responsible lending. There is a downside to any of these developments; our economy in recent years has depended heavily upon burgeoning personal expenditure to maintain levels of activity in the retail and services sectors. To curtail spending habits could produce serious economic disruption.

(vii) **Recognition of the fact that the problem of over-indebtedness is not only the result of the actions of lenders**. Irresponsible *borrowing* lies at the root of the problem and that owes much to the materialistic society in which we live. Changing attitudes of borrowers is a real challenge for our society and simply liberalising bankruptcy law without counterbalancing measures that impact upon the attitudes of borrowers is not the best way to go about things. Again one small step would be to control credit advertising and to produce public service messaging warning of the dangers of credit abuse.

(viii) **A stronger role for the Insolvency Service**. Dealing with personal insolvency is a major social concern that simply cannot be outsourced to the private sector, which quite properly will be driven by the bottom line in delivering its services. But, having accepted that, the Insolvency Service should be made more accountable for its failings. The concept of immunity from suit for Official Receivers as accepted by the courts in *Mond* v *Hyde*[75] should have no place in a modern regulatory system.

---

[72] It is interesting that New Zealand (possibly influenced by developments in Australia) has resisted the temptation to overliberalise discharge rules and instead is sticking to three-year automatic discharge.
[73] The European Commission was believed to be interested in this possibility at one stage.
[74] See Michael Green (op cit footnote 66) at 26.
[75] [1998] 3 All ER 833 (Court of Appeal); [2003] BPIR 1347 (European Court of Human Rights).

(ix) **An Insolvency Ombudsman should be introduced to deal with complaints against practitioners**. It is difficult to argue against this proposal; it is simply a question of minimising implementation costs.

(x) **An Insolvency Court should be established comprising both High Court and county court jurisdictions**. The Cork Committee (paras 1772–1773) recommended this innovation. The US has developed great expertise through its bankruptcy courts. There have admittedly being some difficulties in determining the jurisdiction of these bankruptcy courts but that has much to do with the federal nature of the US State. Some English judges would applaud such a move towards a discrete panel of insolvency courts, whereas other colleagues working in the Chancery Division of the High Court place great value on the variety of work coming before them. Michael Green supports calls for promotion of specialist judicial skills in the insolvency field.[76]

(xi) **Financial incentives to encourage trustees to pursue remedies for the benefit of the estate against inappropriate actions by bankrupts**. The model here would be based on that adopted in Australia (see Chapter 3).

(xii) **Improved data should be made available and funding provided for research on insolvency**. Setting aside the natural vested interest of an academic, it is particularly important to have an understanding on the numbers of those persons who may be described as serial insolvents; this group could become a significant cohort in the years to come with the advent of easy discharge. This research function, coupled with an overview capability, could be carried out by a standing Bankruptcy Reform Committee along the lines of the model found in the USA. If there is reluctance to establish a new body consideration should be given to upgrading through additional investment the valuable functions currently being carried out by the Insolvency Service Policy Unit and by the Research Unit of the Department of Constitutional Affairs.

---

[76] Michael Green (op cit footnote 66) Chapter VI at para 74.

Bibliography

BOOKS

Aitken, J., *Pride and Perjury* (2000, Harper Collins).
Barty-King, H., *The Worst Poverty: A History of Debt and Debtors* (1997, Budding Books).
Blackstone, W., *Commentaries on the Laws of England* (1766) (1966, Dawsons of Pall Mall).
Borkowski, A., *Textbook on Roman Law* (1994, Blackstone Press).
Boyce, W., *Debt and Insolvency on Family Breakdown* (1994, Jordans).
Britnell, R., and Hatcher, J., *Progress and Problems in Medieval England* (1996, Cambridge University Press).
Bunyan, J., *The Life and Death of Mr Badman* (1680, J.A. for Nath Ponder).
Capper, D., *The Enforcement of Judgments in Northern Ireland* (2004, SLS Legal Publications).
Clarke, A., *Current Issues in Insolvency Law* (1991, Stevens).
Cornish, W.R., and Clark, G., *Law and Society in England 1750–1950* (1989, Sweet and Maxwell).
Defoe, D., *Robinson Crusoe* (1719, printed for W. Taylor).
Defoe, D., *The Complete English Tradesman* (1726, printed for Charles Rivington).
de Tocqueville, A., *Democracy in America* (1848) (1956, Mentor Books).
Dicey, A.V., *Law and Public Opinion in England During the Nineteenth Century* (1930) (2nd ed, 1962, Macmillan).
Dickens, C., *Pickwick Papers* (1836) (1986, Clarendon Press).
Dickens, C., *Dombey and Son* (1848) (1970, Penguin Books).
Dickens, C., *Bleak House* (1853) (1971, Penguin Books).
Dickens, C., *Little Dorrit* (1857) (1967, Penguin Books).
Duffy, I.P.H., *Bankruptcy and Insolvency in London During the Industrial Revolution* (1985, Garland Publishing).
Duns, J., *Insolvency: Law and Policy* (2002, Oxford University Press).
Eliot, G., *The Mill on the Floss* (1860) (1979, Penguin Books).
Fehlberg, B., *Sexually Transmitted Debt: The Surety Experience in English Law* (1997, Clarendon Press).
Finnis, J., *Natural Law and Natural Rights* (1980, Clarendon Press).
Galbraith, J.K., *The New Industrial State* (1967, Hamish Hamilton).
Galbraith, J.K., *The Affluent Society* (4th ed, 1984, Andre Deutsch).
Geremek, B., *Poverty: A History* (1994, Blackwell).
Gifford, J., *The Complete English Lawyer* (1823, Whellier).
Gross, K., *Failure and Forgiveness: Rebalancing the Bankruptcy System* (1977, Yale University Press).
Hamilton, A., Madison, J., and Jay, J., *The Federalist Papers* (1788) (1961, Mentor Books).

Harrison, A.R.W., *The Law of Athens* (*Procedure*) (1971, Clarendon Press).

Holdsworth, W.S., *Charles Dickens as a Legal Historian* (1929, Yale University Press).

Holdsworth, W.S., *A History of English Law* (14 volumes) (1923–64, Methuen/ Sweet and Maxwell).

Hoppit, J., *Risk and Failure in English Business 1700–1800* (1987, Cambridge University Press).

Horwitz, M.J., *The Transformation of American Law* (*1870–1960*) (1992, Oxford University Press).

Jackson, T.H., *The Logic and Limits of Bankruptcy Law* (1986, Harvard University Press).

Jenks, E., *A Short History of English Law* (1912, Methuen).

Kelly, F., *A Guide to Early Irish Law* (1988) (Dublin Institute for Advanced Studies).

Kilpi, J., *The Ethics of Bankruptcy* (1998, Routledge).

Lawson, S., *Individual Voluntary Arrangements* (3rd ed, 1999, Jordans).

Lester, V.M., *Victorian Insolvency* (1995, Clarendon Press).

Manchester, A.H., *A Modern Legal History of England and Wales 1750–1950* (1980, Butterworths).

McQueen, J., *Boom to Bust: The Great 1990s Slump* (1994, Bankruptcy Association of Great Britain and Ireland).

Mill, J.S., *On Liberty* (1859, J.W. Parker & Son).

Miller, G., *Family, Creditors and Insolvency* (2004, Oxford University Press).

Moss, G., Fletcher, I. and Isaacs, S., *The EC Regulation on Insolvency Proceedings* (2002, Oxford University Press).

Nash, T., *The Life of Lord Westbury* (1888, R. Bentley & Son).

Niemi-Kiesilainen, J., Ramsay, I., and Whitford, W., (eds) *Consumer Bankruptcy in Global Perspective* (2003, Hart Publishing).

Omar, P., *European Insolvency Law* (2004, Ashgate).

Pound, J., *Poverty and Vagrancy in Tudor England* (1971) (Longman).

Pykett, B., *From Babylon to Bloomsbury* (2000, Insolvency Service).

Rajak, H., *Insolvency Law: Theory and Practice* (1993, Sweet and Maxwell).

Ramsay, I., *Debtors and Creditors: Themes on Issues* (1986, Professional Books).

Rock, P., *Making People Pay* (1973, Routledge).

Rubin, G.R., and Sugarman, D., *Law, Economy and Society* (1984, Professional Books).

Sanfey, M., and Holohan, G., *Bankruptcy Law and Practice in Ireland* (1991, Round Hall Press).

Schofield, G., and Middleton, J., *Debt and Insolvency on Family Breakdown* (2nd ed, 2003, Jordans).

Schofield, P.R., and Mayhew, N.J. (eds), *Credit and Debt in Medieval England 1180–1350* (2002, Oxbow Books).

Shakespeare, W., *The Merchant of Venice* (1596) (1967, Penguin).

Skeel, D., *Debt's Dominion: A History of Bankruptcy Law in America* (2001, Princeton University Press).

Smith, A., *The Wealth of Nations* (1776) (1999, Penguin Books).

Smith, H.L., *The Board of Trade* (1928, Putnam).

Steinmetz, W., *Private Law and Social Inequality in the Industrial Age* (2000, Oxford University Press).

Sullivan, T., Warren, E., and Westbrook, J. *As We Forgive Our Debtors* (1989,

Oxford University Press).

Sullivan, T., Warren, E., and Westbrook, J., *The Fragile Middle Class: Americans in Debt* (2000, Yale University Press).

Thackeray, W.M., *The Newcomes* (1855) (1996, Penguin).

Warren, W.D. and Bussel, D.J, *Bankruptcy* (6th ed, 2002, Foundation Press).

Weiss, B., *The Hell of the English: Bankruptcy and the Victorian Novel* (1982, Bucknell University Press).

West, R., *The Life and Strange Surprising Adventures of Daniel Defoe* (1998, Flamingo).

Wood, P., *Maps of World Financial Law* (3rd ed, 1997, Allen and Overy).

Worthington, S. (ed), *Commercial Law and Commercial Practice* (2003, Hart Publishing).

Ziegel, J., *New Developments in International Commercial and Consumer Law* (1998, Hart Publishing).

Ziegel, J., *Comparative Consumer Insolvency Regimes: A Canadian Perspective* (2003, Hart Publishing).

ARTICLES

Adler, B., Polak, B., and Schwartz, A., "Regulating Consumer Bankruptcy: A Theoretical Inquiry" (2000) 29 Jo of Leg Stud 585.

Allen, M., "IVA: Demand v Supply" [2004] Recov (Spring) 20.

Alsop, J.D., "Ethics in the Marketplace: Gerard Winstanley's London Bankruptcy, 1643" (1989) 28 Jo of Brit Stud 97.

Archer, D., "Insolvency Update" (1998) 142 SJ 596.

Arden, M., "Insolvency and the Courts" [1994] 10 Ins Law 11.

Arora, A., "The Doctrine of Undue Influence and the Protection of the Surety" [1994] JBL 242.

Bacon, A., "At Last, Partnership Voluntary Arrangements – But Was it Worth the Wait?" (1994) 10 IL&P 166.

Baister, S., "The Origins and Operation of Japanese Insolvency Law" (1992) 7 IL&P 181.

Baister, S., "Securing Cooperation: Some Neglected Procedures in Bankruptcy" [2000] Recov (Dec) 16.

Baldwin, J., and Cunnington, R., "The Crisis in Enforcement of Civil Judgments in England and Wales" [2004] PL 305.

Batzel, V.M. "Parliament, Businessmen and Bankruptcy 1825–1883: A Study in Middle Class Alienation" (1983) 18 Can Jo of Hist 171.

Bloxam, P., and Tilbrook, L., "Productivity and Enterprise: Insolvency – A Second Chance" [2002] 5 RALQ 59.

Boardman, C., "What the Standard IVA Conditions Aim to Do" (2003) 19 IL&P 75.

Boshkoff, D., "Personal Bankruptcy in the United States" (1987) 3 IL&P 178.

Boyden, P., "Individual Voluntary Arrangement" [2004] Recov (Spring) 16.

Bragg, R., "Third Parties (Rights Against Insurers) Act 1930 Together with Section 651 Companies Act 1985 (as amended)" [1996] 17 Ins Law 2.

Briggs, N., and Sims, H., "Escaping Bankruptcy – Applications to Annul" [2002] Ins

Law 2.

Brougham, C., and Briggs, J., "Current Issues in Insolvency – Bankruptcy Reform Proposals" [2002] 15 Ins Intell 17.

Brown, D., "Insolvency and the Matrimonial Home – the Sins of the Fathers" (1992) 55 MLR 284.

Brown, S., "Individual Voluntary Arrangements – Limitation, the Appointment of Supervisors and the Doctrine of Estoppel" (2004) 20 IL&P 235.

Capper, D., "Property of the Bankrupt or Personal to the Bankrupt?" [2003] Ins Law 234.

Clements, R., "The Enforcement of Judgment Debts" (1987) 3 IL&P 115.

Clements, R. and Broadbent, G., "The Insolvency Practitioners Tribunal" (1987) 3 IL &P 34.

Cohen, J., "The History of Imprisonment for Debt and its Relation to the Development of Discharge in Bankruptcy" (1982) 3 Jo of L Hist 153.

Condon, R.H., "The Fleet Prison" (1964) 14 Hist 454.

Cooper, S., "Creditors' Remedies Against the Debtor's Home" [1995] JBL 384.

Cretney, S., "Women and Children Last?" (1991) 107 LQR 177.

Davey, M., "Insolvency and the Family Home" [2000] Ins Law 2.

Davis, G., "Insolvency Proceedings in the Age of Woolf" [2000] Ins Law 33.

Dawson, I., "The Administrator, Morality and the Court" [1996] JBL 437.

Dawson, K., "An Extraterritorial Dichotomy?" [2000] Ins Law 81.

Dawson, K., "The European Regulation on Insolvency Proceedings" [2001] 4 RALQ 345.

Deacock, A., and Martin, A., "The Rights of a Trustee in Bankruptcy to the Bankrupt's Pension: Pension Industry v Insolvency Practitioners – A Score Draw" (2000) 16 IL&P 127.

de Berker, P., "Impressions of Civil Debtors in Prison" (1965) 5 Brit Jo of Crimin 310.

Dennis, V.S., "Nothing to Do with Me?" (2000) 16 IL&P 83.

Dennis, V.S., "Bankruptcy Reform – A Start in the Wrong Direction?" (2000) 16 IL &P 179.

Dixon, M., "Combating the Mortgagee's Right to Possession: New Hope for the Mortgagor in Chains?" (1998) 18 Leg Stud 279.

Doherty, N., and Pond, K., "Intelligent Support for Individual Voluntary Arrangements" (1994) 10 IL&P 169.

Doyle, L., "Bankruptcy and Matrimonial Ancillary Relief Orders" [1999] Ins Law 296.

Duffy, I.P.H., "English Bankrupts 1571–1861" (1980) 24 Am Jo of L Hist 283.

Elwes, S., "Transactions Defrauding Creditors" (2001) 17 IL&P 10.

Elwes, S., "Property Which Vests in the Trustee in Bankruptcy" (2004) 20 IL&P 5.

Evans, D., and Pond, K., "Debtor Non-Cooperation in Individual Voluntary Arrangements" (1995) 11 IL&P 95.

Evans, H., "The Wasted Costs Jurisdiction" (2001) 64 MLR 51.

Ferris, F., "Insolvency Remuneration: Translating Adjectives into Action" [1999] Ins Law 48.

Fidler, P., "The Foreign Tax Man Cometh: or Does He? Some Insolvency Cases Revisited" [2000] Ins Law 219.

Finch, V., "The Measures of Insolvency Law" (1997) 17 OJLS 227.

Finch, V., "Insolvency Practitioners: Regulation and Reform" [1998] JBL 334

Finch, V., "Controlling the Insolvency Professionals" [1999] Ins Law 228.

Finch, V., "Is Pari Passu Passe?" [2000] Ins Law 194.

Finch, V., "Regulating Insolvency Practitioners: Rationalisation on the Agenda" [2005] 18 Ins Intell 17.

Finlay, A., "Australian Wives are Special – *Yerkey v Jones* Lives On" [1999] JBL 361.

Fletcher, I.F, "The Insolvency Act 1976" (1977) 40 MLR 192.

Fletcher, I.F., "Bankruptcy Law Reform – The Interim Report of the Cork Committee and the DTI Green Paper" (1981) 44 MLR 77.

Fletcher, I.F., "The Genesis of Modern Insolvency Law – An Odyssey of Law Reform" [1989] JBL 365.

Floyd, R., "The Dinosaur Must Go – Do We Need the Insolvency Service?" (1999) 15 IL&P 85.

Floyd, R., "In the High Court of Justice" (2003) 19 IL&P 216.

Flynn, D., "A Reply by the Insolvency Service to 'The Dinosaur Must Go – Do We Need the Insolvency Service?'" (1999) 15 IL&P 90.

Flynn, D, "Individual Voluntary Arrangements" [2001] Recov (July) 18.

Flynn, D., "Happy New Bankruptcy?" [2004] Recov (Summer) 4.

Frieze, S. A., "Bankruptcy and Pensions" [1999] 12 Ins Intell 76.

Frieze, S.A.,"The Principal Residence – 'Use It or Lose It'" [2004] 17 Ins Intell 106.

Frisby, S., "Making a Silk Purse out of a Pig's Ear – *Medforth v Blake*" (2000) 63 MLR 413.

Frith, S., and Jones, B., "The Insolvent Partnerships Order 1994" (1995) 11 IL&P 14.

Gaines, K., "Applying the May 2002 European Regulation on Insolvency Proceedings" [2001] Ins Law 201.

Gibson, C., "Dealing with Vexatious Litigants: the "New" Range of Civil Restraint Orders" (2004) 25 Co Law 53.

Graham, D., "Shakespeare in Debt? English and International Insolvency in Tudor England" [2000] 13 Ins Intell 36 and 44.

Graham, D. and Tribe, J., "Bankruptcy in Crisis – A Regency Saga" [2004] 17 Ins Intell 85.

Grant, D., "*Landau* – a Level Playing Field" [1999] Recov (Sept) 24.

Grant, R., "Personal Bankruptcy" [2004] Recov (Spring) 32.

Greenstreet, I., "When Can a Trustee in Bankruptcy Get His Hands on a Pension? Post Pensions Act 1995 Position" (1995) 11 IL&P 168.

Greenstreet, I., "Practical Steps to Realise Value from a Bankrupt's Personal Pension Following *Re Landau*" (1997) 13 IL&P 101.

Greenstreet, I., "Pensions and Bankruptcy: Recent Developments" (2001) 17 IL&P 43.

Gregory, R., "Malicious Presentation of a Winding up Petition" [1997–98] 3 RALQ 137.

Griffiths, A., and Parry, R., "Personal Insolvency as a Restriction on Involvement in Company Management" [1999] Ins Law 199.

Griffiths, N., "Voluntary Arrangements after *Somji*" (2001) 17 IL&P 104.

Grundon, T., "SPI Seventh Personal Survey" [1998] (Nov) Ins Pract 20.

Haig, C., "Removing the Stigma from Bankruptcy, or Just Making it Worse?" [2000] Recov (June) 16.

Haley, M., "Mortgage Default: Possession, Relief and Judicial Discretion" (1997) 17 Leg Stud 483.

Haley, M., "Mortgagees and the *O'Brien* Defence: A Developing Jurisdiction?" [1998] JBL 355.

Hall, J.C., "Insolvency and the Family" [1991] CLJ 45.

Hand, C., "Bankruptcy and the Family Home" [1983] 47 Conv 219.

Hankey, G., "The Bankruptcy Advisory Service" [2001] Recov (February) 26.

Harrison, D., "The Insolvency Practices Council" [2002] Ins Law 175.

Hellyer, R.W., "The Early History of the Insolvency Practitioners Association" (1985) 1 IL&P 166.

Hemsworth, M., "Voidable Preference: Desire and Effect" (2000) 16 IL&P 54.

Hiley, C., "Interest in Matrimonial Property" [2003] Recov (Summer) 18.

Ho, L.C., "On Pari Passu, Equality and Hotchpot in Cross Border Insolvency" [2003] LMCLQ 95.

Hosford, D., "Protective Pensions" [2002] Recov (June) 28.

Howells, K., "The Government's Consultation on Proposals for Bankruptcy Law Reform" [2000] Recov (March) 12.

Hughes-Holland, P., "Uncertain Future for IVAs" [2002] Recov (June) 32.

Hunter, M., "Should there be a Separate Insolvency Court?" (1985) 1 IL&P 102.

Ibrahim, A., and Barton, S., "Farm Business Tenancy Schemes: Section 423 Saves the Day for Secured Creditors" (2004) 20 IL&P 163.

Jaconelli, J., "Intercepting a Bankrupt's Mail" [1994] Conv 370.

Jaconelli, J., "Redirecting a Bankrupt's Mail" [1995] 8 Ins Intell 1.

Jackson, T.H., "A Fresh Start Policy in Bankruptcy Law" (1985) 98 Harv L Rev 1393.

Keay, A., "Bankruptcy Law in Australia – the Latest Changes" (1997) 13 IL&P 149.

Keay, A., "Personal Insolvency: A New Option for Debtors in Australia" [1997] 20 Ins Law 10.

Keay, A., "Australian Insolvency Law: Latest Developments" [1998] 11 Ins Intell 57.

Keay, A., "Insolvency Law: A Matter of Public Interest?" [2000] 51 NILQ 509.

Keay, A., "Balancing Interests in Bankruptcy Law" (2001) 30 CLWR 206.

Keay, A., "Pursuing the Resolution of the Funding Problem in Insolvency Litigation" [2002] Ins Law 90.

Korobkin, D.R., "Rehabilitation Values: A Jurisprudence of Bankruptcy" (1991) 91 Col L Rev 715.

Kruse, J., "Home Security – The Impact of Bankruptcy on Collecting Housing Debt" (1996) 12 IL&P 193.

Lawson, A., "*O'Brien* and its Legacy – Principle, Equity and Certainty? [1995] 54 CLJ 280.

Levinthal, L., "The Early History of English Bankruptcy Law" (1918) 66 Univ Penn L Rev 223 and (1919) 67 Univ Penn L Rev 1.

Lightman, G., "The Challenges Ahead" [1996] 16 Ins Law 2.

Loveland, I., "Distress for Rent: An Archaic Remedy?" (1990) 17 Jo of Law and Soc 363.

Marriner, S., "English Bankruptcy Records and Statistics before 1850" (1980) 33 Econ Hist Rev 351.

McCartney, P., "Insolvency Procedures and a Landlord's Right of Peaceable Re-Entry" [2000] 13 Ins Intell 73.

McGee, A., "*Anglo-Manx Group Ltd v Aitken*" [2002] Ins Law 133.

McKenzie-Skene, D.W., "Dealing with Multiple Debt – An Examination of the Proposal for a Debt Arrangement Scheme in Scotland" [2002] Ins Law 212.

McKenzie-Skene, D.W, "Morally Bankrupt? Apportioning Blame in Bankruptcy" [2004] JBL 171.

McQueen, J., "The Hidden Costs of Personal Bankruptcy" (1987) 3 IL&P 81.

McQueen, J., "The Struggles of Small Businesses – the Role of the Bankruptcy Association" (1997) 13 IL&P 197.

Meckling, W.H., "Financial Markets, Default and Bankruptcy: the Role of the State" (1977) 41 Law and Cont Prob 13.

Miller, G., "Transactions Prejudicing Creditors" [1998] 62 Conv 362.

Miller, G., "Applications by a Trustee in Bankruptcy for Sale of the Family Home" (1999) 15 IL&P 176.

Miller, G., "Income Payments Orders" (2002) 18 IL&P 43.

Miller, J.G., "Bankruptcy and Foreign Revenue Claims" [1991] JBL 144.

Milman, D., "Exploitation of a Bankrupt's Personal Assets: The New Rules" (1989) 4 IL&P 71.

Milman, D., "Bankruptcy – The Right of a Debtor to Challenge Proceedings" [1994] 12 Ins Law 5.

Milman, D., "Statutory Demands in Bankruptcy: A Retreat From Formalism in Bankruptcy Law" [1994] Conv 289.

Milman, D., and Davey, M., "Debtor Rehabilitation: Implications for the Landlord-Tenant Relationship" [1996] JBL 541.

Mokal, R.J., "Priority as Pathology: The Pari Passu Myth" [2001] CLJ 581.

Morgan, D., "Unlucky Thirteen" (1980) 43 MLR 221.

Mulligan, M., and Tribe J., "IVA Time Extensions under the Insolvency Act 1986: Uncertainty or Necessity?" (2002) 18 IL&P 190.

Munro, R., "The Release of Co-Debtors under Individual Voluntary Arrangements" (1998) 14 IL&P 230.

Murphy, J., "*Mond v Hyde*: Negligence Immunity for the Official Receiver?" [1999] Ins Law 206.

Oditah, F., "Individual Voluntary Arrangements" [1994] LMCLQ 210.

Oldfield, R., "Cowboys are Still in the Saddle" [2002] Recov (Sept) 20.

Omar, P., "The UNCITRAL Model Law on Cross Border Insolvency" [1999] 10 ICCLR 242.

Omar, P., "The UNCITRAL Insolvency Initiative: A Five Year Review" [2002] Ins Law 228.

Patrick, H., "Scottish Insolvency Reforms" [2003] 16 Ins Intell 65.

Pond, K., "Individual Voluntary Arrangements (Part I) – A Slow Start for a Quick Remedy" (1988) 4 IL&P 66.

Pond, K., "Individual Voluntary Arrangements (Part II) – A Study in Design" (1988) 4 IL&P 104.

Pond, K., "The Individual Voluntary Arrangement Experience" [1995] JBL 118.

Pond, K., "A Decade of Change for Individual Voluntary Arrangements" (1998) 14 IL&P 324.

Pond, K., "New Rules and New Roles for the Individual Voluntary Arrangement" (2002) 18 IL&P 9.

Poyntz, I., "What to Expect from a JIMU Visit" [2002] Ins Pract (Sept) 14.

Preston, D., Morgan, S., and Brown, A., "*Grady* and Beyond – When a Hybrid Action is not a Hybrid Action" [2004] 17 Ins Intell 142.

Prior, M., "The UNCITRAL Model Law on Cross Border Insolvency" (1998) 14 IL&P 215.

Quilter, M., "Daniel Defoe: Bankrupt and Bankruptcy Reformer" (2004) 25 Jo of L Hist 53.

Radin, M., "The Nature of Bankruptcy" (1940) 89 Pen L Rev 1.

Rajak, H., "The Harmonisation of Insolvency Proceedings in the EU" [2000] CFILR 180.

Rajani, S., "JUSTICE Committee Report on Insolvency Law Reform" (1995) 11 IL &P 24.

Rees, K., "Confiscating the Proceeds of Crime – The Effect on Legitimate Creditors and Bona Fide Third Parties" (1996) 12 IL&P 120.

Richardson, M., "Protecting Women Who Provide Security for a Husband's, Partner's or Child's Debts: The Value and Limits of an Economic Perspective" (1996) 16 Leg Stud 368.

Robinson, R., "Bankruptcy – A Fresh Start?" [2000] Recov (Aug) 31.

Robinson, R., "Injustices at Work and Home" [2002] Recov (June) 34.

Salvin, R.F., "Student Loans, Bankruptcy and Fresh Start: Must Debtors be Impoverished to Discharge Educational Loans?" (1996) 71 Tul L Rev 139.

Sargent, P., "9th Personal Survey Report" [2002] Recov (March) 32.

Servian, M.S., "The Influence on and Influence of a Law Reformer: Basil Montagu, A Founding Father of the Modern Law of Insolvency" (1986) 2 IL&P 45.

Servian, M.S., "On the Demise of Acts of Bankruptcy" (1988) 4 IL&P 117.

Sharpe, R.S., "*Ord v Upton*: Some Recent Developments" [2001] Ins Law 182.

Simmons, M., "How Safe are Pensions in Bankruptcy?" (1997) 13 IL&P 98.

Smart, P., St J., "The Rule Against Foreign Revenue Laws" (2000) 116 LQR 360.

Stanley, C., "Excessive Pension Contributions in Bankruptcy" [2002] 15 Ins Intell 68.

Stanner, J., "Insolvency Regulation – Consultation Document" (1998) 14 IL&P 3.

Steiner, M., "UNCITRAL Model Law on Cross Border Insolvency: to Enact or not to Enact" [1997] Insolv Pract (Dec) 18.

Strong, M., "Consumer Debt" [2002] Recov (June) 16.

Sullivan, T.A., Warren, E., and Westbrook, J., "Law Models and Real People: Choice of Chapter in Personal Bankruptcy" (1988) 13 Law and Soc Inq 661.

Sutherland, J.R., "The Ethics of Bankruptcy: A Biblical Perspective" (1988) 7 Jo of Bus Eth 917.

Tamari, M., "Ethical Issues in Bankruptcy: A Jewish Perspective" (1999) 9 Jo of Bus Eth 785.

Tee, L., "The Menace of Retrospective Severance in Bankruptcy" [1996] 55 CLJ 21.

Theobald, K., "The Ferris Report – Insolvency Practitioner Fees and Remuneration" (1998) 14 IL&P 300.

Thomas, M., "Bankruptcy in Occupational Pension Schemes and Personal Pension Schemes: A Dichotomy of Approach" [1998] 62 Conv 317.

Thomas, M., "Bankruptcy and Personal Pensions – A New Dilemma" [1998] 2 CFILR 268.

Treiman, I., "Escaping the Creditor in the Middle Ages" (1927) 43 LQR 230.

Treiman, I., "Acts of Bankruptcy: A Medieval Concept in Modern Bankruptcy Law" (1938) 52 Harv L Rev 187.

von Hirsch, A., and Wasik, M., "Civil Disqualifications Attending Conviction: A Suggested Conceptual Framework" [1997] CLJ 599.

Walker, R., "Trusts Pensions and Insolvency" [1999] Ins Law 3.

Walters, A.J., "A Modern Doctrine of Champerty?" (1996) 112 LQR 560.

Walters, A.J., "Personal Insolvency Law After the Enterprise Act: An Appraisal" [2005] 5 JCLS 65.

Walton, P., "Voluntary Arrangements – The Nature of the Beast" [1997–98] 3 RALQ 277.

Walton, P., "Landlord's Distress – Past its Sell by Date?" [2000] 64 Conv 508.

Walton, P., "Execution Creditors – (almost) the Last Rights in Insolvency" [2003] CLWR 179.

Warren, E., "Bankruptcy Policy" (1987) 54 Univ Chic L Rev 775.

Warrington, B., "The Bankruptcy of William Pickering in 1853: the Hazards of Publishing and Bookselling" (1990) 27 Pub Hist 5.

Weisgard, G., "English Insolvency Practitioners Excluded from Scottish Personal Insolvency Work" [1999] Ins Law 9.

Welbourne, E., "Bankruptcy Before the Era of Victorian Reform" (1932) 4 Cam Hist Rev 51.

Wheeler, S., "Empty Rhetoric and Empty Promises: The Creditors' Meeting" (1994) 21 Jo of Law and Soc 350.

Wilkins, M. "Jersey Insolvency Law and Practice" (1989) 5 IL&P 98.

Wilkinson, L., "Unlicensed Debt Advisers – What are We Smoking?" [2002] Insolv Pract (Dec) 14.

Winder, W.H.D., "The Courts of Requests" (1936) 52 LQR 369.

Wollaston, J., "Injustice in Justice" (1985) 1 IL&P 152.

Wollaston, J., "Working within Insolvency" (1987) 3 IL&P 9.

Wollaston, J., "Bankruptcy and the European Convention" (1987) 3 IL&P 42.

Wong, S., "Revisiting *Barclays Bank v O'Brien* and Independent Legal Advice for Vulnerable Sureties" [2002] JBL 439.

Wood, P., "Principles of International Insolvency" [1995] 4 IIR 94 and 109.

OFFICIAL REPORTS

Bankruptcy: A Consultative Document (1980, Cmnd 7967).

Bankruptcy: A Fresh Start (April 2000).

Blagden Committee (1957, Cmnd 221).

Budd Committee (Ireland) (1972, Prl 2714).

Clyne Committee (Australia) (1962, 8440/62).

Cork Committee (1982, Cmnd 8558).

Crowther Committee (1971, Cmnd 4596).
Hansell Committee (1925, Cmnd 2326).
Harmer Committee (Australia) (1988, ALRC 45).
Insolvency: A Second Chance (2001, Cm 5234).
JUSTICE, A Report by the British Section of the International Commission of Jurists ("Justice") on Bankruptcy (1975).
JUSTICE, An Agenda for Reform (1994).
Muir Mackenzie Committee (1908, Cmnd 4068).
Payne Committee (1969, Cmnd 3909).

RESEARCH PAPERS

Beatson, J., "An Independent Review of Bailiff Law" (2000).
Green, M., "IVAs: Over-indebtedness and the Insolvency Regime" (2002) (Short report available via Insolvency Service website).
INSOL International, "Consumer Debt Report: Report of Findings and Recommendations" (2001).

Subject Index